THE
ADVENTURE
GUIDE
TO
CANADA

Pam Hobbs

D1254843

HUNTER
PUBLISHING INC

Hunter Publishing, Inc.
300 Raritan Center Parkway
Edison NJ 08818
(201) 225 1900

ISBN 1–55650–315–6

Printed in Singapore through Palace Press

Published in the UK by:
Moorland Publishing Co. Ltd.
Moor Farm Rd, Airfield Estate
Ashbourne DE6 1HD
England

ISBN (UK) 0–86190–422–2

Maps by Joyce Huber, PhotoGraphics

ACKNOWLEDGEMENTS

Many thanks to my publisher Michael Hunter and his staff. Also
to *Globe and Mail* travel editor Peter Harris, and former travel
editors Joshua Cohen and Marilyn Dawson, for their support and
generosity in giving me so much space in Canada's national
newspaper. Most especially I want to thank my husband,
Michael. Not only did he put this book together for publication,
but in the past three years drove me more than 18,000 miles in
Canada so I could write new articles and update others.

CONTENTS

INTRODUCTION

1967 was centennial year, Canada's 100th birthday, time we decided to see more of our country. That Spring we took delivery of a new Volkswagen Campmobile with attached tent and started planning. Summer saw us, Michael and I, and our three young daughters, Sarah, Liza and Susan, heading east. We visited Expo '67 in Montreal, vowed to speak French only in Quebec City, learned the value of mosquito repellant in forested campgrounds, took umpteen photos of the girls at Green Gables, lazed on golden beaches, fished and swam in the Atlantic. And hated to come home.

The following year we headed west. North to the rugged terrain around Lake Superior, across the prairies to the Rocky Mountains, through the beautiful Okanagan Valley, on to Vancouver and finally Victoria, B.C. Along the way we explored recreated sites that breathed life into our nation's history for us, watched mounties in training, wore stetsons at the Calgary Stampede. We rode to mountain tops and hiked back down, wallowed in pools fed by hot springs, had our lunch stolen by two baby bears. On the Athabasca Glacier we made snowballs in July. We slept in a dinosaur graveyard, shopped for souvenirs in modern malls and at country fairs.

In other years and bigger motorhomes we took a closer look at our favorite provinces. Since those memorable times of family travel my Canadian adventures have taken me by boat and trains, to stay in castle hotels built by railway giants around the turn of the century, ultra-modern hotels, cosy inns, B & Bs, rustic hideaways in national and provincial parks where it is still possible to get close to nature.

For this book I have chosen a collection of articles originally printed in Canada's national newspaper, *The Globe and Mail.* All travel expenses were paid by the newspaper, all destinations selected by me in consultation with the travel editor. These are trips and places I recommend to friends. All are easily accessible and affordable to the average traveller.

In Canada we have good highways, including one 4,860 miles long which will take you from the Atlantic to the Pacific. Our provincial tourist offices do such a grand job in dispensing free information, we have included their addresses.

During the past 20 years my work has taken me to most of the world's exciting and exotic destinations, yet that first look at Canada from our cramped van and leaky tent is the adventure I recall with fondest memories. I doubt I shall ever tire of travelling in Canada.

Pam Hobbs

Note: All prices are in Canadian dollars. At press time $Can = $US .86 = £ .50.

ABOUT THE AUTHOR

Born in England, Pam Hobbs has lived in Canada since 1950 and written about it for major newspapers since 1968. A *Globe and Mail* travel writer since 1979, she is an award winning journalist and member of the Society of American Travel Writers' Canadian chapter. She lives in Mississauga, Ontario, with her husband Michael Algar.

TO MICHAEL

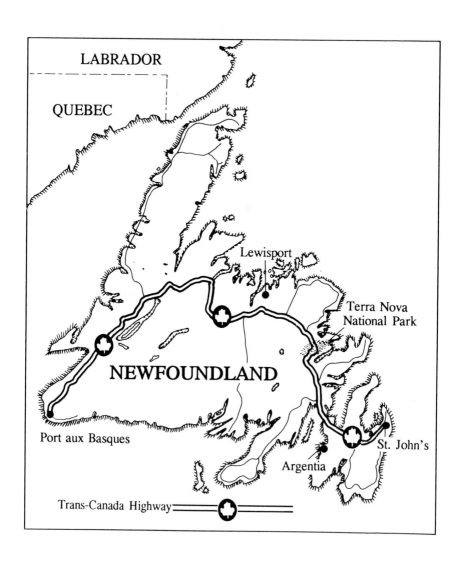

LABRADOR

QUEBEC

Lewisport

Terra Nova
National Park

NEWFOUNDLAND

Port aux Basques

Argentia

St. John's

Trans-Canada Highway

NEWFOUNDLAND

Newfoundland as a tourist destination is one of Canada's best kept secrets. This, our most easterly province, is one of a kind. The first overseas possession of the British Empire, it was the last province to join confederation, becoming part of Canada in 1949. Original settlers, largely from western England and Ireland, gave their communities fanciful names like Heart's Content, Useless Bay, Come By Chance, Blow Me Down and Witless Bay. All these years later you will hear the Irish lilt and idioms of their language. Nowadays when the whole world seems to be on the move, 95 percent of Newfoundland's residents were born here. As a visitor from "away" you will tell yourself time has stood still, and must set your watch to half an hour ahead of our other Atlantic provinces.

Newfoundland comprises the main island of Newfoundland, a few offshore islands and the great northern wilderness that is Labrador. Basque fishermen first came here in the 15th century to harvest the cod on the Grand Banks and a century later established a whale oil refinery at Red Bay. Whales are only for watching these days, but you can jig for cod, try for record-sized bluefin tuna off Conception Bay, Atlantic salmon in more than a hundred rivers, and arctic char in the frigid waters of Labrador. Newfoundland is where you can hunt for big game in the rugged interior, witness colonies of gannets at Cape St Mary's and some of the continent's most magnificent vistas in Terra Nova and Gros Morne National Parks.

Geographical features of Gros Morne (700 square miles) are so striking this wilderness preserve is recognized by UNESCO as a world heritage site. It is a land of Ice Age glaciers, coastal plains, of sandy beaches and sea caves. Birders love the park for its hundreds of feathered species. Climbers come to tackle the 2,644-foot Gros Mountain dominating it all. Terra Nova on the east coast is no less dramatic, with its coastal trails, fresh and saltwater fishing, cottage accommodation and forested interior providing a refuge for wildlife.

Newfoundland's past lives on in old St John's and countless small towns across the province. As the North American shore closest to Europe it has been the scene of many firsts. 1866 brought the first trans-Atlantic underwater cable from Ireland to Heart's Content. St John's received the first trans-Atlantic wireless signal in 1901. Alcock and Brown departed from here for the first non-stop trans-Atlantic flight in 1919. Today similar attempts are being made in anything from tiny rowboats to hot air balloons.

Not that you have to try anything like that. Simply being here fills you with a sense of adventure. Meet the people. Isolation breeds a warmth, traditional hospitality and a wonderful humor you won't find anywhere else. Attend a weekend dance or festival and they will show you "a toime" (good time) remembered long after you get home.

This isn't a province to be rushed through. Sample seafood so fresh it practically jumps out of the pan. Try some flipper pie and cod tongues washed down with a mug of "screech". Sit on an empty beach and be engulfed by its overwhelming isolation. Take a boat ride on Gros Morne's Western Brook Pond, not a pond at all but a majestic fjord with streams cascading down 2,000-foot cliffs into a canyon. Go to Seal Island. Drive north to L'Anse aux Meadows where the first visitors were Vikings around the year 1,000 A.D.

These days Newfoundland welcomes its guests with friendly hotels, picturesque campgrounds and B & Bs where you will be treated as family. The province is served by major Canadian airlines. Year-round ferries operate daily from North Sydney, Nova Scotia, to Port aux Basques. Three times a week, between mid-June and mid-September, there's an overnight trip from Sydney to Argentia. Cabins are available to those who book early. Day-niter seats, a restaurant, movies and children's play rooms help pass the time on board.

Department of Development and Tourism, P.O. Box 2016, St John's, Newfoundland, A1C 5R8, telephone 1–800–563–6353 will send more information. Inter-provincial ferry information is available by telephoning: from Ontario, Quebec and Newfoundland, 1–800–565–9411; New Brunswick, Nova Scotia, Prince Edward Island, 1–800–565–9470; USA, 1–800–341–7981, except Maine which is 1–800–432–7344.

ST JOHN'S, WHERE PAST IS PRESENT

St John's, Newfoundland: The note in the mailbox was welcoming. Along with a room key, it read, "Hello. Your room is on the ground floor. Come on in. Marilyn and Howie." We did, and sure enough, past the lounge furnished to the early 1900s, we came to our room. Formerly the home's dining room, it is now a spacious bed-sitter with its own bath next door. On the mantelpiece another note told us breakfast would be served between 8 and 10 a.m. in the third floor kitchen, and that if we were early risers we could help ourselves.

I found it astonishing that in North America there is still a city where, in the heart of downtown, a homeowner can leave the front door unlocked and invite strangers inside. It set the tone for our few days in St John's, surely the most hospitable city in Canada.

We were lodged at The Roses Bed and Breakfast, one of five heritage properties convenient to downtown, owned and operated by John Koop and Janet Peters (in some instances with partners.) In winter they provide a comfortable home away from home for business people, university lecturers and researchers here for weeks on end. Summer brings tourists, many of whom book from one year to the next, using this as a base for touring St John's and its environs.

At The Roses we had Marilyn and Howie (sister and brother-in-law of the owners) living in a basement apartment. In houses with no resident landlord, guests make their own breakfasts from supplies provided, and a cleaner includes the kitchen in her daily chores. Every guest room has its own bathroom, although not necessarily ensuite. Bright and modern, ours is equipped with an array of toiletries such as I expect of a high priced hotel.

The lounge contains brochures on all area attractions, also magazines and menus from neighborhood restaurants. With its city and harbor view, the kitchen is the sort one likes to hang around in. At eight each morning Marilyn arrived to whip up eggs, pancakes or whatever else we wanted. Cereals, toast, tea, coffee and juice were already on the large pine table. It is a friendly meal. Fellow guests are eager to recommend local excursions, and other B & Bs. (I've learned there is a cult following of Canada's B & Bs. Stay in one and you will learn of three more.) Over breakfast one day I asked our hostess about the wisdom of leaving the front door unlocked. In seven years, she said, not so much as a face cloth has been missing from any of the five properties.

Well rested and nourished, we looked forward to walking around the city each day, beginning always with the historic area in which we were housed. Here, rainbow colored homes march down steep and narrow streets towards the harbor, and Water Street which has been a commercial thoroughfare since the 1500s. With just a pinch of imagination you'll have a good sense of what it was like then, when sailors and whalers crowded the taverns, cod fishermen came home with bumper harvests, money flowed into shops. . . .

A memorial park marks the point at which Sir Humphrey Gilbert came ashore in 1583, claiming this New Found Land for Britain. In doing so, the native of Devon, half brother of Sir Walter Raleigh, gave Britain her first overseas colony. Enterprising merchants of English, Irish and Scottish ancestry built substantial offices and warehouses along the harborside of Water Street, while retailers catered to thousands of traders and fishermen. Some of these buildings are converted to enclaves of boutiques. Others, like the old-fashioned hardware store, have retained gleaming wall cabinets and aromas of times before plastic wrap.

One of North America's oldest cities, St John's was first discovered by John Cabot in 1497 on the feast day of St John the

Baptist. For years, the French and English fought for its possession, until the final victory for Britain in 1762. During the first
half of this century St John's played an important part in the
development of modern communications. It is recorded in the an-
nals of aviation history as departure point for the first successful
non-stop trans-Atlantic flight in 1919. For motorists crossing the
country it is Mile 0 (along with Victoria B.C.) of the Trans-
Canada Highway.

St John's, Newfoundland

On a clear day, the best of city views are to be had from Signal
Hill, so windy when I was there I could hardly keep on my feet. The
hill's earliest record of signalling dates from 1704 when a flag
hoisted on a yardarm told merchants which ships were approaching
the harbor so they could prepare for their arrival. In December
1901, Guglielmo Marconi received the first trans-Atlantic message
in a hospital near the Cabot Tower, and so made communications
history. Now an exhibit in the tower commemorates a new era in
world communications established that day.

By 1900 Newfoundland was the world's largest supplier of cured cod. On historic Water Street the Newfoundland Museum displays 16th-century artifacts of Basque fishermen who came first to fish for cod, and later started a whale fishery here. Models and photographs of ships, descriptions of early steamship services, and a thought-provoking exhibit on the sealing industry will give you new respect for the hardy, often courageous, sea-going men of Newfoundland.

Not that you need a museum to get a sense of the city's past. It is all around you, captured by simply walking the streets. You will find it in churches such as the 19th-century cathedral, repository for ancient treasures in its ecclesiastical museum. And the Basilica of St John the Baptist, built of Newfoundland granite and Irish limestone, once the largest church in North America.

You will find it in traditional Newfoundland crafts and humor, the pubs and fish restaurants. At the St John's Regatta, an annual event first held in 1918, in the picturesque Quidi Vidi Vil-

Street in St John's

lage. (One of North America's oldest houses, dating to the 1700s, is located in Quidi Vidi.) And at Cape Spear, North America's most easterly point, a national historic site since the inauguration by the Prince and Princess of Wales in 1983. On this wild promontory the old lighthouse has been fully restored as a keeper's residence. Footpaths lead you around the park and to the point. Stand there peering into the mist and you can surely see a galleon, or pirate ship, or 17th-century whaler rounding the cape, its crew raring to come ashore and kick up a storm in old St John's.

IF YOU GO: St John's is served by major Canadian airlines, as well as by Marine Atlantic ferries. The Roses Bed and Breakfast, 9 Military Road, St John's, Newfoundland A1C 2C3 (telephone 709–753–6036), has single rooms $44, double $54, including tax and cooked breakfast. St John's Tourist Information guide (from City of St John's, Economic and Tourism Development, P.O. Box 908, St John's, Newfoundland, A1C 5M2) lists more B & Bs, small and large hotels.

THE ROAD TO THE ISLES

Grand Falls, Newfoundland: It became our bible of sorts, the little blue Newfoundland and Labrador Auto Guide available from the province's information centers. Twenty-two tours are described therein, leading motorists to sandy beaches, rocky headlands and magnificent mountain vistas in national parks. With its help you will be directed to sleepy fishing outports on secluded bays, to cod jigging and whale watching excursions, and to places with tantalizing names like Blow Me Down Park and Gooseberry Cove, Butter Pot, Plum Point, Cow Head and the Bay of Exploits.

We chose tour # 12, Road to the Isles, and had our eyes opened to a way of life worlds from our own. The drive proved all the itinerary promised, except for icebergs which in August had disappeared. Tours are designed so that you can travel just a portion, or all of a three-day trip such as this. For ours, an overnight in Grand Falls (in roughly the center of Newfoundland) brought us to Norris Arm, from where we continued around Notre Dame Bay towards the group of islands off its north shore.

Provincial parks along the way are jewels, whether you're camping or simply looking for a brief stop. Visitor accommodation is provided at small motels, hotels and B & B's in tiny harbors where life is ruled by tides rather than time. And photographers be warned. You will use twice as much film as anticipated, because seascapes are so compelling.

The first sizeable town on this route is Lewisporte, the Marine Atlantic terminal for ferries to northern Newfoundland and Labrador. Town history is explored in a museum operated by the Women's Institute. Handicrafts (including unique Christmas decorations) are for sale on the ground floor, while upstairs rooms contain household, farming and fishing artifacts donated by local families. Most outstanding is a wall tapestry, 30 feet long, recording a century of community history from 1876. A work of love and community pride, it was designed by one woman and stitched by three more. Amazingly, to me if not them, they completed their task in three months. Represented are Lewisporte buildings, transportation from early sailing schooners to arrival of the railway and automobiles, two World Wars, industries and more.

Notre Dame Bay's main industries are fishing, farming and lumbering, all of which are in evidence as you drive from one hamlet to the next. Tourism isn't so obvious, and we found ourselves detouring often to walk on sandy beaches with no footprints other than ours. Four causeways connect the mainland to New World and Twillingate islands, for which you require another two full days.

Twillingate is one of the most rewarding stops on tour # 12. Merchants from Poole on England's southwest coast established trade here in the mid 1700s. Unlikely as it seems now, the new town prospered so it had 1,000 residents, could support its own newspaper, "The Twillingate Sun", and by the 1800s even had a championship cricket team. Now every July brings the Twillingate Fish, Fun and Folk Festival during which visitors are treated to songs, dances, and recitations originating from Dorset in southwest England. "Crafts, baked goods, picnics and a lively party spirit," are advertised for the festival.

The community's rich history is relived in a former Anglican Rectory. While the ground floor is furnished as an upper class residence, bedrooms are given over to various exhibits including one on sealing from the fisherman's point of view. Should you feel you've seen enough of these folk museums, you will still find this one worthwhile for coverage of the controversial offshore seal hunts. The exhibit starts with Archaic and Beothuk Indians' arrow heads and axeheads. Photos show steamship sealers setting off from Twillingate. Up-to-date exhibits deal with public outcry over clubbing of the seal pups.

The museum's craft shop has a large selection of local pottery, knitted hats and sweaters, paintings, wood carvings and whatever other crafts have kept the Bay's men and women busy during their long winter evenings.

At Long Point, according to our guidebook, one can witness the world's most beautiful sunsets and huge mountains of ice floating in from the Labrador Sea to melt in warmer waters south of Newfoundland. We saw neither, but did discover Wild Cove where we sat on a beach to eat a pan-fried cod lunch from a local cafe.

From Twillingate, you can turn south to Gander and be there before nightfall. Or you can cross a causeway to Boyd's Cove, then drive north again to Farewell and Change Islands. Despite the name, little has changed in Change Islands (connected by road and incorporated as one community) during the past hundred years. Motor vehicles arrived in 1965, but still lifestyles are of another era. Narrow clapboard homes nest in neat gardens, fishing stages and stores are painted a traditional red. At a general store you can buy the makings of a picnic, and the deserted Puncheon Cove is a grand place in which to eat it.

Fogo Island, 15 miles long and nine wide, was first settled in the 1600s by fishermen who sought refuge from French raiders terrorizing the east coast. Because it remained isolated well into the 20th century, descendants of early inhabitants have retained traces of their old English dialect. Ancient customs and folklore, too, have survived here. During the 12 days of Christmas, for example, costumed mummers go from house to house performing skits and songs.

More coves and fishing villages, herds of wild ponies and, if you are lucky, caribou are to be seen on the way to the Bay's northeastern tip. Sandy Cove, aptly named, is a beautiful conclusion to the Road to the Isles tour.

IF YOU GO: From Sandy Cove, the return journey is via ferry to Farewell, and around Gander Bay or directly south to Gander—best known for its international airport, and departure point for the little blue book's Tour # 13.

OCEAN WATCH IN TERRA NOVA NATIONAL PARK

Terra Nova, Newfoundland: In these depressed times when so many young people pull up their Newfoundland roots for transplanting elsewhere, it is refreshing to meet a couple who have deliberately chosen this as the place in which to build their home. For seven years Fraser and Mark Carpenter, both qualified sea captains, operated wildlife and natural history tours in the

On the Road to the Isles

Caribbean aboard their boat *Morning Star.* A native of Sable Island, Nova Scotia, Mark has spent most of his life at sea. Fraser is from southwest England, and like Mark was delivering boats to various world ports when they met in Fort Lauderdale.

Their decision to leave the Caribbean was mutual. Both wanted more than a regular charter service; both were discouraged by demanding tourists who really weren't interested in nature, and both wanted to settle down in a permanent home. A worldwide market survey focusing on natural resources and wildlife attractions put Newfoundland at the top of their list. They met with Terra Nova officials and agreed on a marine interpretation program, through expeditions to the park's outer reaches. A new boat, *m/v Northern Fulmar,* was custom built for the purpose. Last summer, during the Carpenters' first season I watched them turning away would-be passengers rather than spoil things because of crowding.

Terra Nova National Park

Dedicated to introducing us to local wildlife, the couple conducts tours of different lengths. An all-day trip includes whale, iceberg and bird-watching as well as cod jigging and an on-shore guided walk. During the hike a lunch stop allows you to cook your own "catch of the day" and swim in a forest pond. Operating twice a week, such day trips cost adults $65, children half price. An evening fjord tour (departing 7 p.m., fare $16) takes passengers to watch the sun set against towering cliffs at Mt. Stamford. It also provides a shuttle service for campers at Minchin Cove.

Our four-hour afternoon trip was as pleasurable as it was informative, and bargain priced at $23. The scenery is as awesome as I've seen anywhere. In places the water is a translucent turquoise. Backed by forested cliffs, basking under a warm sun, it is reminiscent of many an island in the Caribbean. We stop at a tickle to look for bald eagles, but see little more than a pile of lobster traps left by fishermen at the end of the season. For those of us from "away" it is explained that a tickle is a community on an inlet of water on this side of the island. Sadly, although the sea is an important part of the national park, only one percent of thousands of visitors who come here annually will ever see this area.

Mark explains the ebb and flow of marine and birdlife as they follow shoals of capelin in spring, herring and squid in autumn. Our August visit is between seasons. Late June and July is the best time to see minke and humpback whales. Then, pilot whales, dolphins and porpoises are spotted regularly near the dock.

We learn that icebergs are made of snow, not ice, and that eel grass is real grass with seeds and flowers and all. On-board posters tell us about various seaweeds, Irish moss, sponges and Atlantic fish. Others illustrate fishing methods used by Newfoundlanders, from baitless jiggers through lines and trawls to stationary fish traps and salmon nets.

At a second stop we can clearly see eagles nested on the cliffs. Perhaps because it spots our boat, a bald eagle flies towards us. An extraordinarily graceful creature, white headed and tailed, with a wingspan of six to ten feet, it swoops for fish tossed by

Fraser. Soon a second adult appears. The air is so still, the water so calm, we can hear chicks screeching in the nests. A young boy is more curious about jellyfish alongside the boat. Obligingly, Fraser nets one, explains the differences between red and white species and shows the delighted lad how it breathes.

At a particularly rugged spot with Mt. Stamford a ponderous backdrop, we are taken close to shore for soft sandstone caves—and land bridges created by waves. A lone cormorant stands nonplussed before our clicking cameras, drying its wings—a necessary gesture we're told, because its feathers are easily water-logged. Dozens of little terns appear from nowhere. Delicate looking birds, but oh so clever. Upon returning from their annual trip to the Antarctic each bird lodges on the very same crevice it had last season.

Minchin Cove is eerily quiet now where it once resounded with the noise of lumbering and ship-building. A dock allows us to go ashore for a brief walk, to desolate signs of habitation. Wilderness campers are invited to this idyllic site, but there are few takers. With the season nearing its end, only two parties had camped here all summer. Nature enthusiasts don't know what they are missing.

The hour has come for us to try our luck at that old Newfoundland tradition, cod jigging. Each passenger is given a spool and line and told how to jiggle it a few inches from the ocean floor. The man beside me is an expert from St John's who has brought his Californian sister for a day in the park. He urges me to write to my Member of Parliament, complaining about the lack of decent sized fish off Newfoundland's shores. Several passengers do catch sizeable fish, but I am unsuccessful. Before setting off Mark warned us we probably wouldn't catch anything today. He offered a refund to anyone aboard expressly to fish, but nobody accepted.

Had I realized that this is one of Canada's loveliest parks I would have planned on staying overnight. As it was we had a room reserved in St John's, a four hour drive away. Another time I might rent a housekeeping cottage in the park, giving myself time to walk some of the 60 miles of hiking trails, rent a bicycle, join an escorted nature session.

When I voiced my reluctance to leave the park Fraser offered us use of their house at Squid Tickle, since she and Mark would be sleeping on the boat. It is a new house they built last winter. Neighbors have a key. This is a couple we met just half an hour before the boat tour. I knew nothing about them or the tours until I stumbled over Fraser photographing her husband on the dock. She knew nothing of me. A generous spirit and sense of old fashioned hospitality appear to be inbred in the people of Newfoundland. From the brief time spent with the Carpenters, I would say they are truly home at last.

IF YOU GO: Terra Nova National Park is 50 miles south of Gander, 150 miles north of St John's via the Trans-Canada Highway. Housekeeping cottages, restaurant, laundry, and gear rentals are located near Newman Sound. For information and campsite reservations, contact the Superintendent, Terra Nova National Park, Glovertown, Newfoundland, A0G 2LO, telephone 709–533–2801. Ocean Watch Tours (Doryman Marine, Squid Tickle, Burnside, Newfoundland, A0G 1K0, telephone 709–533–2801 or 709–677–2327) operate mid-June through mid-September.

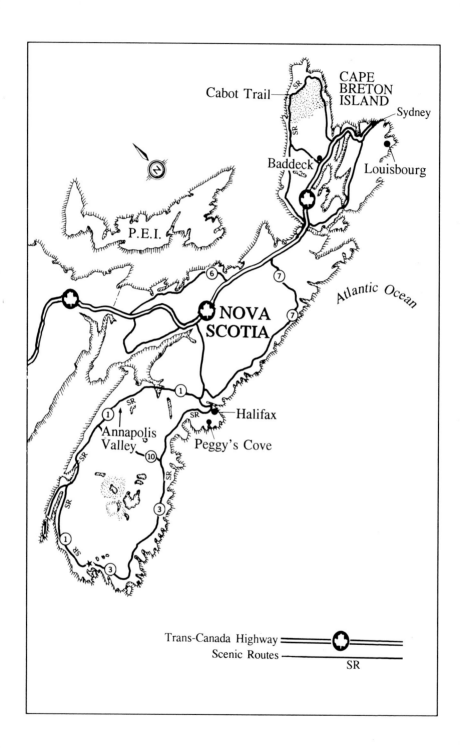

Cabot Trail

CAPE
BRETON
ISLAND

Sydney

Baddeck

Louisbourg

P.E.I.

Atlantic Ocean

NOVA
SCOTIA

6

7

7

1

SR

Annapolis
Valley

SR

Halifax

Peggy's Cove

1

10

SR

SR

3

SR

1

SR

3

Trans-Canada Highway

Scenic Routes

SR

NOVA SCOTIA

For good reason Nova Scotia license plates tell us that this is "Canada's Ocean Playground." Joined to the rest of the country by a narrow isthmus, it is surrounded almost entirely by a sea that is never far away because nowhere is the province wider than 80 miles.

The rugged coastline, particularly on Cape Breton Island, contains some of the world's most remarkable scenery. Sailing enthusiasts enjoy huge natural harbors such as Halifax and Sydney, and the protected waters of the Bras d'Or lakes. Diminutive fishing communities attract artists and photographers. As for beaches you have your pick of wide strands slapped by thundering Atlantic rollers that thrill the surfers, and tranquil bays where time slips by unheeded.

Nova Scotia enjoys a unique heritage. Chartered as Britain's first colony by James I of England (who was also Scotland's James VI) it was named by its Scottish founder Sir William Alexander for his homeland. Today 35 percent of "New Scotland's" population is of Scottish ancestry. More trace their roots to French speaking Acadians, Loyalists from New England, Germans and other European immigrants. Almost all cultures are reflected now in towns and villages around the province.

In some places Nova Scotia is more Scottish than Scotland. At least it seems that way when we are welcomed across the provincial boundary by a kilted bagpiper. Cape Breton Island terrain is as rugged as any in the Scottish Highlands. Wild lupins brush the landscape with the mauve of heather, and in St Ann's tartan kilted students attend North America's only Gaelic college. Cafés do Scottish teas; gift shops are crammed with as many souvenirs from Bonnie Scotland as you will find in their Edinburgh counterparts.

The Acadian influence is a little more subtle. This is a heritage recalled in the tranquil Annapolis Valley and Evangeline's tragic plight in Longfellow's poem. Acadian artisans sell crafts on which they have practiced ancestral skills. Restaurants serve traditional Acadian food.

Tourism has the province divided into nine different routes. The most spectacular is the Cabot Trail, one of five on Cape Breton Island joined to the mainland by causeway. Another takes you through the Annapolis Valley. Each of the drives is a comfortable day trip, whether your choice is for seafaring and fishing communities on the south coast (where seafood is the greatest and lobster is king), or Fundy's shores and a region steeped in tales of MicMac Indians.

Aside from all that sea, sports enthusiasts have 3,000 lakes and countless rivers, many teeming with fish. Golfers complain that courses are in settings so beautiful the scenery distracts from their game. Camping is as good as it gets in the province's two national parks. On the north shore, Cape Breton Highlands National Park has campsites a brief walk from area beaches, and a short drive from the most magnificent mountain vistas. On the south coast Kejimkujik attracts summer canoeists because of its gentle lakes and rivers travelled by MicMac Indians long ago. Both parks have beaches, hiking paths and nature programs.

History is revived in recreated settlements such as Port Royal which acquaints visitors with the oldest European settlement in Canada. The Fortress of Louisbourg, an awesome French bastion and important fishing and trading center in the 1700s, is now acclaimed as one of the best living museums on the continent. Maritime museums in Halifax and nearby Lunenburg are so well presented they interest even the non-believers. And while on this part of the coast be warned of those sleepy little villages. Stop for the catch-of-the-day lunch, and you will find yourself sticking around for afternoon tea.

Nova Scotia receives more than its share of perennial visitors who, like the seabirds, return to their own little niche each year. Alexander Graham Bell loved the Bras d'Or lakes at the foot of the Cabot Trail. A museum here devoted to his genius is one of the province's most interesting. The newly opened Anne Murray Center is at Springhill where the entertainer was born and returns every summer. On the south shore Chester, first settled by

New Englanders, is a favorite summer place for Americans. There are even hopeful souls who come each year to Oak Island, determined to uncover Captain Kidd's legendary treasure.

For Nova Scotia's free "Doers and Dreamers Complete Guide," contact Nova Scotia Tourism, P.O. Box 130, Halifax, Nova Scotia B3J 2M7. Telephone: central or southern Ontario 1–800–565–7140, northern Ontario and western Canada 1–800–565–7166, Maritimes 1–800–565–7105, Quebec and Newfoundland 1–800–565–7180, US 1–800–341–6096 (Maine only 1–800–492–0643).

HALIFAX, A CAPITAL PLACE TO TOUR ON FOOT

Halifax, Nova Scotia: After expressing surprise at meeting me again, the Bostonian exclaimed, "I do so love your capital cities. They are such a manageable size." Coincidentally we were both staying in Halifax's Haliburton House Inn, and three days before had shared a table in a Charlottetown B & B. From here she was off to the Cabot Trail and I to New Brunswick, so we didn't see each other again. Still I thought of her while walking around Halifax and later Fredericton, and decided she was right. A big plus with our Atlantic provinces' capital cities is that they are easily explored on foot.

Because of its great harbor, Halifax was one of the first English settlements in Canada. Back in 1749, colonel Edward Cornwallis came from England to build the fortress city that would be the leading naval and military location in British North America for over a hundred years. Now its seafaring past is so attractively presented, visitors find themselves pursuing it for days on end.

My first stop was the massive hilltop fortress, the fourth to be built on this site, started in 1828 and completed some 30 years later. Now a national historic park, the Citadel has a 50 minute orientation movie recalling Halifax history in four segments with special effects produced by sound, lighting and artifacts. On any summer's day you will find something going on here, whether it's a lone piper on the parapets, musket drill or ceremonial firing of the noonday gun.

Edward, Duke of Kent, earned himself quite a reputation while stationed in Halifax for six years from 1794. A stickler for punctuality, he ordered the large clock on Citadel Hill. Ticking away ever since, it didn't so much as slow down during the 1917 explosion that levelled much of the city.

Until Hiroshima this was the world's largest man-made explosion, putting two square miles of land to waste, and felt 50 miles away. It happened on December 6th at around breakfast time when the ammunition ship *Mont Blanc* and the Belgian relief steamer *Imo* collided in Halifax harbor narrows. The ensuing fire ignited the volatile cargo and 2,000 lives were lost, 9,000 people injured. Property damage alone was estimated at over $50 million.

A series of visitor-activated videos in the Maritime Museum of the Atlantic (located on the city's waterfront) tell of the explosion and other disasters at sea, including sinking of the *Titanic*. The city's role in this tragedy was to send rescue ships to the scene. One hundred and fifty four of the 1,500 victims are buried in Halifax.

The museum is a must if you are to appreciate the city's past, so inexorably bound up with the sea. A ships' chandlery, lifesaving vessels, detailed models of submarines, corvettes and cruise ships are displayed, the age of steam and days of sail represented.

Outdoors, *H.M.C.S. Sackville,* a corvette used for escort duty during World War II, is now a museum. On board we are transported in time to 1943, in the crew's quarters with songs by Vera Lynn and Doris Day and in the canteen with cigarettes for 10¢ a package and chocolate bars for a nickel.

For a livelier experience in maritime history, summer visitors can sail on *Bluenose II,* replica of the schooner featured on our dime. Under full sail she makes three trips a day (except Mondays), and 40 of the 80 spaces can be reserved in advance by calling 422–2678. If *Bluenose II* is off on a tour as Nova Scotia's goodwill ambassador, you might settle on a harbor cruise. It will include the site of that dreadful explosion, the dockyard established in 1758, and Point Pleasant Park leased to the city for a shilling a year.

The *Bluenose II* slip is next to a waterfront restoration area known simply as Historic Properties. Here former warehouses and commercial buildings are reborn as boutiques and craft shops, restaurants and pubs. Offices of the Nova Scotia and Halifax tourist organizations are housed in the Old Red Store, an auction house for war prizes in the 1812 war. Enos Collins, considered the wealthiest man in British North America in his time, owned many of these buildings. His partner, Samuel Cunard, did just fine too, thanks very much. (Born in Halifax in 1789, Cunard established a fortnightly sailing to Liverpool with his paddle steamer *Britannia,* and founded what became one of the world's largest shipping companies.)

In a city so well endowed with historic structures there are probably a dozen or more old churches of merit. One to catch my imagination is Our Lady of Sorrows Chapel, built in 1843 by 1,800 men in a single day. Another is St Paul's, Canada's oldest Protestant church, constructed of oak brought from Boston in 1749. This is the city's only church to entirely escape damage from the great explosion. Well almost. A window (third along, on Argyll Street) shattered in an unusual fashion leaving a silhouette of a human head.

Tree-shaded squares, parks, waterfront seats and benches— there is always somewhere to sit and ponder in this attractive city. Parade Square, in front of St Paul's Church, has plenty of summer entertainment, especially at weekends. For a quiet rest, find yourself a bench in the Halifax Public Gardens, uninspiring in name only. On summer Sundays traditional concerts are conducted in its Victorian bandstand. At any time this is an enchanting place, lovely in early evening when tall shadows creep

Public Gardens, Halifax

across the lawns and old ladies empty plastic bags of crusts for the pigeons. And smartly dressed young people can't resist the temptation to walk in stockinged feet on the grass as they hurry home briefcase in one hand and shoes in the other.

Halifax has excellent hotels in all categories, convenient to the waterfront and other visitor attractions. Looking for something special, I was happy to find Haliburton House Inn, close to the Public Gardens and shops of Spring Garden Road. Nineteenth-century home of Sir Brenton Haliburton, it has luxurious rooms and suites, a courtyard where you can relax over Afternoon Tea, an excellent dinner menu, and attentive service. Rates are approximately $65 to $80 per double room, $110 to $130 for a suite, including breakfast and tea.

Tourists arriving in Halifax should try and stay long enough to take one or two out-of-town excursions. Peggy's Cove is the province's most photographed fishing village. Lunenburg deserves a whole day, with stops along the way.

IF YOU GO: For more information on the city, contact Tourism Halifax, P.O. Box 1749, Halifax, N.S. B3J 3A5, telephone 902–421–8736. The Haliburton Inn's address is 5184 Morris St., Halifax, N.S. B3J 1B3 (telephone 902–420–0658).

PEGGY'S COVE, FAIREST OF THEM ALL

Peggy's Cove, Nova Scotia: I had no intention of visiting Peggy's Cove, most photographed hamlet in maritime Canada. The editor didn't want a story; *Globe and Mail* files were doubtless bulging with pictures. But I was shamed into it by a Haligonian. To visit his city without seeing Peggy's Cove, he said, was like a Maritimer not bothering with Niagara on his trip to Toronto.

So I drove for some 30 miles west of Halifax in late afternoon and probably saw the famous scene at its best. The tour busses had gone for the day, the car park contained only three or four cars, and the sun was high enough for a nice picture. First thing I saw was the massive project of former resident artist William E. deGarthe. It is a large mural carved from local granite in his garden. Started in 1977 and coming to an end with his death in 1983, this 100-foot monument to local enterprise and heroism depicts 32 fishermen along with their wives and children. The artist's two murals in St John's Anglican church here are said to be quite as spectacular. To see them you must obtain the church key from the house next door.

What makes Peggy's Cove unique is its picture-postcard perfection. Not only has it all the requisites of a "quaint fishing village" but they are composed as an artist would have them. There's the lighthouse, perched dramatically on the rocks, with waves crashing against them to send up almost constant sprays. On a stormy day, that's the violent side of Peggy's character. Then there is the cove, tranquil but no less perfect, with fishing boats tied up against docks and decks, and suitably weathered fishermen on hand.

Peggy's Cove

Even the rocks are picturesque, worn smooth by the elements over millions of years. They are horribly slippery when wet, especially around the lighthouse. Signs are posted telling of the dangers, but not every tourist heeds them.

Peggy's Cove, named for an early resident, is reasonably unspoiled and will remain that way under the protection of the Nova Scotia government and residents—who numbered well under 100 at last count. There is a gift shop and restaurant, and pastel colored houses scattered across the landscape. And the lighthouse doubles as a post office, where your mail will be stamped with its picture. You can see it all and be back in Halifax within three hours of leaving your hotel. The trouble is you won't want to. Peggy's Cove may be the most famous, but there are more equally attractive fishing villages along this stretch of coast. It's a bit like eating cookies. There's no way you can stop at just one.

IF YOU GO: For the scenic route from Halifax, take Highway 103 to exit 5, then 333 beside St Margaret's Bay to Peggy's Cove. Then, continue along 333 and back into Halifax.

EVANGELINE COUNTRY

Annapolis Royal, Nova Scotia: It is known as Evangeline Country, this fertile valley along the Annapolis River, soaked in history, human drama and tragedy so poignantly described in Longfellow's Evangeline. It was here in this valley that the first permanent settlement north of Florida took root in 1605, two years before Virginia's Jamestown. In this remote setting Canada's first social club was organized; the first formal theatre was a play written about and performed for Samuel de Champlain at this habitation in 1606. Apples were introduced to this land by Acadians who brought them from their native France. Grandchildren and great-grandchildren of those farmers were driven from their homes, but the apple trees continued to prosper.

On a crisp September day we explored the Annapolis Valley, for the most part following a highway marked as the Evangeline Trail. It took us into little towns mellowed with age, their streets graced by enormous maple trees. We passed mile upon mile of orchards and emerald green fields; trim white houses set in gardens prolific with hollyhocks and lupins, dahlias and roses encouraged by a maritime climate. Butterflies are big in these parts—wooden butterflies, attached like colorful limpets on the sides of houses—presumably as decorations.

Signs tell of homemade quilts and antiques for sale. And Digby chicks, not chickens at all we discovered, but tiny herrings, offered to eat in or take out. Names on mail boxes indicate farmers of French and English ancestry living side by side. At last all is peaceful in this beautiful valley.

In 1603 the Sieur de Monts received permission from France's Henri IV to colonize this part of the New World. He came with fellow noblemen, priests, artisans, criminals and captain-cum-navigator Samuel de Champlain, who drew up plans for habitation here in a sheltered basin at the mouth of the Annapolis River. Three hundred and thirty five years later Port Royal was reconstructed from local wood cut and adzed, and pinned together with wooden pegs for authentic replication of the real thing.

This is one of Canada's more dramatic recreations. Bounded by high palisades, somber looking buildings are huddled around a patch of green. Pigeons fluttered prettily above the entrance, coo-ing at our approach. Student guides bantered with a carpenter fearful of working on a steep-hipped roof. But it really isn't a light-hearted place. One is very aware that the colonists lived under constant threat of disease, that winters were cruel, the isolation probably worse. It was to raise the low morale of his men at Port Royal that Champlain started his Ordre de Bon Temps (Order of Good Cheer) in which members took turns in preparation of lavish dinners, each one destined to outshine the feast before.

Of necessity Port Royal was self-contained. It had its own bakery and blacksmith's shop, a fur trading room where Indians would bring fox furs and beaver pelts to exchange for European goods. Homemade remedies in the apothecary include jars of barberry, rhubarb and peach blossom syrups neatly lined up on a shelf. The Governor's House, built on St Croix where the group spent its first disastrous winter in the New World, was brought to Port Royal as Champlain's residence. Considering the year and the location, Champlain achieved a surprising degree of comfort in this wilderness. His living quarters, warmed by a fire in a massive stone hearth, have solid wood and leather furnishings. While others slept on crude little bunks, his was a sizeable four poster bed, hide canopy and all. And beneath the house, his cellar was stocked with good French wines.

The idea of Good Time feasts was brilliant, since available provisions allowed for inventive dishes made of moose meat and beaver tails, caribou steaks, wild goose and fresh trout. Breads were baked in their own ovens; French wines served in fine goblets. And once every fortnight at least, some of the men felt closer than two months' journey from home. It didn't last. In 1613, an English expedition from Jamestown raided the habitation. Finding almost everyone out working in the fields, they took what they could carry and set fire to everything else.

Years later the French built a second Port Royal five miles away at the junction of the Allain and Annapolis rivers. Nothing like the earlier tight-knit community, this one changed hands often until the British took permanent charge, renaming it Annapolis Royal for their queen. For several years (from 1713 until Halifax was founded in 1749), Annapolis Royal was the capital of what had become Nova Scotia. Costly restoration of historic houses along the waterfront is under way. Beside the Allain river, the Annapolis Royal Historic Gardens represents regional horticulture from Indian times to the present day. Covering 10 acres, these botanical gardens include historical themes such as an Acadian garden complete with replica of their dyke system, the 18th-century Governor's Garden, and a Victorian garden. The rose garden shows the species' development over time.

All that remains of the original Fort Anne is a storehouse, and a magazine which the British found too damp for powder, so they converted it to a military prison. Officers' quarters have been restored as a museum. Contents now concern both of the early settlements, as well as the Acadians who farmed the region. In a mixed bag of mementoes you will see exhibits that include an 18th-century prayer book, a copy of Queen Anne's speech to Parliament, homemade ice skates and dinky velvet chairs belonging to midgets born in Hampton, Nova Scotia.

At Annapolis Royal we saw a pale, cracked stone wheel. Brought from France in 1610, it ground some of the earliest grain grown by white men in North America. Acadians from western France tilled this particular soil in the 17th and 18th centuries. As immigrants they were unique at the time in that they didn't rob the land of its fur-bearing animals. Instead they created arable land from existing marshes. With large earthen dikes along the shores to keep out Fundy's high tides, they soon had herds of cattle grazing on former marshlands. They grew prodigious crops of grain and wheat, established productive orchards and vegetable gardens. And they bothered no one.

Henry Longfellow, with his "Evangeline of Grand Pre", has publicized the Acadians' plight more widely than any history book. In Grand Pre National Historic Park expect no grave for Evangeline, or reconstructed house "with frame of oak and of hemlock such as the peasants of Normandy built . . . " because she is the poet's creation. Her story, though, probably relates to a certain Acadian girl whose groom was deported from Grand Pre on the couple's wedding day.

In the park a bronze statue of Evangeline is the work of Canadian sculptor Philippe Herbet and his son Henri, descendants of one of the first Acadian families to settle here. Behind her, St Charles' Church, on this site from 1689 to 1755 and now reconstructed as a museum, documents the tragedy of Grand Pre's Acadians. On St Charles' front steps, that September 5, 1755, the British commander, Lt Colonel John Winslow read the deportation order. His ultimatum was clear: Acadians must sign allegiance to the British crown, or leave this land settled by their families a century before.

In that one year 6,000 Acadians were expelled from their farms. In all some 14,000 were deported, usually to British colonies in the south. When peace returned, so did some of the Acadians, only to find their homes taken over by British immigrants.

On our visit, we found Grand Pre alive with tourists. Like them we sought out traces of the "dikes that the hands of farmers had raised with labor incessant," and strolled in the park's informal gardens. We walked clockwise around the tragic

Evangeline to see if, as promised, she aged before our eyes, then pursued the saga of her people in St Charles' Church.

The park gift shop sells pendants made from wild flowers pressed in glass, the ubiquitous wooden butterflies, Indian belts, and Longfellow's Evangeline in paperback. Continuing our journey to Halifax I saw little of the surrounding countryside, but much of Acadia through poet's eyes. . . .

> "In the Acadian land, on the shores of the Basin of Minas,
>
> Distant, secluded, still the little village of Grand Pre
>
> Lay in the fruitful valley. Vast meadows stretched to the eastward,
>
> Giving the village its name, and pasture to flocks without number . . . "

IF YOU GO: Driving from Digby to Halifax along Highway 101, we covered 145 miles. The three national historic parks are open between April 1 and October 31, while the grounds are open all year. Admission is free. There is a modest admission charge for the Annapolis Royal Historic Gardens. More information on the Evangeline Trail is available from Nova Scotia Tourism.

DRIVING THE CABOT TRAIL

Ingonish, Cape Breton: This time we did it right, driving clockwise from Margaree so as to keep on the land side of the road. Last time around we took it in the other direction from Baddeck, hugging the cliff's edge for most of the 190 miles—and that's not terribly comfortable when you are driving a 24-ft motorhome on Cape Breton's mountainous Cabot Trail.

Without doubt this is one of North American's most magnificant drives. Every turn in the road brings a new vista, as it winds around forested mountains, across grassy plateaus and plunges down to the sea on inclines so steep they could alarm timorous drivers.

It is possible to drive the trail in half a day, but that would be a crime. Picturesque fishing villages cry out to be photographed. Picnic areas are reserved above perpendicular cliffs, with a swirling sea way down below. And part of the trail loops through Cape Breton Highlands National Park, safeguarding for posterity the region's most prized scenery in a 366-square-mile preserve.

The trail is named for explorer John Cabot who came this way in 1497. Portuguese fishermen arrived soon after, followed by French and Scottish settlers whose influence is strong still in both language and traditions.

Alexander Graham Bell, who chose Baddeck at the foot of the Cabot Trail as his summer home, is quoted as saying that he travelled around the globe, saw the Canadian and American rockies, the Andes, the Alps and the Highlands of Scotland, but for simple beauty Cape Breton outrivals them all. I too have seen all those places, and agree with him wholeheartedly.

Half an hour or so from Margaree we stopped for lunch above a scenic cove and watched what we thought were two whales cavorting a few hundred yards offshore. After 15 minutes, when they hadn't moved on, we had to admit the "whales" were black rocks and that the waves, not they, were being playful. Never mind, it was a heavenly spot carpeted with honeysuckles permeating the air with their sweet perfume. And the sea birds were for real.

There were so many stops in the next three days. Neil's Harbour is a favourite with photographers for its lobster traps piled high on the dock and fishing boats alongside. The traps were being unloaded when we happened by. Most of the lobsters were around two pounds each. One five pound monster was offered us for $12.

Coastal scene on the Cabot Trail

At Cheticamp harbor, deep sea fishing and seal watching excursions are popular. An ideal base from which to explore Cape Breton, Cheticamp has a golf course, good seafood restaurants, shops specializing in Acadian crafts. The handsome St Peter's Church here was built in 1883 with stone taken from Cheticamp Island and hauled by horse drawn sleigh over winter's ice.

The national park has seven campgrounds. At Ingonish our fully serviced site was a joy, close to well maintained showers and kitchen shelters, and a five minutes walk from the beach. There we could swim in the sea or a freshwater lake, play a game of tennis, set off on nature trails. The Highlands Golf Course was half a mile away, the Keltic Lodge twice that distance. Operated by the Department of Tourism and Culture, the lodge is perched on a stunningly beautiful site above the sea. Accommodation is in a main lodge, the White Birch Inn, or two- or four-bedroom cottages. All are within walking distance of golf course, tennis courts, heated swimming pool and beach.

Wild flowers beside the Cabot Trail are unforgettable in summer. For years I have tried without success to grow lupins, yet here they are in great profusion alongside the highway. Twenty eight walking paths within the park are designed to lead you to more of its natural treasures. Some of the trails provide no more than a 10 minute stroll, others offer a "challenging wilderness experience." A Parks Canada booklet from one of the information centers will tell you which ones lead to lakes and streams and historic sites settled by early Acadians; which are flat and which are steep, and how to reach the most exciting lookouts.

Our final stop on the Cabot Trail was St Ann's where at around 8:45 one morning the sound of bagpipes hurried our approach. Reward for our haste was the sight of kilted students being piped into morning classes at North America's only Gaelic college.

St Ann's was originally settled by immigrants from the Highlands of Scotland. Back in 1851 more than half the population of St Ann's emigrated to Australia and then New Zealand with a Rev Norman MacLeod who had brought them from Scotland. Now every year, visitors from New Zealand come here in search of their roots.

The Gaelic College stands on 400 acres of the original 1,000 granted the Rev MacLeod. At its summer school, students learn Highland art and crafts, bagpipe playing, clan lore and Gaelic singing, Highland dancing and hand weaving of clan and family tartans. During the first week of August the Gaelic Mod is a seven-day festival of Celtic culture and a gathering of the clans.

On campus, the Hall of Clans has visual displays on the history of the clans and tartans. One exhibit features Angus McAskill, a Scottish giant nearly eight feet tall who lived and died in St Ann's.

IF YOU GO: The Cabot Trail begins and ends just south of Baddeck, about 50 miles northeast of Port Hastings on Highway 105. To follow the clockwise route, turn onto the Trail to the left of the highway just north of Nyanza, where signposted.

THE MOTORHOME MODE

I can't think of a better way to tour this country—to smell it, feel it, taste it—than to travel by motorhome. Camping friends may sneer at the power-steering and on-board comforts that can include a home entertainment center, microwave oven, ice machine and even a wall safe if you can't leave home without one. But the reality is, had we tented our way through the Maritimes last year, preparing meals over open fires, setting up shop in different locales each day, we wouldn't have seen much more than campgrounds.

Motorhomes are for touring. The only similarity between this mode of travel and camping is that you carry your own shelter and usually park at a campground each night. Literally mobile homes, they allow you to travel with whatever home conveniences you want. Personally I love the freedom they afford. I like to pack just once for a two- or three-week trip. I like having my clothes hanging handily in a wardrobe, should I decide to get changed halfway through the day as mood and weather indicate. I prefer my cooking to the fast food of highway cafeterias, and I like being self-contained when it means passing up crowded public washrooms. I like spur-of-the-moment decisions to stay or move on, unfettered by hotel reservations. And I like the way these vehicles effortlessly gobble up the miles.

For families travelling with babies and young children there are untold advantages. Like the very old, the very young are happiest with their own things around them. Some even bring their pets.

Europeans are discovering Canada by motorhome as never before. Often they collect a vehicle in one province and drop it off in another. Several told us they were seeing Canada at a rate of one or two provinces per year. Good highways, clean cities, and the vastness of this land and beauty of our national parks are of tremendous appeal to them.

My first long trip by motorhome was with young children on a three-week Maritimes tour. It remains one of our favorite family vacations. Certainly it is one I recommend for novices inasmuch as the only boring day (when driving from Toronto) is the long haul between Quebec City and New Brunswick. After that there are exciting stops, ferry boat rides, beaches and an ocean to keep everybody happy.

Following a similar route last year, we chalked up another winner, totalling 3,502 miles in little more than two weeks. Our vehicle was a 24-foot motorhome from an Ontario dealer chosen for several reasons. One, we were assured our vehicle would be less than two years old. After a disastrous trip in a wreck of a rented motorhome the year before, this was important to us. We particularly liked the layout wherein a back bedroom could be curtained off. Not only is such privacy welcome when one person is resting and others require the lights up front, but it doubles as a changing room more spacious than the tiny bathroom. Also this dealership rents by the day, so we could have our motorhome for $2^1/_2$ weeks, and start the trip on a Wednesday which suited us better than the weekend.

It was a memorable trip. Our longest day's drive was the 435 miles between Quebec City and Caraquet, N.B. Our itinerary

Cape Breton fishing village

allowed for a full day in Quebec City. We explored two national parks and the re-created Acadian village in New Brunswick, drove Nova Scotia's magnificent Cabot Trail and toured Fortress Louisbourg. In Canada's smallest province we joined a deep-sea fishing charter, attended a traditional lobster supper, enjoyed the musical Anne of Green Gables for the umpteenth time and made the pilgrimage to Green Gables at Cavendish. We walked for miles on beaches and hiking trails, swam in the ocean that surprised us with its warmth, met some very nice Maritimers whose warmth didn't surprise us at all.

In mid-summer, height of the tourist season, we had no difficulty finding campsites. National park campgrounds tend to fill up by early afternoon. If our schedule called for a late arrival, we checked into a nearby commercial campground for the night and presented ourselves at the national park next morning.

Most campgrounds we stayed at provided fully serviced sites, meaning we could plug into their electricity, water outlet and if necessary air conditioning. When such services were not available we simply switched to the motorhome's batteries and propane supply. One of the pleasures of motorhome travel is that appliances, hot water heater, furnace and lights are operable without campground services. Average cost of a serviced campground site with picnic table and barbecue grill is $12 a day. Private parks lean toward swimming pools and recreation rooms. National and provincial parks are definitely more esthetic.

Our motorhome was designed to sleep four adults comfortably, or a family of five or six with small children. We had our own bathroom with tub, sink and toilet, and constant supply of hot water. Storage cupboards were so generous that we stocked up with staples from home, purchasing fruit and vegetables from farmers' stands along the way and fresh fish from the boats once we reached the coast. Most campgrounds have laundrettes and convenience stores.

Our motorhome cost $2,200 for 17 days' rental, including tax and insurance. We paid $745 for gasoline and propane. Tolls, ferries and national park permits were $50. Campsite fees totalled $175. In all we paid out CAN$3,200 plus museum admissions, food and personal items. Had we split expense between four friends, our motorhome vacation would have cost well under $1,000 per person, less during the shoulder or low seasons.

THE VERSATILE ALEXANDER GRAHAM BELL

Baddeck, Nova Scotia: It's a fascinating museum about a fascinating man, as it examines the awesome genius, scope and humanity of Alexander Graham Bell. Many places claim him as one of their own: Edinburgh where he was born in 1847; and Brantford the southern Ontario town from which he made the first long distance telephone call; Boston, where he was a teacher of the deaf; Baddeck, chosen for his summer home because it reminded him of Scotland.

At Baddeck, overlooking the scenic Bras d'Or Lakes, Bell lived at his estate called Beinn Bhreagh—Gaelic for "beautiful mountain." He and his wife Mabel are buried on the estate; their grandchildren continue to spend summers here. Bell and associates conducted many successful aeronautical experiments in this little town. Now these and others are spelled out in a most interesting fashion at the Alexander Graham Bell National Historic Park.

Countless exhibits illustrate Bell's lifelong commitment to speech therapy, and invention of the telephone. Its patent, No. 174,465, is displayed along with his pass to the U.S. Centennial Exposition in 1876, where he showed the world his Electric Telephone and Multiple Telegraph. That same year he founded Bell Telephone Company.

Bell first went to Boston in 1871 to teach in a school for deaf students. At night he worked with tuning forks, wires and magnets. His experiments with the transmission of sound by light beams were a forerunner of fiber optics and lasers. In Boston he first met his wife Mabel Gardiner Hubbard, who came to him as a deaf pupil at age 16. The couple had four children, two of whom died of respiratory disease soon after their births. This tragedy led Bell to develop the first form of iron lung, known as a vacuum jacket.

His research into speech therapy alone would have over-taxed most men, but not this one. He worked on production of drinking water from breath, fog and seawater, for use by sailors stranded at sea. At one time he attempted to breed perfect sheep.

Bell's aeronautical experiments are illustrated in the museum's movies, storyboards and exhibits. Soon after he moved to Baddeck around the turn of the century, he began conducting experiments that led to invention of various winged flying devices. He formed a group known as the Aerial Experiment Association, with leading American and Canadian scientists as members.

On a February morning in 1909, local member J. A. D. McCurdy piloted their Silver Dart above the frozen lake. At a height of 30 feet it flew for 90 seconds, making aviation history as the first airplane flight in the British Commonwealth. During the following month, the Silver Dart made some 30 more flights over Bras d'Or. Ten years later, another Bell invention, a cigar-shaped hydrofoil called the HD–4, put Baddeck under the international spotlight again by racing across the lake at a stunning speed of 70 miles per hour. It was a world record that stood for a decade.

The museum is laid out in sequence of Bell's life, starting with his childhood in Scotland where he recalls his earliest memory as being lost in a field near Edinburgh. We are told that in Brantford (Ontario) he applied his father's system of visible speech to learn the Mohawk language, becoming so fluent he was initiated into the Nation with full ceremony. Outstanding photographs on the mezzanine level were given Parks Canada by the National Geographic Society, of which Bell's father-in-law was a co-

ING

The second exhibit area, Bell the Experimenter, deals largely with Bell's work in the field of aviation and medical science. His widely used probe for metal detection led to an honorary doctorate in medicine from Heidelberg University. He also worked on the use of radium in cancer treatment years before its actual application. In the Hydrofoil Hall we are shown remains of the original cigar-shaped HD–4 hydrofoil, along with a full-sized replica as it was in 1919 after modifications.

The museum itself is architecturally striking, based on the tetrahedron form Bell used for his flight test kites. From its roof you can look out over the lakes and understand why this man chose to spend his last 35 summers here. On a clear day its beauty is haunting.

IF YOU GO: Located at the bottom of the Cabot Trail, Baddeck is an attractive community, and a good overnight stop before setting off on the trail. East of town on Highway 205, Alexander Graham Bell National Park is open daily throughout the year. Guides are on hand to answer questions between mid-May and mid-October. Admission is free.

LIFE AND TIMES IN NEW FRANCE

Louisbourg, Nova Scotia: When I was stopped for questioning at the Dauphin Gate, my French was a little lacking. Worse than that, I spoke English with an accent akin to that of a dastardly Briton. At first I was promised a spell in the jail, and told I wouldn't be grinning if I knew what it was like there. But then

the soldiers relented, and I was released into the French stronghold of the Fortress of Louisbourg for an interesting day in one of
Canada's finest re-created historic townsites.

Louisbourg was founded in 1713 as a maritime stronghold for
the French after the Treaty of Utrecht which saw Newfoundland
and Acadia ceded to the British. It was demolished in 1760 at the
end of France's military power in North America, and reconstruction by Parks Canada started in 1961 based upon archeological
investigation and extensive records. The re-creation illustrates
life in the town during summer of 1744. Although only a third of
the original community has been rebuilt, it leaves you with a
lasting impression of those times.

Military and government officials set the tone of everyday life,
in what was originally a very busy town. Nearby fishing banks
and an ice-free harbor were inducements for settlers. It was a
major port of call on the sea lanes between France, Canada, New
England and the West Indies. Ambitious merchants used the ad-
vantageous location to develop a trading center which ranked
third in North America after Boston and Philadelphia. Curren-
cies of many nations changed hands in well-stocked shops; along
the quay the inns resounded with voices of sailors from many
nations.

Now employees dressed as townspeople and soldiers represent
those who actually lived here in 1744, the only noticeable differences being that today's "residents" are bilingual. Visitors are
encouraged to talk to them and learn about their day-to-day
lives. Officers and men of the French army, colonial officials, sailors, clerks, merchants and fishermen from Newfoundland made
up most of the population. Tradespeople and innkeepers found a
ready market for their services. By the 1740s, 2,000 people lived
at Louisbourg, with more in adjoining outports.

Every spring, fleets of Basques, Bretons and Normans came to
join the fishermen. One of the first houses we enter belongs to
the enterprising fisherman-owner, George Des Roches. His house
and garden, and fish flakes for holding drying cod, are typical of
their time. Not so typical is George, who at 28 married a 69-year-
old widow in order to get her house. When she died he turned
part of it into a tavern.

Sentries at Louisbourg

George tells me his boat is an open shallop capable of holding 3,000 pounds of codfish. And that 30 million pounds of salted cod are exported annually from Louisbourg, its value being two or three times that of Quebec's fur trade.

Some of the fort's citizens are as entertaining as they are informative. In the Royal Storehouse a rueful Basque fisherman is doing a few odd jobs. Looking down on his luck, he explains in French how his boss had sent him out to fish and it was a little boring jigging the line, oui? He happened to have a bottle of rum with him, so went on a "merrigot" with his friends. His story that the fish weren't biting didn't hold water, because other boats returned with a better-than-usual catch. Now he has no credit, no place to live and his belongings have been confiscated. His only hope is to make a deal with a ship's captain to work his passage back to France. Meantime, he works in the storehouse to pay for some food.

There are several such characters in town. One disreputable man, missing his front teeth, tries to sell me his bread ration so he can buy rum. Then there is the elegantly coiffeured merchant in his office-living room enjoying a glass of wine. A little plaintive in his views of life in Louisbourg, he complains there is nothing to do in the evenings other than play cards or cribbage. He wants me to know that he does not drink the common man's spruce beer, inasmuch as he imports brandy and wine from France.

Watching the comings and goings from the merchant's front porch, a sea captain comments that he is very proud of the town's importance as a seaport. Although he is originally from France, he regards Louisbourg as his home. His ship takes codfish to Guadaloupe and Martinique, returning with sugar, cocoa, rum, cotton and coffee. It is a good life, he says, even though he is nowhere near as wealthy as the town's 36 merchants.

Clothes are key to the social scale at Louisbourg. Merchants and their families are decked out in beautiful brocade and silk and fine lace, enhanced by expensive European accessories. Property owners are well dressed, too. Servants and tradespeople who would have made their own clothing in the original fortress are dressed in coarse durable clothes. As at the first fortress, a lot of skills go into the dressing of its citizens.

The Citadel, once seat of government, is in a walled compound. Information about it is relayed via wall telephones in various rooms. Here both civilians and soldiers worshipped in the rather spartan military chapel. Several officers and two governors were buried beneath the floorboards. The body of Governor Duquesnel, who died here in 1744, was exhumed more than 200 years later showing he had suffered from abscessed teeth, arthritis, arteriosclerosis and other miseries. Officers lived in fair comfort in houses around town, but soldiers were so cramped in their citadel quarters (12 to 16 per room, two to a bed) one wonders how they managed to sleep at all.

Taverns serve traditional dinners and snacks. My hefty meal of sausage, carrots, cabbage and bread pudding with custard came to less than $10. One large spoon is the only cutlery provided. If you want a knife, you must bring your own, as did the soldiers and other patrons of taverns in the 18th century Fortress of Louisbourg.

IF YOU GO: Allow several hours so you can stop and talk to residents who are very convincing in the roles they play. Fortress of Louisbourg National Historic Park, Louisbourg, Cape Breton, Nova Scotia, is 290 miles from Halifax and 22 miles south of Sydney on Highway 22. Hours of operation are from 10 a.m. to 6 p.m., June and September, 9 a.m. to 7 p.m. in July and August. There is a modest admission charge.

PRINCE EDWARD ISLAND

If you believe the best things in life come in little packages, you will love Canada's smallest province. Separated from the mainland by the Northumberland Strait, this is considered the Birthplace of Canada. MicMac Indians knew it as Abegweit, or Land Cradled in the Waves. Upon discovering it for France in 1534, explorer Jacques Cartier described the island as "the fairest land 'tis possible to see." And for most people who flock here in summer prime attractions are beaches that seem to stretch forever, an ocean claimed as the warmest north of Florida and Anne of Green Gables.

Agriculture is the prime contributor to island coffers. Farms resemble miniatures such as we had as kids, the sort with red barns and white wooden houses, black and white cows at the trough, ducks on mirror ponds. The main crop is potatoes. Drive through the countryside and you will be struck by the depth of color: the brilliant green meadows and dark green of potato plants against brick red soil. The second largest industry is commercial fishing. Local lobsters, oysters and clams are the greatest.

The island's most famous character is a red-haired freckle-faced orphan who continues to win the hearts of new fans more than 80 years after she first burst on the scene. Cavendish, located within the national park, is author Lucy Maude Montgomery's Avonlea. Sent to live with her grandparents as a child, she visited elderly cousins in what we know as Green Gables. Now a museum, the green and white farmhouse is everything you want it to be—comfortably cosy, set in picturesque gardens close to Anne's haunted woods and Lover's Lane.

Crescent shaped, with the capital Charlottetown a little east of the center, the island has three scenic drives mapped out on brochures provided by the tourist office, and recognized en route by color coded signs. Lady Slipper Drive is described on pages 56–59.

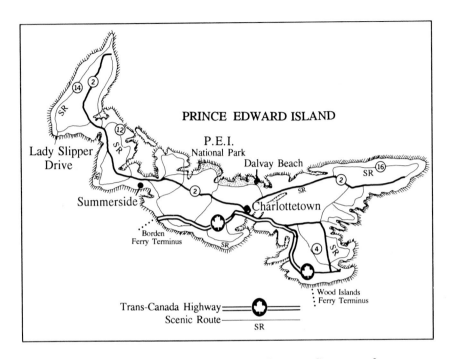

Blue Heron Drive (120 miles) around Queens County takes you into the national park, past the north shore's mile upon mile of beaches, an 18-hole golf course and Green Gables. Kings Byway (235 miles) to the east, leads to high red cliffs and golden beaches, a fisheries museum and prosperous looking farms.

Charlottetown is known as the Cradle of Confederation since the 1864 conference here resulted in formation of the Dominion of Canada three years later. (Ironically PEI didn't join until 1873.) Now the Confederation Center of the Arts commemorates that important occasion. As part of the center's annual summer festival the musical, Anne of Green Gables has been a winner since its first performance 26 years ago.

The 1864 conference took place in neighboring Province House, where the second floor Confederation Chamber is furnished to period. The city's old sector has handsomely restored buildings housing specialty shops and restaurants. The 40-acre waterfront Victoria Park is an oasis on a warm evening.

Island entertainment runs the gamut from sophisticated musi-cals in the Confederation Center to homespun festivals and tradi-tional lobster suppers. Recreated communities represent MicMac Indians, Acadians and pioneers.

If all this isn't enough you can gather oysters, learn to wind-surf, study the life cycle of the oyster, go fishing, watch harness racing, take a tour in a double decker bus. Try some roller skat-ing, watch the stars at the university's planetarium, take the kids to Fairyland. Still, when all is said and done, on the sunny days you will want to do no more than pack a picnic and head for those sensational beaches.

Two ferry services operate between Prince Edward Island and mainland Canada. Marine Atlantic sails between Cape Tourmen-tine (New Brunswick) and Borden (PEI). Northumberland Ferries crosses between Caribou (Nova Scotia) and Wood Islands (PEI). Reservations are not necessary, but do get to the terminal early in the summer. For ferry times telephone 1–800–565–9470. Is-land information is available from Visitor Services, P.O. Box 940, Charlottetown, PEI, C1A 7M5. Telephone: 902–368–4444. Or toll free numbers: from the Maritimes, 1–800–565–7421 in summer; from Ontario, Quebec and Newfoundland 1–800–565–0267; from eastern USA 1–800–565–9060.

CHARLOTTETOWN, BIRTHPLACE OF CANADA

Charlottetown, Prince Edward Island: This is where it all began—the courting of maritime colonies by Upper and Lower Canada that resulted in the union, and ultimate birth of one

Canada. The year was 1864, the event a five day conference to put forward proposals for confederation. Originally governments of Nova Scotia, New Brunswick and Prince Edward Island had planned to meet in Charlottetown to discuss unification of their colonies. Then Ontario, and Quebec asked to attend, bringing proposals for a united British North America. For the 23 delegates gathered in Province House, it must have been a gruelling week, arriving at history-making decisions by day, attending a constant round of parties at night. (Upper Canada's Prime Minister John A. Macdonald reputedly brought champagne valued at $13,000 to assist his cause.) Proposals, basically agreed upon in Charlottetown that September, were finalised at conferences in Quebec a month later, and London in 1866. On July 1 1867, as every Canadian schoolchild knows, the Dominion of Canada was born.

Charlottetown's visitors can learn more about these Fathers of Confederation, and events leading to the unification, at a slide show presented in historic Province House. Handsomely restored to its original appearance, the building has some offices furnished to the 1850s. Most impressive is the elegant Legislative Council Chamber, in which tables and chairs are those used by the 1864 delegates. A close second is the Lieutenant Governor's office.

Charlottetown was established approximately 100 years before that famous conference. Under the French, Port La Joie had been the island capital. When the British took over, they chose this new site for its safe harbor, and named their new town in honor of Queen Charlotte, In 1768 the deputy chief surveyor for Nova Scotia, Charles Morris, arrived to lay out the town's streets. It is his original grid plan with broad parallel streets, that makes it so easy for strangers to find their way around the city today.

A walking tour of Charlottetown is described in a pamphlet distributed by P. E. I. Tourism. More comprehensive descriptions of historic buildings are contained in a little green book, Walks in Charlottetown, by Irene Rogers, available in local bookstores. This author not only suggests two routes but gives such detailed accounts of the original owners and tenants of 19th-century homes along the way, you almost expect them to be standing in the doorways.

More pleasant walking is promised in Victoria Park which at 40 acres is the city's largest park. In addition to sports facilities, and walking paths, an open-air bandshell provides an enjoyable setting for summer church services and concerts.

It's my guess that most vacationers stay close to island beaches, and come into town once in a while, perhaps when it rains. If that's the case, you may not get to wander about the waterfront area, but do at least find time for the two main buildings in Confederation Square. On this former market place, the aforementioned Province House offers guided tours for visitors. Before the building was completed in 1847, politicians met first in taverns and private homes, and then in a small courthouse here in the square. In 1839 an architectural competition was held throughout the Maritimes. It was won by a Yorkshire-born man, Isaac Smith, whose proposals were for this three-storied building which would become a showplace for social functions as well as a political arena.

Dominating the square is the Confederation Centre of the Arts, opened by Queen Elizabeth II in 1964 to commemorate the Charlottetown Conference's centennial. Its Memorial Hall exhibits documentation on the conference and confederation, and a model of the s. s. *Queen Victoria* which carried delegates to Quebec for the second conference in October 1864. The art gallery has a large and interesting permanent collection, as well as travelling exhibits. Still, for most visitors, the Confederation Center means the Festival Theater, home of that perennial favorite production, Anne of Green Gables. Choreographed as a musical by Allan and Blanche Lund, the ever-popular Anne was first presented here over two decades ago and has played to full houses ever since.

Because this was primarily a city of wooden buildings in the 19th century, fires were disastrous, often wiping out whole streets. Pownall Street in central Charlottetown was completely destroyed by fire in 1866, and rebuilt soon after. Local businessman Parker Carvell built a very comfortable family home at 200 Pownall in 1903. Later converted to a guest house, it has more recently been lovingly restored and furnished to period, and is now known as the Dundee Arms Inn. Rooms are tastefully decorated and furnished to the early 1900s yet equipped with ensuite baths, television and telephones.

The inn's Griffon Room is generally acknowledged as one of Canada's finest restaurants. Theatre-goers are served early here, so they can stroll over to the Confederation Centre by curtain time. As you might expect, the menu includes lots of delectable seafood dishes. I can tell you first hand that the lobster pie is fantastic. So is the snow crab in mornay sauce—and the chocolate Cointreau mousse—and the grasshopper pie. In fact, anyone in town without theatre tickets can still have a lovely evening, over an unhurried meal in the Griffon Room with after dinner drinks in the adjoining Hearth and Cricket pub.

IF YOU GO: The Dundee Arms Inn is at 200, Pownall Street, Charlottetown, P. E. I. CIA 3W8, telephone 902–892–2496.

THE SHORES OF RELAXATION— P. E. I. STYLE

"Compressed by the inviolate sea, it floats on waves of the blue gulf, a green seclusion and haunt of ancient peace."

Lucy Maude Montgomery, writing of P. E. I.

Prince Edward Island National Park: It isn't the largest or the oldest park in our system, but Prince Edward Island National Park, hugging the tiny province's north shore is certainly one of the most popular. While European farmers settled this coast as early as 1777, and vacationers discovered its wonderful beaches a century later, it wasn't until 1937 that 13 square miles along the Gulf of St Lawrence were contained in a national preserve. Its purpose, as every visitor will appreciate, is to protect the delicate sand dunes, red sandstone cliffs already in danger of crumbling, marshlands home of so many bird species, natural ponds and some of Canada's finest sand beaches.

There is no real hub to the park, no main town with shops and restaurants clustered around country club amenities. Nor is any needed, because all along the coast you will find vacation and leisure facilities. It is a place where big-city people can wash away a year's accumulated stress, and retirees enjoy leisurely summers. Families love it because there is plenty to do. In good

North shore, Prince Edward Island

weather the beaches are heaven blessed (some have wash and change rooms, snack bars and lifeguards.) If it rains, shops, museums, restaurants and theatres are only 15 miles away, in the tiny provincial capital of Charlottetown.

The park has something for everyone. Accommodation runs the gamut from campgrounds and cottages to a gracious old hotel where some guests have been returning every summer for thirty years. There are fish to catch and birds to watch, golf and tennis and windsurfing for the energetic. You can find a quiet cove for your picnic lunch, or eat at a wooden table in a busy harbor. Drive through a landscape so colorful it looks unreal, and past ocean views that exhaust your film supply in no time at all.

Nature enthusiasts have a lovely time. Many are retired people, here for the season. Bronzed and fit, they stride along the beaches and cycle the seafront for pleasure and exercise. They set up easels and paint the scenery, buy food supplies direct from farmers and fishermen, form their own hiking and nature study groups and are regulars at park interpretive programs.

Every national park has interpretive programs designed to illustrate its special features. On Prince Edward Island we learn a lot about the sand and sea. An evening slide show at Stanhope proved disappointing, because of its amateurish presentation and pictures. On the other hand beach hikes and campfires were enthusiastically attended. At a talk on sand dunes we learned about a wide variety of wildlife they support. Seafood cooking demonstrations, given by staff of the Provincial Department of Fisheries at both Stanhope and Cavendish campgrounds, are as useful as they are entertaining.

One fine morning I joined bird lovers at a wetland marsh area where park personnel arrived with tripod-mounted telescopes so we could study some of the 200 bird species inhabiting this region. Several great blue herons were obligingly close, majestic creatures standing motionless, knee-deep in water, waiting for their lunch to swim by. We didn't see the elusive piping plovers, and didn't really expect to. The park has an estimated 25 pairs which is two percent of the world population. Most years fewer than 15 percent of their eggs survive to maturity here, and so intense is a program to preserve the species, beaches where they nest may be closed during the breeding season.

I found myself wandering about Covehead harbor most days, usually to buy cod fresh from the boats, and to watch leisure fishermen return triumphant. On an afternoon when the sea was particularly calm, we joined six others for a fishing excursion (four hours, $15 a person) and came home with a respectable haul of cod and mackerel. Fellow passengers who had no means of cooking their catch gave us more, so we had three or four dinners in our motorhome freezer when we eventually left the island. Deep sea fishing jaunts, scenic boat rides and even seal watching are popular with visitors all around the coast. Rods and tackle

Green Gables

are provided. Skippers have a saint-like patience with novices who tangle their lines.

Of the park's three main regions Cavendish is most popular for its 18 hole golf course, grand beach and Green Gables—home of that ever-popular red-haired, freckle-faced orphan Anne. The 19th-century wooden farmhouse, sparkling white with green trim, was originally owned by elderly cousins of author Lucy Maude Montgomery. Rooms are furnished according to descriptions in Anne of Green Gables, since visitors want to believe she actually lived here. In mid-July, height of the tourist season, I sat on the grass outside waiting for a line-up at its front door to shorten, only to see it grow as one busload of tourists after another arrived.

If you are staying in the park, a better bet is to join an interpretive walk covering Anne's favorite haunts. At the Cavendish cemetery Lucy Maude Montgomery's remains are buried in a plot she selected, "because it overlooks the spots I always loved, the pond, the shore, the sand dunes and the harbor."

There is no disputing Anne's success since she burst into the world eight decades ago. The book is translated into 17 languages. Plays, films and TV shows are based upon the story; a musical in Charlottetown is deservedly sold out every summer. Less publicized events, also traditional to the island, can be worthwhile. Ask at any tourist information center whether a scallop, blueberry or potato blossom festival is scheduled during your visit. Or join a lively *ceildidh,* held weekly at Orwell Corner Historic Village.

Lobster suppers have become an island tradition since the first was held as a church fund raiser in 1964. By now the suppers have outgrown volunteer cooks and waitresses, but the downhome atmosphere prevails. Even at St Ann's where the licensed restaurant serves close to 300 customers on an average summer's evening. Cost is about $18 for a full dinner. That's for a one pound lobster (chops and steaks are also available), with juices, mussels, salads, and assorted homemade desserts. Seconds of everything except the entrees are offered. At our table comment cards read "excellent value for visitors", "typical island hospitality," and "will definitely be back." The same could be written about Prince Edward Island.

IF YOU GO: Prince Edward Island National Park is between 35 and 50 miles from the Borden ferry terminal, depending on your destination, via Highways 1 and 15. For more information on the park, write to the Superintendent, c/o P.O. Box 487, Charlottetown, P. E. I. C1A 7L1, telephone 902–672–2211.

DALVAY-BY-THE-SEA

Little York, Prince Edward Island: I have just the place for a Murder Mystery Weekend. When the organizers are through with Northern Ontario's Minaki Lodge, Toronto's Casa Loma and the Orient Express, I urge them to take a look at Dalvay-by-the-Sea, an imposing summer hotel on the north shore of Prince Edward Island. The rain lashes at my windows, and the wind howls, and I hear scuffling outside my door when there is nobody there. Beyond the wind-bent trees and flowers, the sea heaves and retches like a woman with morning sickness. Indoors and out, during a storm, a spookier place would be hard to find.

Converted to a hotel some 60 years ago, Dalvay-by-the-Sea was built as a summer cottage in 1895. The entrance is magnificent, its broad staircase leading to 26 guest rooms along two upper galleries. Public rooms are lavishly panelled in polished maple. Almost everywhere you look there's gleaming wood—the walls, ceilings, doors, and floor where not covered by bright red carpeting. Exception is the lounge, very light in contrast to everything else, because its walls are plastered and painted in refreshingly delicate pink.

One of the island's most interesting dwellings, Dalvay was built by businessman Alexander MacDonald (vice president of Standard Oil and partner to John Rockefeller), who emigrated

Dalvay-by-the-Sea

from Scotland to Ohio. While vacationing on Prince Edward Island with his two little grand-daughters, he decided to build a sumptuous summer place here, and named it for his former Scottish home.

They must have been idyllic times for the family and their invited friends. The home was furnished with expensive imports from all over the world. They entertained in a grand manner, and at the end of each season held a dance for their servants and the local tradespeople. They kept horses for sport as well as transportation, and several different types of carriages and coaches.

It still resembles a wealthy family's summer home. Enormous armchairs are placed cosily around fireplaces in both entrance hall and lounge. Log fires burn there, and in the dining room. Shelves are stocked with books for every taste. Parlor games are left out on side tables.

Cheerful students serve in the dining room, where meals are tasty enough though not spectacular. For resident guests, breakfast and dinner are included in the rent. When I was here we had a choice of shrimp cocktail, marinated mushrooms, cold fruit soup or a hearty leek and potato. Entrees included beef, turkey and fillet of sole in wine sauce, followed by trifle sorbet and baba desserts. Dalvay seems a popular dining spot for islanders and their guests so, unless you are staying here, reservations are essential.

Recreational facilities are pretty much the same as when it was a private estate: tennis courts, a lawn bowling green, canoes and boats on the private lake. Manicured lawns surrounding flower beds are studded with tall trees, beneath which you could happily spend an hour or two. And of course there's the beach, broad and long and smooth, some 200 yards from the hotel.

Guests come often to Dalvay for the entire summer, booking for next year before they leave. My room here is large and well furnished, with bay windows facing the sea. Accommodation in the main hotel consists of twin and single bedded rooms and meal plans include breakfast and dinner. Rent this summer will be $150 to $260 per couple in a twin room with private bath, breakfast and dinner included. Single rooms with two meals are $115 per day. There are also two attractive cottages, one of which was built for wartime Field-Marshall Viscount Alexander, the last British Governor General of Canada.

IF YOU GO: Dalvay-by-the-Sea is open in summer only. From Charlottetown, take Highway 2 north for six miles and turn left on Highway 6 to the hotel. Address is Dalvay-by-the-Sea, P.O. Box 8, Little York, P E I, C0A 1P0, telephone 902–672–2048 in summer, 902–672–2546 in winter.

LADY SLIPPER DRIVE

Summerside, Prince Edward Island: If there comes a time when you feel the need to escape Green Gables, Matthew's Market, Marilla's Pizza, Anne's Tea Room and assorted kindred spirits scattered in and around Cavendish, you could be ready for the Lady Slipper Scenic Drive on the quieter western part of the island. Starting and finishing in Summerside, it will take you for 180 miles past some of the province's most productive potato fields, lovely little fishing villages, provincial parks, uncrowded beaches and coves sheltered by high red cliffs.

You will learn something of island history you probably didn't know before, encountering industries and cultures pertinent to the region. The direction you travel is unimportant. Either way you will drive a figure eight, marked by signs bearing the island's floral emblem of a delicate pink Lady Slipper Orchid.

Before setting off, do call into the information center at Wilmot, a mile or so east of Summerside on Route 11. Here you can preview the drive's highlights through photographs, artifacts and storyboards, and pick up your easy-to-follow brochure detailing the route.

Almost immediately on leaving Summerside, we are into country where tall trees line the roadside and rich green leaves of potato plants on brick-red soil stretch to meet the sky. Introduced by settlers in the late 1700s, high quality potatoes thrive in the island's temperate climate. And now, 30,000 acres here in Prince County produce half of the province's renowned crop.

As we reach the coast, scenery changes. Now we are into Acadia's French speaking communities such as Mont Carmel and Cap Egmont where great twin-spired churches look disproportionate in size to the towns they serve, and headstones in cemeteries often appear larger than houses passed along the way. Throughout the Atlantic provinces we have come upon Acadians, striving to keep their culture and traditions alive. When their ancestors arrived two centuries ago this was Ile St-Jean, named by French explorer Jacques Cartier in 1534. When the British took over, they called it the Island of Saint John and later renamed it for their own Prince Edward. All who wouldn't pledge loyalty to the crown were expelled. Some took to the woods, others left the country, but gradually they came back. At this time approximately 15,000 Acadians live in fishing communities around this part of the coast. Several work in the recreated village representing 19th-century Acadia, three miles beyond Mont Carmel.

Reaching the pioneer village around 11:30 on a weekday morning we found little happening, but were told that between 1 and 4 p.m. costumed interpreters are on hand to explain life in early Acadia. Meantime we could tour the buildings and read descriptive plaques (in French). Last year a hotel opened on the property. Bicycles are available for leisurely rides to neighboring communities. The village's award-winning restaurant serves local seafood, super-fresh of course, as well as traditional Acadian dishes. In the adjoining bar-lounge, I understand, nightfall brings Acadian style entertainment.

Provincial parks along the west coast are among the island's finest, usually with beach frontage and recreational facilities, and at least one has a hotel. Photographers will find themselves stopping often along these shores. At West Point, for the century-old lighthouse that continues to guide freighters past the headland. And at Cape Wolfe, named for Britain's General James Wolfe who stopped off on his way to Quebec where he defeated the French, and so changed the face of Canada.

On these shores farmers and fishermen gather Irish moss, the purplish seaweed tossed loose by wind and waves. I didn't see any, but that doesn't mean you won't, as they load their harvest onto horse-drawn carts or tractor-pulled trailers to transport it to drying plants. (Carrageenin, an emulsifier extracted from the moss, is used in the manufacture of toothpaste, ice cream, wine and cough syrup, among other things.) According to my guidebook, almost half the world's supply of Irish moss is derived from Prince Edward Island.

North Cape, meeting place for Gulf of St Lawrence tides and those of the Northumberland Strait, is the island's most northerly point. From this windswept corner our homeward journey is past jagged red cliffs shaped by the sea, and more delightful provincial parks. At Alberton a 19th-century courthouse has become a folk museum telling of farm life in that era. Additional exhibits tell of the island's Micmac Indians, and the silver fox industry which prospered here until the 1930s.

Biggest surprise for me is Green Park Provincial Park, not for its campgrounds, beach frontage and pleasant parkland for day visitors because I have come to expect these things of Prince County, but for its commentary on the island's shipbuilding industry I knew nothing about. At one time, because the region's wooded lands were considered an impediment to settlers, trees were cut down and the lumber sent to Britain's shipbuilders. Almost every type of wood was useful: birch, beech and maple where strength was required, softwoods such as pine and spruce for hull planking, decks and masts.

Yeo house

The original French settlers carved their fishing boats from island timbers of course, but really P.E.I.'s shipbuilding industry began in 1818 when master shipwright William Ellis and two young helpers arrived from England to set up shop. In the modern interpretive center now, plans, tools and models of ships built in their yards are displayed. In 34 years from 1830, close to two and a half thousand ships were built and launched at these yards—an average of 70 a year. The island's most successful shipbuilder perhaps was James Yeo. Arriving from Cornwall in 1819, he was soon one of the island's wealthiest men. His son did even better as a banker, farmer, property owner with 20,000 acres, lumber baron, owner of 20 ships at sea, and member of the provincial legislature. As well as the museum and interpretive center, a shipyard has been recreated down by the river, and James Yeo Jr.'s comfortable home is open to the public.

A widow's walk in the James Yeo Jr. house affords a good view of neighboring Malpeque Bay, our final stop on the tour. This is home to the succulent Malpeque oysters, which all but disappeared from the bay in the early 1900s because of a deadly disease. Then in a rather unbelievable turn of events, the oysters developed an immunity to the killer and began to re-populate. Now, 10 million are harvested annually through modern techniques at Malpeque farms.

Throughout this drive you will be tempted by attractive little restaurants, canteens serving freshly caught fish to be eaten at picnic tables on the wharf, quiet and cosy dining rooms in former private homes.

We made two stops, one at the Acadian Village for a snack, and a second for a late lunch in Tyne Valley at the Studio and Tea Room. Lobster rolls, bread with wildflower honey, cheeses, gingerbread carrot cake, fruit pies, herb teas and cider are all made on the premises. As are sweaters, candles, preserves and pottery in the gift shop. Next door, the Doctor's Inn looks most inviting. Like the valley, it smacks of a gentler era that is very appealing today.

IF YOU GO: Summerside, the start of the Lady Slipper Drive, is 17 miles west of the Borden ferry terminal, and 45 miles from Charlottetown, but longer if you follow the coast along the equally scenic and interesting Blue Heron Drive.

THE ISLAND'S SMALL INNS

Summerside, Prince Edward Island: For a province this small (139 miles long by 3½ to 40 miles wide), Prince Edward Island has a surprising variety of vacation accommodation. If junior believes that milk grows in bottles and potatoes in sacks, a farm stay can be an enjoyable learning experience. Island campgrounds offer resort facilities along with fully serviced sites within steps of golden beaches. Rental cottages hug prime beach frontage in the national park. Large homes have been converted to gracious inns, some of which are as luxurious as Britain's country house hotels yet offer rooms at motel prices.

On this visit I elected to stay at three inns, chosen partly for their locations, and took a new look at this island I thought I knew so well.

Silver Fox Inn, Summerside. Often referred to as the island's western capital, Summerside on the south coast has a population of 8,000. A 15-minute drive from the Borden ferry, it hosts an annual lobster carnival in July, numerous sports events and excellent lobster suppers. My home here was Silver Fox Inn, built in 1892 as a private residence for a local judge, and later sold to a farmer whose sudden wealth came from the breeding of silver foxes. Owner Julie Simmons lived in the neighborhood for years before moving to Montreal and Halifax. Regaled by her father's stories about the silver foxes, she decided to name her inn for them.

The capacious home was designed by architect William Critchlow Harris, responsible for many such dwellings on the island around the turn of the century. (His artist brother gained even more fame with his Fathers of Confederation painting hanging in the Charlottetown Confederation Center.)

The inn provides warm hospitality for 12 guests in six large rooms, each with ensuite bath, and furnished to period. Mine is an elegant room with a double and single bed, desk and bureau and comfortable chairs in front of the window looking out on a secluded residential street. Both lounge and dining room are also furnished to period, with pieces from Julie's family and others gleaned at sales and auctions. Breakfast—homemade muffins and breads, juice, cereal, tea or coffee—is set out on the best of china. It is all graciously presented.

In Summerside I had a grand time pottering about the harbor, museums and shops a short walk from Silver Fox Inn, in an area of great old buildings included in a printed walking guide of Summerside. The one-day Lady Slipper Drive tour starts and ends in Summerside. And if you are wondering about yellow ribbons tied to car aerials, trees and lamp-posts, they are to remind us that the local armed forces base has been ordered closed, resulting in a loss of over 1,300 jobs.

Silver Fox Inn is open all year round. Rent is $53 double, $48 single. For more information and reservations, contact Julie Simmons, Innkeeper, 61 Granville St., Summerside C1N 2Z3, telephone 902-436-4033.

Strathgartney Country Inn, Bonshaw. Roughly half way between the Borden ferry terminus and Charlottetown, this heritage farmhouse has been home to five generations of the Stewart family originating from Scotland. Built in 1842 it isn't difficult to visualize it as a family homestead which friends would visit by boat from Charlottetown then horse and buggy from the dock. In 1961 the home became a museum, and later an inn. More recently Gerry and Martha Gabriel purchased the property stripped of fixtures and furnishings, and devoted themselves to its authentic restoration. Now Strathgartney has eight bedrooms in the main house. I was lodged in the carriage house, where Gerry was putting finishing touches to four new bedrooms each with ensuite bath.

The guest lounge and dining room are reminiscent of times when this was a comfortable farm house. During July and August dinner is served in the licensed dining room. There isn't a great selection, but food is fresh and service friendly. Gerry cooks the muffins and breads for breakfast, spiking the jam with cognac so you start the day right. Although open only a couple of seasons, the Gabriels already have guests booking from one year to the next. The inn's workshops in creative writing, photography, painting, island music and folklore and nature appreciation are popular weekend and week-long sessions. Whether you join a group or not, the 320 acre property offers great potential for artists.

For me this was a chance to discover neighboring Victoria, described by Gerry as "an atmosphere, the essence of the island rather than a tourist attraction." Certainly it is a picturesque little community, with a good summer theatre, handicrafts, antiques and hand-dipped chocolates sold in tiny shops. A seafood restaurant on the wharf offers lobsters packed for travel.

For more information, contact Gerry or Martha Gabriel, Strathgartney Country Inn, Bonshaw, R.R. #3, C0A 1C0, telephone 902-675-4711. The inn is open June 1 to October. Rates for B & B are $42 per double room with shared bath, $55 with bath ensuite.

Elmwood guest house

Elmwood, Charlottetown. In an exclusive residential area within walking distance of the provincial capital's downtown, this is exceptional accommodation provided by Jay and Carol MacDonald in a century-old home built for shipowner Samuel Cunard's son-in-law and, like the Silver Fox Inn, designed by William Harris. Originally set in seven and a half acres, the house took its name for 71 elm trees planted here. Today the grounds are reduced to a park-like one acre and 38 of those original elms still stand.

The MacDonalds purchased Elmwood as a home five years ago and set about restoring one guest room for visiting friends. But then a local friend who has a B & B sent them her overflow and they found themselves with paying guests all summer. Now the second floor, with its own entrance, has two suites and one double room around a bright comfortable lounge. (Since the suites have their own sitting areas, guests in the double room usually have the lounge to themselves.) My double room is handsomely furnished with a queen sized bed, antique desk and bureau, wing backed chairs and ensuite bath. One of the suites has a queen sized bed, sitting area and bath plus a single bedroom for a third person. The second suite is more like a cottage, with living room, bed, bath and full kitchen. A sumptuous breakfast is served in the dining room. Fruit, freshly squeezed juice, muffins and breads (three types of cream and milk for the diet conscious) are served on family silver and china.

Best of all I can walk into town, to restaurants and shops, to the Confederation Center for the Arts, the historic area and the rest. I walked to the theater for a performance of Anne of Green Gables (celebrating a quarter of a century this year), lunched on fresh lobster on the waterfront, and dined in historic restaurants come nightfall.

B & B for the double room is $75, in the two-bedroom suite $95 for two people, $105 for three. Rent for the self-catering suite is the same. Both suites have fireplaces, handmade quilts and period furniture. For more information and reservations contact Jay and Carol MacDonald, Elmwood, P.O. Box 3128, Charlottetown, P.E.I. C1A 7N8, telephone 902-368-3310.

IF YOU GO: The Prince Edward Island Department of Tourism will send you booklets on all accommodation, festivals and events, theater, parks, and anything else to help you plan your vacation on their favorite island.

SILVER FOXES OF P.E.I.

Summerside, Prince Edward Island: Have you heard the one about the little foxes? Perhaps you know about the phenomenal success of certain board games for their Canadian inventors. And the rags to riches tales of 19th-century adventurers in Canada's northwest are legend. But if you haven't heard about the silver foxes that brought fame and fortune to a wily group of dirt-poor farmers here on Prince Edward Island, do lend an ear . . .

It began in 1894 when islanders Charles Dalton and his partner Robert Oulton decided to breed foxes. Their experience as trappers taught them that a litter of wild red foxes occasionally produced a silver-black cub. They also knew such a pelt would fetch $100 in London, when beaver skins were selling for $2.50 apiece. But to breed the little beauties wasn't a simple matter.

Some 20 years earlier the island's first pair of black foxes used for breeding in captivity were dug out of the ground by a New Brunswick fisherman and sold to an islander for $3.25 and one cow. The new owner kept them on Charles Dalton's farm, and while Dalton got them to breed, the resultant litters were all crosses. Over the next few years Dalton acquired more silver foxes, and some did mate, but the cubs weren't good enough to start an industry. When they ceased to breed, Dalton decided he must re-create their natural environment. Enter Robert Oulton, a fishing and hunting buddy who lived on a fairly isolated part of the island. Together they replicated red fox dens in hollow pine logs, and proceeded to breed large litters of healthy silver fox cubs year after year.

In 1900 one of their silver fox pelts sold for $1,807 in London, by which time Prince Edward Island fox furs had become a symbol of high fashion. For 10 years the two men shared the secret of their successful methods, and the breeding foxes, with only four neighbors. It was agreed that they and their heirs would sell only the furs, and never the live foxes. Then, in a serious breach of pledge, one of the six sold a couple of foxes to his ambitious nephew. He in turn sold two pairs, for $5,000 a pair, to merchant Robert Holman.

The flood gates had been opened. One of the six originals took his breeding foxes to Europe for sale. At home, island farmers mortgaged farms and homes and anything else of value for a single share in a breeding fox. These were people used to selling eggs at eight cents a dozen and hogs for four cents a pound, now engaged in an industry in which a top breeding fox could fetch up to $20,000. In the year 1910 the Dalton and Oulton pelt harvest of 25 skins brought a total of $35,000. That's an average of $1,400 a pelt when a hired hand earned $27 a month. $26,000 was offered, and refused, for "Sir Charles", the famous sire of the Oulton and Doulton partnership.

During the 1920s it was commonplace to see buyers from London and New York making deals with fox farmers on Summerside's Water Street. It remains a community where tree-shaded sidewalks are lined with capacious old houses, built by fox farmers while the rest of the country struggled through the Depression years. Within a short time of buying into the industry, fox breeders of formerly modest means owned 14 room houses with spacious bathrooms and electrical wiring—30 years before the public utility reached rural Prince Edward Island! Many of these homes were designed with upper verandahs supported by Doric columns, a style that told the world they were built with fox money.

One such house, originally owned by breeder and merchant Robert Holman, has become the International Fox Hall of Fame. Established by the Greater Summerside Chamber of Commerce, and opened in 1987, it tells its story through displays of farming artifacts, ranchers' portraits, pictures and clothing made from furs. Its commercial room is devoted to the island's original breeders. Through "Fox and Fashion" exhibits we learn that in medieval Europe, royal decrees proclaimed just who was permitted to wear furs. Only royalty could wear ermine, for example, while sable, beaver and black fox were highly prized by noblemen. Russian Czars favored fur of the silver fox. Napoleon kept silver foxes as pets.

But the boom was soon over. By 1935 there were too many people in the business, some of whom were producing second-rate pelts. World War II brought shipping problems and prohibitively high insurance, and already mink had overtaken the silver fox in popularity. In the early 1960s island fox pelts were selling for $10 each; tails had become cheap souvenirs for car aerials and bicycles.

However, all is not lost. Driving around the island you will often see farms with cages on stilts containing foxes, and I am told the industry is on the upswing. Even if it weren't, this is still a success story. The island benefitted tremendously from the generosity of those original six breeders. As for Charles Dalton, the farmer-cum-trapper who started it all, his perserverence paid off in more than mere wealth. He became Sir Charles Dalton, and was made Lieutenant Governor of Prince Edward Island.

IF YOU GO: The International Fox Hall of Fame is at 286 Fitzroy Street in Summerside. Admission is free.

NEW BRUNSWICK

Largest and most westerly of our mainland Atlantic provinces, New Brunswick is separated from Prince Edward Island by the Northumberland Strait and from Nova Scotia by the Isthmus of Chignecto. Surrounded by water on three sides, this is our "picture province". Here you will find a natural beauty in the fertile farmlands of the Saint John Valley, phenomenal tides (some among the world's highest), and seaside villages that change little from one century to the next, miles of golden beaches and often forests for as far as you can see. It is a province with grand resorts and elegant little inns, wharfside restaurants serving fiddlehead greens and berry desserts and seafood second to none.

In the early 1700s the French were well established here. Following America's War of Independence Loyalists arrived. Both have left their mark on French-speaking communities around the north shore, and towns steeped in an English influence are very much in evidence today.

Provincial economy is based on natural resources. Four fifths of the land is forested. Commercial fishing, fish processing, agriculture, and mining all contribute. Tourism is of major importance too.

Leisure fishermen will tell you it is everything they've dreamed of, as they try for salmon in the Miramichi and bluefin tuna in the Bay of Chaleur. Trout, bass and landlocked salmon crowd numerous rivers and streams, in settings so scenic they appear unreal. Camping can be idyllic too, in the province's two national parks: Fundy on the south coast, Kouchibouguac on the east. While Fundy's high tides are legend, there are also islands to be explored in the Bay. Campobello (linked by bridge to Maine, by ferry from New Brunswick's Deer Island) is where the late President Roosevelt summered in a 34-room "cottage" which is now a museum. Grand Manan is endeared to all who discover it. Artists are so inspired they sometimes decide to stay. Deep sea fishing, seal and whale watching excursions are known to create life-long enthusiasts. For birders binoculars are part of their everyday apparel.

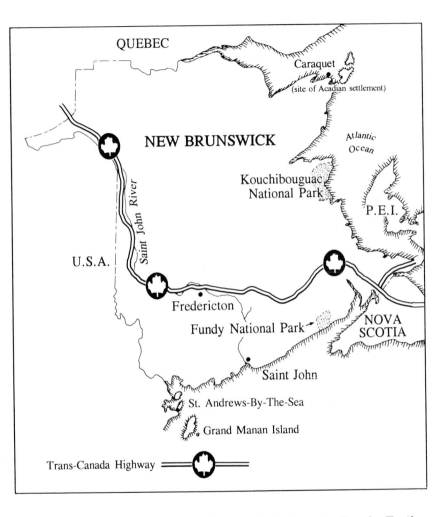

In New Brunswick you will want to follow the Fundy Trail where 50-foot tides are awesome. (The tourist office will send you a tide timetable.) And stop at Hopewell to see giant flowerpots sculpted by the sea.

New Brunswick will leave you with special memories—the majesty of Grand Falls, or the fabled Restigouche, or a farm stay in the Saint John River Valley. They will stay with you in unique crafts made with caring hands and skills of former generations—

in holiday pictures of Loyalist Days, Acadian and Lobster Festivals, Sugarloaf where a chairlift takes you up the mountain and you get to slide back down. New Brunswick is remembered for its heritage sites marked by the sign of a key, and covered bridges, and the thrill of being close to whales off Grand Manan. For the vacation that had you gathering seashells, watching the sun go down from the dock at St Andrews-by-the-Sea, nibbling on dulse and Skiddaddle Ridge cookies, and admiring picture-perfect scenery just about anywhere you looked.

Information on New Brunswick is available from Tourism New Brunswick, P.O. Box 12345, Fredericton, New Brunswick E3B 5C3. Telephone 506-453-2377, or toll free 1-800-561-0123 in Canada and USA.

ST ANDREWS-BY-THE-SEA

St Andrews-by-the-Sea, New Brunswick: It is one of those neat little towns of sterling character, nestled around a harbor on New Brunswick's southwestern coast. The type of community where mainstreet shops sell English china, Welsh weaving, hand knitted woollies and whatever else is dear to the store owner's heart. Where you can dine in cool, dim, wharfside restaurants on seafood that's second to none. And where some 200 19th-century homes are lovingly maintained, so they look better now than when new.

The first settlers came here from Maine following the American Revolution. Choosing to live under British rule, they packed their fine furnishings, linens and good silver, and sailed across to this picturesque peninsula on Passamaquoddy Bay. Some even brought their houses, re-assembling them on streets laid out by British engineers. By the spring of 1784, 90 families lived around this little harbor in the town they named St Andrews.

Tourists discovered St Andrews in 1907, when it became linked to Quebec by rail. With a regular train service in operation, Canadian Pacific next purchased an ailing hotel overlooking the bay. They renamed it The Algonquin and, when it burned down, constructed another which is more popular than ever today.

In the years before World War II, St Andrews was a favorite summer place for wealthy families. Some moved into The Algonquin for the season. Others built their own estates. Canadian

St Andrews-by-the-Sea

Pacific Railway president, Sir William Van Horne, put his stamp of approval on the area by opening a summer home here, then other CPR directors followed suit. The attractions were simple: golfing on a rather splendid course, fishing excursions, family picnics and parties on a quiet and scenic part of the coast.

That's really about the size of it now. The summer people come to cottages inherited from their grandparents. The Algonquin seldom has an empty room at the height of the season. After your first visit you will want to return whenever in need of rest and recreation.

In pursuit of area history, the Block House is as good a place as any to start. One of three such defenses built in St Andrews during the War of 1812, it contains town plans drawn up in 1784 from which you'll see that cross streets are named for King George III and his 12 children.

Almost all of St Andrews can be explored on foot, but not the Huntsman Laboratory on the outskirts of town. "Please touch" exhibits here include a sea peach and potato, and similar goodies. A section devoted to lobsters has one specimen called Clyde who weighs 27 pounds and Bonnie who's about 10 pounds lighter. The largest lobster caught in Canadian waters we learn was found off nearby Campobello Island. It weighed in at a whopping 37 pounds. At 10 a.m. and 4 p.m. resident harbor seals are fed. And if you like to hike, look for a pleasant enough trail out back.

Personally, I preferred walking about town, beneath voluminous old trees shading residential streets, past gardens overflowing with lupins and dahlias and climbing roses. Within an area of roughly nine blocks by five, you will pass no fewer than 35 buildings eligible to be called historic sites. Most are 19th-century dwellings. Some, still lived in, date from the 1700s. For example, there's the town's first two-story building at the corner of Edward and Water Streets since 1784. A little frame dwelling at Montague and Adolphus is one of the original houses brought from Maine, where it was built in 1770. The Church of England Burying Place tells its own grisly story, through tombstones recording infant deaths and youthful sons lost at sea.

Greenock Presbyterian isn't the oldest church in town, but is certainly the most attractive. In the early 1800s a local man, Captain Christopher Scott, decided the people of St Andrews should have a Presbyterian church and so built Greenock (named for his one-time Scottish home town) at great personal expense. Interior upper galleries are faced with mahogany and supported by 10 pillars of solid maple. The mahogany pulpit is a masterpiece, constructed without benefit of nails or screws. Some of the original furnishings, communion chalices and huge pulpit bible imported from Scotland are still in everyday use. As for the distinctive green oak trees painted on the tower's white exterior, this is a traditional Greenock emblem.

The exact spot where loyalists are believed to have stepped ashore in the Fall of 1783 is claimed by a wool shop in Harbor Square. In this same square you'll find the tourist office, practically bursting at the seams if a tour bus is in town. Here also is access to the pier, a handy viewing platform from which to spot crabs and sea urchins and an occasional sand dollar on the mud below.

For identification of treasures picked out of the mud, or if you would like to participate in an escorted beach walk, call into Sunbury Shores Arts and Nature Centre on Water Street. There a resident naturalist will explain the coral found on these shores was brought in as ballast on trading ships from the West Indies, while colored pebbles are actually flint dumped from British ships. She will invite you to accompany her on hikes across the salt marshes and early morning bird walks. And she will urge you to go to Deer Island Point at high tide to witness harbor porpoises and seals and multitudes of birds.

IF YOU GO: On the southwest coast of New Brunswick, St Andrews is 18 miles east of Calais, ME, or 60 miles west of Saint John via Highway 1, then south on 127. A nice day trip from town is via the free ferries, first to Deer Island then continuing to Campobello where the late President Roosevelt's summer home is now a museum. The return trip can be by road, over the bridge to Lubec, ME, and north to Calais, crossing back to Canada at St Stephen.

THE ALGONQUIN HOTEL

St Andrews-by-the-Sea, New Brunswick: It has all the speed and precision of a well-rehearsed military exercise. At a given signal they rush from the lobby, kilts flying as they go, and hurry back staggering under their loads. Next, names and numbers are barked out, to be checked off on the leader's list. That done everyone disperses to assigned floors, and as the last kilt swirls into the elevator, we clap. Drill practice by fortress guards? A royal tattoo? Not at all. A tour group has arrived at the Algonquin Hotel. Bell boys, aiming to beat their own record, have not only delivered luggage to rooms before some 40 guests amble in from the bus, but have completed the operation in less than five minutes. It is an entertaining display of efficiency effected with youthful exuberance, and contributes to the cheerful atmosphere permeating this renowned New Brunswick resort.

A grand hotel has stood on this hill above the Passamaquoddy Bay since 1889. Six years earlier some Bostonians built it as a private club which, proving economically unsound, went public as The Argylle Hotel. In 1907 the Canadian Pacific Railway Company, with a rail connection between St Andrews and Quebec, purchased the property and renamed it The Algonquin. As with so many of these large hotels, The Algonquin was constructed of wood and eventually burned down. The blaze occurred in 1914. A new concrete hotel, along the same architectural lines, was completed in time for the opening of the following season.

By now St Andrews was an established summer resort, receiving the same well-to-do families year after year. But the staid hotel's popularity didn't last much beyond World War II. The 1950s saw modern hotels built in glamorous destinations. A new generation spent its old money abroad in exciting, action-packed vacations. The Algonquin, burdened by antiquated amenities, dowdy furnishings and a demoralized staff couldn't hope to compete. Sporadic attempts were made to renovate and modernize, but costs were high and returns dismally low.

The turning point came in 1970 when a group of local businessmen purchased the hotel. During the next four years the New Brunswick government leased, then bought the property from them. With the wedding of provincial ownership to management by CP Hotels Ltd., The Algonquin has since prospered.

The resort is a relaxed and friendly place these days. Almost all of the staff is hired from universities and community colleges across Canada. Their enthusiasm for The Algonquin spills over

Algonquin Hotel

to guests you'll meet in the public lounges, the library bar where drinks are named for the classics. And gardens, wonderful last summer with roses, marigolds and carnations growing in colorful profusion, alongside beds of tousle-headed dahlias the size of young cabbages.

Of The Algonquin's 190 rooms and suites we found our "standard" room nicely furnished but very small. Public areas on the other hand are so spacious, the resort seems sparsely populated even when we know it to be full. There are two dining rooms. The Passamaquoddy Room offers excellent table d'hote and a la carte lunch and dinner service. The atmosphere is less formal in the Chart Room downstairs. Reservations for either room should be made early.

Guests tend to get acquainted on the front porch, or sitting about the grounds. For a little action, there is a large swimming pool (with adjacent changing rooms) and tennis courts. And those who know it first hand tell me the 18 hole golf course nearby is a treat.

The days slip pleasantly by. We walk to Katy's Cove where children play on a small beach, and ocean swimming is supervised by the hotel's youthful staff. We poke about the wharf, talk with proprietors in shops in buildings of historic note, stroll along residential streets lined with English-style gardens. We cycle into town for morning coffee on the verandah of Canada's oldest summer resort and for lobster lunches overlooking the sea. I guess a sing-along in Sir William's lounge is not the same as an old-fashioned party at the Van Horne estate. Other than that, things don't change much at St Andrews-by-the-Sea.

IF YOU GO: The Algonquin Hotel's season is from late May to October. Rooms are about $130 per night double, plus 11 percent tax. MAP plans are available for approximately $200 per night, plus tax, double occupancy. For reservations, contact The Algonquin Hotel, St Andrews-by-the-Sea, New Brunswick, E0G 2X0. Telephone 506-529-8823. Or use CP Hotels' toll free numbers: In the US 1-800-828-7447; Ontario & Quebec 1-800-268-9420; elsewhere in Canada 1-800-268-9411.

WATCHING WHALES, A SPECTACULAR SPORT

Grand Manan Island, New Brunswick: The fog was disconcerting. It hung like a wet, grey blanket between us and the sea, reaching out to dampen our spirits more as each minute ticked loudly by. We were a mixed bunch sitting around the cluttered parlor: two school teachers with their three children from Belleville, a University of Toronto student, a couple of young campers from the neighboring park and, from time to time, Jim Leslie, owner of the Marathon Inn and partner in Ocean Search with Dr. David Gaskin, professor of marine biology at the University of Guelph, director of Ocean Search.

Jim peered through his binoculars yet again, and conferred with Dr. Gaskin again before announcing, "No whaling today." There were groans all around. Still, everyone, except the campers who were leaving the island that night, agreed to return tomorrow. Meanwhile, to keep our appetites whetted, we were invited to watch a film about whales inhabiting these Bay of Fundy waters.

Of several species in this area the right whale, hunted almost to extinction until protected by law as an endangered species, is what we are after. Whalers so named these whales for several reasons. As slow swimmers they are relatively easy to pursue. When harpooned, they float where other species sink. Their bodies contain huge quantities of high quality oil and numerous baleen plates. Hanging like hairy ribbons in their throats to filter out plankton on which they feed, these were the source of whalebone once used to manufacture corsets. All of which made these the right whales to hunt.

Although the ponderous creatures seem to lack a sense of self preservation, they have some rather human traits I found endearing. A calf for example, seldom strays more than a length from its mother. Mum, in turn, often tucks her infant under her flipper while swimming. The whales embrace each other with their flippers. They snore and get burned when dozing off in the

sun. They consume millions of tiny shrimps, but because of their baleen filter system, can't manage big things like people. Definitely my kind of whale.

Next morning dawned as if the world's windows had been washed clean over night. The air was crisp and clear, giving good visibility for miles across the flat sea. Excitement was obvious as we trooped down the hill between inn and harbor. When gathered aboard the 44-foot fishing boat, our little group comprised a dozen paying passengers, five members of Ocean Search (including Jim Leslie and David Gaskin), skipper Ivan Green and his mate.

About 90 minutes out to sea our first right whale sighting was roughly two miles away. A partly submerged head and body, it looked more like a hippopotamus than a whale until it fluked— that is submerged with a cheeky wave of its tail before disappearing from sight. Within minutes two more appeared on the boat's other side, still too far off to be photographed without a telephoto lens. Gaskin studied all three, then decided we should move on. This was mating season, he told us and the loner who "wasn't getting any" could prove unpredictable.

We had been out a little over two hours and spotted eight or nine different whales. Each time we approached they would dance around, go sailing with only their flukes above water, slap the water with a thunderous sound—seemingly for the pure joy of it. Always they moved off as we moved in to within 200 feet.

One never sees an entire whale this way. It just isn't possible for a creature weighing 40 to 50 tons to leave the water supporting it. At most one will breach, repeatedly lifting its head and upper torso from the water. Other than that, you will see humps of backs, lots of heads and tails. Gaskin and his assistants recognized all of the whales they saw, some from their encrusted "bonnets", others from individual tail markings.

Lunch was great, sitting on deck beneath a warm midday sun. The skipper and his mate made us a thick fish chowder from scratch. There were plenty of fresh rolls, cheese, fruit, cold meats

Whale watching off Grand Manan Island

and soft drinks on hand. Gaskin was telling me of his life-long work with whales in various parts of the world when it happened. Like some pre-historic monster—I swear no more than six feet from where we stood—this head emerged from the water. Upright as if it was standing on its hind legs, it stared at us through one piggy eye, before sinking back into the sea. It was spy-hopping, as it does most days, apparently as curious about us as we were about it. I cursed the fact that I was holding a soup bowl instead of a camera, but then, I couldn't have gotten a picture because its enormous bulk would have filled my lens. This was, after all, 40 tons of whale, 60 feet long and some 15 feet wide.

Warmed as I felt towards the massive, gentle creatures, I still have to say right whales are ugly. I mean, forget those sleek dolphin-like killer whales performing at Marineland. These have rough old hides, and heads encrusted with callosities—bumpy configurations, infested with yellowish parasites.

When two or more whales were sighted playing in the distance, our 17-foot dinghy was lowered so we could be taken, in pairs, for a closer look. Came my turn, both whales had disappeared. We rowed for a bit. The silence, except for the sound of oars slicing a glass smooth sea, was eerie. When we drifted on the endless sea, I felt as if we had been shipwrecked and turned for reassurance that the mother boat was behind us. Dr. Gaskin chose this moment to tell how he had sat here, like this, two days before, and a whale had playfully surfaced under the boat lifting it clear from the water. I chose this moment to tell him I couldn't swim, and rather than waste a nice afternoon like this, maybe we should be getting back. I had seen the spy-hopping and enjoyed the ride. . . .

A dreadful odor of rotten eggs and gas engulfed us. I stared at my fellow whale watcher. He stared straight ahead. "Whale feces," Gaskin shouted excitedly, scanning the water for a sample to take back to his lab. Mission accomplished, his excitement over the secrets it might reveal was not shared. Next, he told us that this being mating season we should be patient. They were, remember, very large creatures. Someone said he knew a sea captain who had a golf bag made from a whale's penis. My turn to scan the sea.

Our lesson on whale anatomy and sexual habits was cut short when the two graceful, beautiful-ugly mammals crashed through the water's surface within 20 feet of us. In slow motion they swam, floated, weaved under and over each other. It was an unbelievable sight. "Power without aggression," Gaskin termed their performance. One slap with a giant flipper and we could have been tossed into the sea, or worse. But there was no sign of hostility. These gentle, placid whales were, I felt sure, entertaining us. The experience of watching them at such close range was so overwhelming I almost offered to carry the bucket of samples, by way of thanks to Dr. Gaskin for his personal introduction into this whale world.

An estimated 100 right whales inhabit waters around North America's east coast. Thirty live offshore from Grand Manan, and of these we have seen 11 or 12 in those few hours.

For a family, closely supervised whale watching such as this is expensive, but it is worth saving for. The excursions are limited to about eight weeks, and to continue this personal service, a limited number of people are taken at one time. Chances of getting close to a whale are excellent, because the Ocean Search people are up early to confer with returning fishermen as to the whales' present location. If none have been sighted, a plane is chartered to locate the whales before a boat sets out, so no time is wasted wandering about empty waters.

IF YOU GO: Off the coast of Maine, Grand Manan Island is reached by a two-hour ferry boat ride from Black's Harbour, 40 miles west of Saint John on Highway 1. Ocean Search is based at the Marathon Inn. Whale watching programs operate between mid-July and mid-September. Cost is $69 per person. The operators suggest you put aside two or three days for your whale safari so as not to be disappointed by fog or bad weather on any one day. Besides, the island, with its pretty little villages, coves and headlands, seals and 275 species of birds, is well worth the stay. More details are available from Ocean Search, P.O. Box 129, North Head, Grand Manan Island, N.B., Canada, E0G 2M0, tel 506-662-8144.

FUNDY
NATIONAL PARK

Alma, New Brunswick: If you think of our national parks simply as wilderness preserves, where one forfeits creature comforts for the sake of scenic phenomena, then Fundy on New Brunswick's southern coast will be a welcome surprise. Not only does this park encompass rugged scenery and the world's highest tides, but its visitor facilities match those of the finest country club. Frankly, I can't think of a private resort with its own golf course, tennis courts, lawn bowling green, heated pool, stables, boat rentals, art classes, 50 miles of walking trails, beaches, licensed restaurant, and very affordable chalets. Yet you will find all this and more at Fundy National Park.

Established in 1948, the 80-square-mile park extends inland for some nine miles over grassy hills 1,000 feet above the sea. Its forests, still recovering from a century of logging, are home to 87 different bird species. Speckled trout are plentiful in rivers and streams, as are Atlantic salmon during late August. Eight miles of coastline skirt the park, its high cliffs being washed by colossal tides which rise somewhere between 30 to 55 feet twice a day.

Man-made facilities aside then, this is one of our loveliest and most interesting national parks. Take Point Wolfe, at the mouth of the Wolfe River. Its only landmark is a covered bridge built in 1909 to replace a former suspension bridge, and the dam constructed a few years earlier. But in the early 1900s this was a thriving little community, with sturdy log homes for 25 families, a post office, saw mill, and schoolhouse attended by 42 pupils.

Shortly after the 1812 War, British soldiers and settlers from Nova Scotia were given land around the river. From spring through fall, they would work their farms, then come winter moved to lumber camps in the surrounding bush. Following the spring drive, with logs safely on the holding pond here at the dam, there were joyous celebrations at this point. Now it is

Fundy National Park

deathly quiet, except for the birds and sound of running water. According to tradition, you should "make a wish or steal a kiss" when walking through the covered bridge. A footbridge leads from the 35-foot-high dam to the river, and wild raspberries grow all around.

Logs assembled at Point Wolfe were loaded aboard the tall ships anchored in neighboring Alma. No more than a hamlet at the park's entrance these days, Alma was once a lively port and ship-building town. European vessels used to put into port here for food supplies and repairs, as well as their cargoes of lumber. Nowadays the international flavor is provided by tourists, usually from the park, and they too come to replenish their larders and take care of the chores. Small though it is, Alma has everything for self-catering vacationers. The bakery sells fantastic bread, savory pies, cakes and pastries. Lobsters are available cooked, or fresh from the sea. There is a post office, laundrette, supermarket, gift shops and restaurants. Even a stuffed moose to be photographed next to. Beside the bridge, an interpretation center has free pamphlets describing those years when Alma was a noisy sea port. Here too, you will hear of Alma's favorite daughter, Molly Kool. "Call me Captain from now on," read the telegram she sent home in the 1930s, upon becoming the first woman in North America (and second in the world) to obtain her master's papers.

In Alma, you will stock up on groceries, do your laundry, and perhaps wander about the mud flats gathering shells and brightly colored pebbles. But most of your days will be spent within the national park.

Understandably, the park is popular with families because every age group is catered to. The heated salt-water pool is supervised, which means you can drop off your young swimmers and take to the tennis courts or golf course with a quiet mind. At the summer headquarters of the New Brunswick School of Arts and Crafts, long or short term projects are designed for adults and children. You can hire a boat on Bennett Lake for half a day. Equipment for golf, tennis and lawn bowling is available for a small charge.

All national parks have interpretive programs. Many have amphitheatres, but none surely so aesthetic as Fundy's which is surrounded by velvety lawns and lovely flower beds. Here, one breezy evening, a naturalist told us of deer, moose, red foxes, hares, beavers, otters, raccoons, porcupines, skunks and other creatures inhabiting the park. Wintry slides showed personnel rescuing deer from snow drifts, tracking a moose, and taking inventory of animal residents by counting their droppings. It was explained how we too could detect who's been where by examining droppings for undigested plants, fur and other bits and pieces. (How's that for holiday fun, guys?) Another evening we learned about the massive tides of Fundy, in reality just beyond the amphitheatre.

IF YOU GO: Fundy National Park is 80 miles northwest of Saint John, N.B., via Highways 1, 2, and 114. The park is open all year round, with seasonal facilities. For more information contact the Superintendent, Fundy National Park, Alma, New Brunswick E0A 1B0. Telephone 506-887-2000.

NEW BRUNSWICK'S ACADIAN PAST

Caraquet, New Brunswick: It is noon on a pleasant summer's day in the 19th-century Acadian village. Farm hands are busy in fields and workshops, children help with the chores, and in her log house Madame Doucet prepares lunch over an open fire. Being Friday, fish is on the menu and for dessert there's blueberry cake baked in an iron pot. Any minute now, Monsieur Doucet and some of the children will be in for lunch. Seated at the worn wooden table they will have cod and onion stew with thick slices of bread. Then it's back to the fields for Doucet and his helper, and for the youngsters an afternoon session in the one-room school. As for Madame Doucet, she will welcome visitors who want to know how she manages so well without the aid of modern technology.

There is a convincing authenticity to the Acadian Historical Village on the Baie des Chaleurs in northern New Brunswick. Not only are "residents" costumed to the period, and well versed in the skills of their forefathers, but children stay for a week each summer. Dressed in traditional clothes they arrive each morning before the village opens. Their lunch is cooked and served in the farmhouses. Taught to help with the chores, they are seen pumping water, assisting in kitchens and around the farms. Each afternoon they learn about this period in their history, during lessons at the local school. Most important for us, they enhance the illusion that we have truly walked into the Acadia of 200 years ago.

Essentially French settlers of the Maritime provinces, Acadians were deported in 1755 for refusing to swear allegiance to the British crown. Some went south of the border, others to Europe or the French territories. But they came back. By the beginning of the 19th century approximately 8,000 had returned to live in isolated villages on the fringes of Maritime society.

Religion played an important role in their otherwise bleak lives. Irregular education was provided by itinerant teachers. With the economy controlled by Jersey companies who exchanged trade goods for the fishermen's catch, there was little chance for Acadians to get ahead. But, as their numbers increased, they were gradually heard. In 1867 the Moniteur Acadien became the Maritimes' first French language newspaper. Fourteen years later the Acadians' first annual convention was attended by 5,000 people. The 1900s brought cooperatives and credit unions, and hope for a better life.

The recreated village, which spans a century from the year 1780, gives testimony to the perseverance of these people. Most of the costumed "residents" are descendants of the Acadians driven from their homes. Houses are of necessity simple. The 1783 Martin House is a crude log cabin with dirt floor and primitive furniture. Most are two-storied log or clapboard homes, in which a family would live on the ground floor and use the upper for storage. By the early 1800s they were reasonably comfortable.

Efficient Acadian women were skilled in producing nutritious meals from heavy iron pots over open fires. Some houses have stone and cast iron stoves.

The Godin House (1880) is a carpenter's pleasure, with fine wooden furniture, shelves and cupboards, and a handsome staircase to the second floor. One of the more luxurious homes belonged to the Blackhall family who brought certain refinements and furnishings from Scotland in 1830.

Acadian Village, Caraquet

Workshops are as busy now as they were in the 1800s: the carpenter, broom maker, wheelwright, smithy and other trades keep the village supplied. In the Jersey-owned warehouse, a clerk passes out samples of dried cod, as fishermen mend their nets and salt the fish. The aromatic village store is crowded with jars of pepper, ginger, sugar, coffee and other goods which had to be purchased. Panes of glass and tools that couldn't be made at the forge were sold here.

The Acadians were industrious farmers. By the 1800s they were harvesting a variety of fruit and root vegetables, which along with fish and poultry provided a decent diet. A flax crop brought them linseed oil and linen. Working bees were part of village life, helping to get the more tedious work done with company from neighbors. A frolic, similar in its group involvement, had traditional and ceremonial overtones. At the milling frolic, for example, cloth was milled (shrunk) by some half a dozen men pushing and pounding the cloth in a trough of hot water and soft lye soap. Rhythmic songs kept the pounding going and, when the first six men tired, a second group took over. Women cooked and set out a great meal, so that instead of a workday it became a happily anticipated celebration.

Frolics are no longer part of village life, but you can sample traditional Acadian cooking at the community's Table des Ancestres. On this Friday, codfish and chicken are the main dishes. Wanting less than a full meal I ordered poutine rapée, a boiled ball of potato flour stuffed with minced pork and doused with molasses, which was delicious. Enormous portions of gateau bluette were served for dessert. Beer and wine are available. Elsewhere in the village, Post Houses sell sandwiches and snacks, and a cafeteria serves cooked lunches.

IF YOU GO: The Acadian Historical Village, six miles west of Caraquet on Highway 11, is open seven days a week, June to September. There is a modest admission charge. Do plan to stay in this area for a few days. Caraquet is New Brunswick's oldest French settlement and very picturesque.

KOUCHIBOUGUAC, NEW BRUNSWICK'S *OTHER* NATIONAL PARK

Kouchibouguac, New Brunswick: It is New Brunswick's best kept secret. Every visitor touring this province wants to stay in Fundy National Park, because of the phenomenally high tides, country club facilities and cottage accommodation so convenient for non-campers. But how many know about New Brunswick's other National Park: Kouchibouguac, in scenic Acadia where the Northumberland Strait meets the Gulf of St Lawrence?

Kouchibouguac, a MicMac Indian name meaning River of the Long Tideway, is a 150-square-mile preserve safeguarding a special part of Canada's natural heritage. An integral blend of coastal and inland habitats, it includes beaches and sand dunes, salt marshes, bogs, rivers and forest—all of which helped to shape the way of life in this corner of Acadia.

Descendants of three cultures share the region. MicMacs were hunting and fishing long before the Europeans arrived. French speaking Acadians cultivated the salt marshes here over 300 years ago, and by the late 18th century the British were farming these lands. Now, outside the park information center three bronze figures characterize the three cultures. Often they are photographed with a fourth at their table, by way of a park visitor having a bit of fun.

Locals know all about Kouchibouguac. On a sultry weekend last summer with temperatures in the 90's, day visitors poured in with their picnic coolers and chaises and beach umbrellas. Still there was plenty of room on the supervised beach, while along the coast we were practically alone.

The beaches are sensational. Broad and smooth, trimming warm waters of the Northumberland Strait for 15 miles, they are reached via boardwalks straddling sand dunes spiked with sea grass. Even Kellys Beach, most popular for its amenities (snack bar, change rooms, toilets and showers) and lifeguards posted on the sand, is remarkably clean. By noon on Saturday this central hub became uncomfortably crowded, but 10 minutes walk brought us to a deserted spot where shorebirds dashed about on seemingly urgent errands and noise was the sound of a pounding surf.

Park interpretive programs usually start beneath a large yellow umbrella on the boardwalk to Kellys Beach. Here you can read storyboards describing the fragile nature of surrounding dunes and plant species thriving in them. Because of their protected status, wildlife in the park is abundant. Along the coast (a half mile from Kellys Beach), Tern Island is home to one of the largest tern nesting sites in North America.

Lagoons and salt marshes house tens of thousands of shore birds, geese and ducks. You may even see the endangered species of plover and the osprey which is adopted as the park's symbol. Gray harbor seals, nicknamed "horse face" by local fishermen, often guard the mouth of the St Lawrence River. These bull seals have spent much of the winter defending harems of perhaps a dozen females and their young. Now, like the rest of us, they enjoy basking in the summer sun.

Less developed than Fundy and other well known parks in our national chain, Kouchibouguac is unhurried, uncrowded for the most part because it is off the tourist route, and an altogether ideal place for us to get in touch with nature. If all 219 campsites are taken when you get there, don't give up. On a sweltering Friday evening in July, we arrived to a No Vacancy sign at the entrance, camped overnight in a nearby commercial campground and returned to the park next morning at 8 o'clock. Third in line, I barely had time to make coffee when our motorhome's number was called. Within half an hour we had settled into a site scooped from the forest, and headed for a swim in what is acclaimed as "the warmest water north of the Carolinas."

Fifteen miles of cycling trails give an intimate view of the park. (In winter these are groomed for cross-country skiing.) Additional walking paths are designed for short or long hikes to particularly interesting areas. The Pine Trail, for example, loops through majestic white pines with colorful mushrooms growing at their feet. A Salt Marsh trail winds through one of the park's most productive habitats. Tweedy Trail features picturesque river bank picnic areas, and from a tower on Bog Trail's boardwalk you might well see a moose or two.

Ours was an enjoyable weekend at Kouchibouguac. On my early morning walks I saw nothing as intimidating as bears or moose, but did spot an osprey. Also two grey seals in a lagoon at Kellys Beach. At the information center we learned about the park environment from a slide show and exhibits, and inquired about escorted walks piquing the curiosity with names like "Foul and Loathsome Creatures", "Marine Mysteries", and "Flying Mammals of Kouchibouguac". Deciding the escorted tours would take too big a chunk of my time, I hired a bicycle instead and pedalled in the cool shade of forest paths.

Three rivers flow through the park. I was told that any one of them is reason enough for fishermen to come here, while clams in the lagoons are free for the taking. Boats, canoes and fishing gear (also bicycles) are for hire at Ryan's center. On this occasion though, we didn't attempt to catch our supper. With temperatures still uncomfortably high we succumbed to the air conditioned comfort of the park's licensed restaurant, Bon Accueil. After a day of nature study it seemed almost obscene to sit beside lobsters clambering over each other in the confines of a tank. Without a sporting chance of avoiding their fate, they were unceremoniously fished out, slung into a pot of boiling water and served to drooling diners.

Outside the park Acadian communities offer cottage and motel accommodation, traditional crafts, antiques and home baking. Deep sea fishing is advertised at $10 per person. For us this proved a delightful stopover, affording a chance to stock up and get sorted out before tackling the Cabot Trail.

IF YOU GO: Easier to find than pronounce, Kouchibouguac is on Highway 11 about half way along New Brunswick's east coast, 60 miles from Moncton. Serviced campsites, on a first-come basis, cost about $8, according to location. Wilderness sites reached on foot or by canoe are free. For more information, contact the Superintendent, Kouchibouguac National Park, Kouchibouguac, N.B., E0A 2A0. Telephone 506-876-2443.

FREDERICTON, A HAPPY BLEND OF PAST AND PRESENT

Fredericton, New Brunswick: It's different. Unlike other provincial capitals of Atlantic Canada Fredericton wasn't chosen for its harbor, and its citizens are not dependent on the sea. Instead of sailors and whalers in centuries past, Fredericton had its military men and Loyalists and a prestigious university, all of which reflect in the air of gentility pervading its tree-lined streets today.

A French military community established in 1692 where the Nashwaak River empties into the St John was destroyed by the British. During the early 1700s a few British settlers trickled in. More came in 1783 as loyalists fled the United States, and two years later Fredericton (renamed for George III's second son) became New Brunswick's elegant little capital.

Tourists can readily find the military and Loyalist past so carefully preserved. Make your first stop the City Hall because here, if you arrived by car or camper, you can collect a sticker entitling you to unlimited free parking. You won't need wheels again until you leave town. While at the City Hall do pop up to the second floor to see the council chamber, which as a guide points out is fashioned after the one in Toronto's City Hall. More impressive are giant tapestries created by two local artists to commemorate 200 years of city history. The scenes are so detailed, at a glance you might think they are worked by brush and oils. Even more remarkable is that one of the artists was 79 years old when he started this project.

Along from City Hall (as directed in a pedestrian guide distributed there), past the Justice Building, the Soldiers' Barracks is a solid looking stone structure completed in 1827 to house the British army. Renovated a few years ago, one room is equipped as it would have been in the 1800s. That is to say 19 soldiers can be crammed into 19 tiny beds, while wooden pegs and shelves must suffice for their belongings. Tours of the Soldiers Barracks are conducted in summer by guides from the Guard House around the corner. It too is open in summer, restored to period.

Knots of tourists in Officers' Square alerted us to an imminent Changing of the Guard ceremony, performed daily at 11 a.m. by youthful red coated recruits. Beyond its colonial arches, Officers' Quarters now house the York-Sunbury Historical Society's museum portraying an excellent capsule of Fredericton's past. At the close of the American War of Independence, thousands of people choosing loyalty to the British crown abandoned everything and emigrated to other British colonies. Many found their way to St John, then came inland by river to Fredericton. Now we can see pictures of the 19th-century river boats, artifacts, documents written by loyalist arrivals.

In a despairing moment one of these immigrants wrote, "I climbed to the top of Chipman's Hill and watched the sails disappear. Such a feeling of loneliness came over me, that although I had not shed a tear through all the war, I sat down on the damp moss with my baby on my lap and cried." She is identified as a Mrs. William Frost who became grandmother of Sir Leonard Tilley, a Father of Confederation. Military exhibits, tales of hardships, even splendidly furnished rooms are serious stuff. Yet I am told some visitors come to the museum for a chuckle. They have heard about the Coleman Frog, a gigantic bullfrog which weighed approximately seven pounds when first discovered in a lake near the city, and eventually grew to an unbelievable 42 pounds. (Had it been discovered by a beautiful maiden, this story would have had a happier ending.) In any event the frog was fed by Fred Coleman during his fishing weekends, and when it er-um, croaked, Fred took the body to his friendly neighborhood taxidermist. Now this gross frog sits at the top of the museum stairs smirking at visitors as they come and go.

The "square" outside is actually a pleasant park with a fountain and flower-beds, and a bronze statue of Lord Beaverbrook—the former Max Aitken who became a newspaper magnate and a British peer but never forgot his New Brunswick home, and was very generous to Fredericton's cultural scene. One of his gifts is the Beaverbrook Art Gallery, practically deserted on this weekday morning. Beaverbrook often said the best picture here is the view of the St John River through its window. Most of us would disagree, saving our gasps for the huge Salvador Dali painting "Santiago el Grande" purchased for the gallery's opening in 1959 after the exhibition at the Brussels World Fair.

The permanent collection comprises some 2,000 works. Many are from Britain, including Turner and Constable landscapes, portraits by Hogarth and Gainsborough. Artists from Atlantic Canada are well represented of course. Several of Beaverbrook's friends donated art to the gallery. The Dali paintings were given by his pal Sir James Dunn, in whose memory a marble fountain was brought from Buckinghamshire to grace The Green.

The Green is a tree-shaded treasure stretching down river from the Beaverbrook Art Gallery. Following Loyalist history I attempted to find the Loyalist Memorial and cemetery, described as being beyond the railway bridge at the far end of The Green. The walk was pleasant enough but I had no success in locating either one.

Every Fredericton visitor should take the 22-mile drive west of the city to King's Landing, a community created with dwellings and workshops from Loyalist times to turn of the 20th century. It is very well done. Traditions and cultures are brought to life by costumed employees in the 11 homes and attendant buildings. Here countryside echoes with sounds of cart horses plodding along winding dirt roads and creaking wheels of wagons they pull. The view from the saw mill is the type we admire on Canadian calendars.

In the houses women dressed to period perform everyday chores. There is a general store, busy workshops, a school, even a four-seater outhouse once owned by a provincial chief justice. Children live in the village for five days at a time, helping their pioneer "parents", attending school, wearing clothes and playing games of their 19th-century counterparts.

The King's Head, built as a private home around 1840, is now a pub and restaurant. Its dining room serves tasty lunches with folksy names like Squire Ingraham's crackling roast pork, Mrs. Long's chicken vegetable pie, and Captain Jones' baked ham with sugared turnip. Smaller dishes such as Cornish pasty, pickled herring and chowder are also offered.

Whether at King's Landing or in downtown Fredericton one is uncommonly comfortable slipping in and out of the past, here on the banks of the St John.

Maybe that's why I felt so at home at the Carriage House Bed and Breakfast which marries old-fashioned graciousness to modern comforts. It is located in a quiet residential area close to The

Green and downtown attractions. Built in 1875 for one of Fredericton's former mayors, it has seven guest rooms and comfortable lounges. Breakfast is a sunny affair in an arboretum. 1990's room rates are $40 single, $45 double with shared bath, $50 and $55 with private facilities, cooked breakfast included. In summer owners Joan and Frank Gorham turn 12 to 15 would-be guests away every day, so if you are interested do write or call ahead for reservations.

IF YOU GO: For general information on Fredericton, contact the Visitors Information Center, City Hall, Queen Street, P.O. Box 130, Fredericton, E3B 4Y7. Telephone 506-452-9500. The Carriage House Bed and Breakfast is at 230 University Avenue, Fredericton, E3B 4H7. Telephone 506-452-9924.

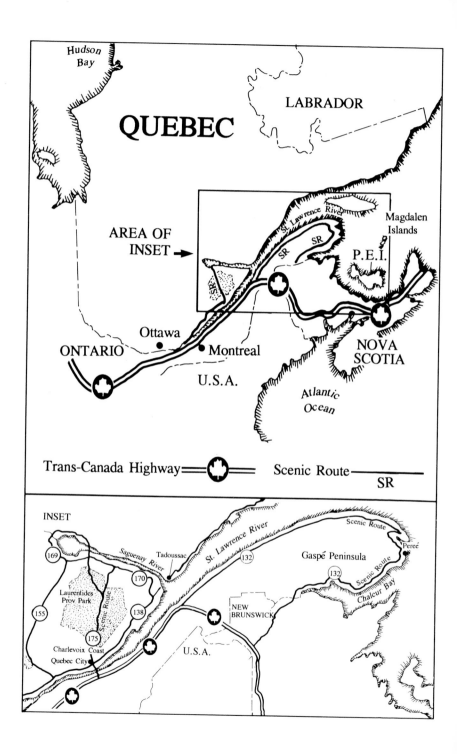

Trans-Canada Highway ⊕ Scenic Route ────── SR

QUEBEC

Quebec is special, often our favorite province with visitors because it is so unmistakably French. Over 80 percent of Quebeckers are French speaking. Names on shops, streets and highway signs are in French only where a few years ago they were bilingual. But it isn't only the language that appeals. The culture, cuisine, art and history, festivals and even the countryside at times have you thinking you are in France.

This is our largest province (almost 600,000 square miles), twice as big as Texas, three times the size of France, with most of the population in a small portion of the south around the St Lawrence River. At its height, France's North American domains covered half the continent, stretching from the Arctic to the Gulf of Mexico and to the foothills of the Rocky Mountains. Now the walled Quebec City is one enormous memorial to the history of French culture in the Americas, filled with reminders of 16th-century explorers, soldiers, priests and traders. A two-tier city beside the river, it is considered by tourists to be the finest jewel in the Quebec collection.

In 1535 explorer Jacques Cartier sailed along "the road that walks" (as the Indians knew the St Lawrence River), landed in Hochelaga and planted a cross on top of the mountain he named Mont Réal. Now Canada's second largest city, and second largest French speaking city in the world, Montreal becomes more French with every passing day. An exciting city, it draws visitors to old world cultures in a modern environment, to French restaurants and smart boutiques, gracious dwellings from earlier centuries, showcase buildings from a world exposition and Olympics. Underground Montreal extends for miles, creating a climate-controlled subterranean city where walkways lined with shops and eateries connect to office towers, subway stations and hotels. (Rumour has it that in winter some apartment dwellers in this city never go outdoors.)

Attractions for first-time visitors usually include Ile Nôtre Dame, site of Expo '67 and now a leisure park. Romantics will want to tour Mount Royal by horse-drawn carriage. Nôtre Dame Cathedral is a wondrous setting for orchestral concerts, St Joseph's Oratory so revered by some they climb its 99 steps on their knees. Montreal's rich religious heritage is nurtured in more than 400 churches, its joie de vivre celebrated in jazz and similar festivals, and numerous summer happenings in the Old Port.

For weekend escapes from city stress Montrealers head for the Laurentians less than two hours' drive from home. Here they ski in winter, hike and swim in summer. In any season, focus your visit around Lac Tremblant and you will have at least half a dozen resorts to choose from, all offering family plans, special packages and a delightful French ambiance. Windsurfers, weekend sailors and golfers love this area. So do mountain hikers and canoeists following the wilderness routes of the 2,574-square-mile Mont Tremblant Park.

Drive the province's oldest highway (Le chemin du Roy) on the river's north shore between Montreal and Quebec City, and you will be in a realm of historical homes and farms established in times when narrow strips of land allowed everyone access to the river. This is Charlevoix, a choice vacation region peppered with historic inns and resorts. Explore the Eastern Townships close to the American border. Referred to in government brochures as the French version of New England, the area has a quiet beauty, comfortable inns, gourmet restaurants and the largest aggregation of golf courses in La Belle Provence. Take a cruise on the mighty Saguenay, and drive around the rocky Gaspé peninsula. Visit the wood carvers of Saint-Jean-Port-Joli, the gannets on Bonaventure Island, whales at Tadoussac and the Mingan archipelago.

Fly from Quebec City or take a ferry-boat from Prince Edward Island to the Iles de la Madeleine. I hate to disclose Quebec's best kept secret, but would be remiss if I didn't tell you about the Magdalens. Here's where you come to get away from the places others go to to get away from it all. Where you like to get up early to meet fishermen returning with their catch, wander on 150 miles of practically empty beaches, stay in an island home, dine on sea bass and lobster and local berries, and lose all sense of place and time.

For more information write Tourisme Quebec, P.O. Box 20,000 Quebec, PQ, G1K 7X2. Toll free telephone numbers: Ontario 1-800-361-6490, Quebec 1-800-361-5405, US 1-800-363-7777.

STROLL THROUGH MONTREAL'S CENTURIES

Montreal: For a while, on that bleak Sunday morning, mine were the only footsteps to echo on narrow streets of the old city. Eventually, a steady clop-clop-clop of horses' hooves and the grating of wooden wheels against the cobblestones overtook me. Bonjour, madam. Bonjour monsieur. Beneath the shapeless rain cape and hood there was no telling what century the driver was from. His caleche complemented our setting, and the horse wasn't tarted up with pompoms as some of them are. And so I could continue along the streets of Vieux Montreal, my illusion of walking in centuries past unshattered.

Not long ago laborers ripped up the 20th-century asphalt paving of Old Montreal and discovered these original cobblestones beneath. Surrounding 18th- and 19th-century buildings were fully restored or updated for modern use. Now these physical features combine with the predominantly French-speaking population to create a delightful patch of New France on the fabric of Old Montreal.

This particular morning, while the streets were still deserted, it was easy to lose myself in the times of Champlain and Maisonneuve and Claude de Ramezay. But the night before was another story. Then the old city had all the gaiety of Paris over a holiday weekend. Music and laughter were everywhere. Sight-seers thronged the squares and narrow lanes, pausing in convivial groups to watch street entertainers and artists at work. The flower sellers were kept busy, as were purveyors of nonsensical souvenirs. Sidewalk cafés were packed, often overflowing. And it didn't cost a cent to stroll in the warm evening air, soaking up that marvelous joie de vivre.

There were no street musicians and flower sellers to greet Jacques Cartier when, in 1535, he became the first white man to visit this largest of the group of islands in the upper St Lawrence. Even so, his welcome at the fortified village of Hochelaga, in the area of today's McGill University, was a hospitable one. By the time Samuel de Champlain arrived 75 years later and set up a temporary fort, both Hochelaga and its 3,500 inhabitants had vanished. The founding of Montreal as a permanent community goes back to May 17, 1642, on which day Paul de Chomedey, Sieur de Maisonneuve, came ashore with 40 men and women. On the site of Champlain's Place Royale they built a settlement called Ville Marie de Montréal. Later the name was shortened to Montreal.

Maisonneuve and party represented the Société de Nôtre Dame, whose primary objective was to bring Christianity to the natives of New France. (It was widely believed that the North American Indians were the lost tribe of Israel, and their conversion to Christianity would speed up the Second Coming.) The settlers' life here was harder than most. For starters, shortly after their arrival, a flood all but swept Ville Marie away. And until a treaty was signed in 1701, Indian wars took a constant toll.

The 1763 Treaty of Paris, giving Britain rights to lands east of the Mississippi River, saw the end of French rule in Montreal. Under the British, the fur business boomed as Montreal traders travelled into the interior for pelts to be sold in Europe. By the mid-19th century Montreal had been incorporated as a city, and for eight years was the capital of Upper and Lower Canada.

However, it isn't size or commercial importance that sets Montreal apart these days. It is the French culture which has survived the centuries against all odds. Montreal is now the largest

French-speaking city in the world, after Paris. Two-thirds of its population is of French descent. And nowhere is the Frenchness more appealing than in the old part of the city.

A booklet called "A Walking Tour of Vieux Montreal", complete with map, is available free from Quebec and Montreal tourist offices. Most of the restored area is contained within 94 acres, which means you will be covering eight blocks in one direction and roughly four in the other, sloping down to the waterfront from Nôtre Dame Street. With your guidebook in hand, here are some of the more interesting sites to look for.

The most impressive landmark by a long shot is Nôtre Dame Church, recognizable from a distance by its twin towers Patience and Perseverance. Architect of this 19th-century masterpiece was a former Irishman from New York, James O'Connell, who died before the towers were in place and is buried in the church's basement. There were two earlier Nôtre Dames: one a small chapel built in 1642 and a larger church constructed for an ever-growing congregation 30 years later. The present church is an architectural gem, superbly decorated with 14-karat gold leaf, rich wood carvings and 40-foot-high stained glass windows by Limoges presenting scenes from early Montreal. And, interestingly, because the church rests on a hill its floor slopes gently towards the river.

Designed for a congregation of 3,500 to 4,000, Nôtre Dame holds audiences of close to 6,000 when classical concerts are held there on summer evenings. The 1672 Nôtre Dame church was built by a religious order founded in Paris in 1641 and known as The Gentlemen of Saint-Sulpice. Once established in Montreal they purchased seigneurial rights and responsibilities from the Societé de Nôtre Dame. Their seminary is the city's oldest building; the garden behind it one of the first to be cultivated in Ville Marie. Two hundred years later, this is a Sulpician residence still.

Montreal's oldest church, Nôtre Dame de Bonsecours, is a little gem built in 1772 on the site of another dating back to 1657. Overlooking the river, it is fondly known as the sailors' church because so many prayed here before going off to sea. Its museum

recalls the founder of the Congregation of Nôtre-Dame, Marguerite Bourgeoys. Already 51 when she came to New France in 1671, she became Canada's first woman saint. The rooftop observation deck offers a fine view of the river and old city.

The old city has many museums, of course. One you are bound to come to sooner or later is the Château Ramezay, a few steps from Place Jacques Cartier. Restored and furnished in the style of the early 1700s, it reminds us of times when de Ramezay, as the 11th governor of Montreal, held lavish parties and receptions in his home. Now guided tours are conducted in summer months, while at certain times of the year it provides an elegant setting for art exhibitions.

Scene of much summer frivolity, Place Jacques Cartier sweeps down to the river from Nôtre Dame Street. Near the top, horse-drawn carriages wait in line to carry passengers on a leisurely tour. At the bottom you can hire a bicycle for your self-conducted tour. But first stand at the top of the hill by Nelson's monument and visualize the vista before you, not as the 19th-century fruit and vegetable market it used to be, or the hub of tourist activities it has become. Think of it instead in grander times when, during the early 1700s, the Marquis de Vaudreil had his chateau down here facing the river and splendid gardens stretched all the way to Nôtre Dame Street.

Vieux Port, a park at the foot of Place Jacques Cartier, has more organized entertainment. Entry to sports and most theatrical events is free. (Exceptions are live shows presented on the Big Stage.) Last summer, top performers and dance troupes gave a total of 250 performances in 80 days. In addition to these, daytime entertainment ranging from jazz ensembles to puppet shows for children is free.

Along the riverfront, past Rue du Port, the courtyard of D'Youville Stables is a lovely backdrop for more free concerts. Here, tucked away from crowds in the old city's core, we thoroughly enjoyed a string quartet with our noontime aperatif. The adjoining building has a nice little bar in the cellar, while upstairs Gibby's is one of Montreal's more popular restaurants.

City Hall, Montreal

Throughout these few city blocks, it seems that every available space, on rooftops and patios, in back alleys and courtyards, is set with a few tables and chairs where you can enjoy a drink or a meal. If our experience is anything to go by you will receive attentive service and well-prepared food, and nobody will expect you to eat and run. This is true whether you stop for hot chocolate and croissants in a simple café on a damp Sunday morning, or a light lunch at a sidewalk table. Or settle into a classy little French restaurant for an evening of good food, music, candlelight and wine.

As in most cities you can pay a little or a lot for an enjoyable meal. Selecting dinner from the fixed price side of the menu and staying with house wine, will, of course keep costs down. The same can be said of city hotels. The lively St Denis Street district has many modest small hotels. At the other end of the scale, you can be wonderfully pampered in Montreal's luxury hotels. The prices here are comparable with most big city deluxe hotels, and special packages are available.

IF YOU GO: For a calendar of events, walking tour and accommodation guide, or general information on the old city, contact the Greater Montreal Convention and Tourism Bureau, 1010 Ste Catherine Street West, Montreal, Que., H3B 1G2, telephone 514–844–5400.

CHATEAU FRONTENAC: BASTION OF THE BEST

Quebec City: He wore a purple and yellow vest and hat smothered with shiny tin buttons, and his exaggerated back-slapping "Bonjewer Monsewer," caused me to cringe. Not so the venerable recipient of this greeting. He simply smiled and said to have a good day, sir, then turned his attention to somebody else. I had expected him to at least shake his head in mock disbelief, or stare straight ahead as Whitehall horseguards do when tourists take liberties with their mounts. But as a bellhop these past decades I guess he's seen them all—movie stars, royalty, sugar daddies, loudmouths, and run of the mill tourists—and as guests of the Château everyone is attended to with civility.

Towering over Quebec City, a historic landmark so renowned it requires no name above its portals, the Château Frontenac is not only a very civil hotel, it is one of the world's finest. They say that to know the old city is to know the Château and vice versa. It's true. The two are as inextricably intertwined as vines from a single root—planted in the rich soil of New France 350 years ago.

Even without a hotel on it, this site qualifies as a historic landmark because of all that has happened here. Samuel de Champlain, first governor of New France in 1608, started a settlement by the river and a fort on the cliff 200 feet above it, on this site. Members of Canada's first social club, founded by Champlain in Port Royal three years before, continued to entertain each other with sumptuous feasts here.

On this site, Canada's first ball was held in the Château St Louis. A glittering, glamorous affair, it was reminiscent of an event at Louis XIV's court, yet this was Quebec in 1667. Indian chiefs assembled here in 1658 to discuss trade with the governor; allied leaders in 1943 to plot the course of the Second World War. The fiery Comte de Frontenac for whom the hotel is named, lived and died here while governor of New France. And just a stone's throw away, in 1759, generals Wolfe and Montcalm gave their all on the Plains of Abraham.

For 18th-century settlers, sight of the Château St Louis meant blessed civilization after weeks at sea. Twentieth century immigrants arriving by ship were no less impressed. From the decks of a liner approaching Wolfe's Cove, this ponderous castle-like structure is the passenger's first image of Canada.

A property of Canadian Pacific Hotels Ltd. now, the château's construction was initiated by a group of private citizens who real-

Château Frontenac, from the Dufferin Terrace

ized the potential of a good hostelry in this city. In 1892, they
formed the Château Frontenac Company, and with the CPR's
president, William Van Horne, as guiding force, it was full steam
ahead. Ground was broken in May, 1892. Nineteen months later
the hotel welcomed its first guests.

Van Horne saw the new hotel as a luxurious stopover for Europeans en route to the rest of Canada and the Orient. Legend has it that he went by canoe to the middle of the St Lawrence River, looked to the top of the 200-foot-high Cape Diamond and declared, "This is where we build our hotel." Some hotel! On December 20, 1893, the Château Frontenac's official opening was celebrated with the grandest ball this city had ever known. Rich in elegant trappings imported from France, its guest rooms were furnished in oak, tower suites with expensive antiques. What's more, 94 of the 170 rooms had private baths. Added to several times between 1899 and 1924, the hotel's last expansion was the Great Tower. Seven stories high, it brought the total number of rooms to 640.

Resembling some great castle or fortress, the irregular, horseshoe shaped Frontenac is a wondrous assortment of turrets and towers, capped with steep copper roofing, distinctively green. Entrance is via a secluded courtyard in the rear, designed to keep traffic from the Dufferin Terrace. As well as the hotel itself, this 2,200-foot-long boardwalk offers a marvellous view of the original settlement below (now being restored,) and beyond it the river with its dinky ferry boats crossing to Levis.

By 1974 the Château, pretty much unchanged for 50 years, was ready for the costly overhaul which took several years to bring to completion. Walls were demolished and entire rooms lost, so that each of the 500 remaining bedrooms is large and comfortable, with private facilities. The public rooms weren't neglected either.

I could sit in the front lobby for hours, beneath a portrait of the dashing Count Frontenac, watching world travellers come and go. Thirty years ago, when transatlantic liners docked so frequently down below, this lobby would suddenly fill with people and piles of steamer trunks.

Now, guests arrive in ones and twos, and even those from far-off lands bring no more than carry-on baggage. Some wear name tags and pour themselves coffee in styrofoam cups outside the ballroom. Soon they will be engrossed in slide presentations and talks on sales growth at one of several conventions booked in this week.

What would Louis de Buade, Comte de Frontenac, think of it all? I wonder. One of New France's most durable governors, he was past middle age when first sent to the colonies. Before he was through he had fought off the Iroquois and the British, was recalled to France and then—because his successor couldn't manage the Indians—returned to Quebec.

Those 17th-century governors are easily remembered at the Château. Chevalier Charles Huault de Montmagny, who followed Champlain as governor, was a member of the Order of St John of Malta. A stone carved with the order's crest in 1647 is set in the hotel's entrance archway. It was discovered among the ruins, following the 1759 battle of the Plains of Abraham.

Champlain, of course, is everywhere, or appears to be since his statue, close to 50 feet high, towers over the terrace. The hotel's main dining room is named after him, in the hope of promoting the atmosphere he created with his L'Ordre de Bon Temps.

While you can't have the Good Cheer gang's beaver tail specialty, today's menu includes quail, pheasant, and roast duckling typical of their fare. Faultless service in the dining room and throughout the hotel is enhanced by employees who have been there for decades; like our affable bellhop, Johnny Sheridan, on the job for 43 years when we met a few years back.

Johnny recalled when a room here cost $3.25 a day, dinner 75 cents, and he used to eat breakfast with longtime Quebec premier, Maurice Duplessis. He remembered times when ladies wore hats and white gloves to visit the Château, and a promenade on the terrace followed by afternoon tea was a highlight of every young couple's week. He was on duty during visits of Queen Elizabeth II and Prince Philip, Queen Juliana of the Netherlands and the King and Queen of Siam. And he told how the Château was emptied to accommodate Churchill and Roosevelt during the Second World War. (These two leaders lodged at the nearby Citadel, but held their conference at the Frontenac.)

Between May and October, when the city is awash with tourists, the Château enjoys 90 percent occupancy. Early spring and late fall bring conventions by the dozen. Christmas here is so magical some families have been celebrating it at the Château for generations. Highlight of the year though, according to Johnny, is Winter Carnival time.

IF YOU GO: For further information, contact the Château Frontenac, 1 rue des Carrières, Quebec City, Que., G1R 4P5. CP Hotels' toll free numbers are: US 1-800-828-7447; Ontario & Quebec 1-800-268-9420; elsewhere in Canada 1-800-268-9411.

SAVORING CHARLEVOIX'S RICHES

Baie Ste Catherine, Quebec: At the coastal Marine Center, young Marie Colomb was apologetic. She had shown us model whales, a movie about whale hunting and the skeleton of a beluga recently washed ashore. But then, after lugging her telescope to the station's upper deck for the grand finale, she could point out nothing livelier than a lighthouse in the grey water.

It was, she said, most unusual, because at least 10 species of whales inhabit this region where the St Lawrence and Saguenay rivers meet. The mighty blue whales arrive in July and stay through fall. Approximately 350 belugas are known to live here the year round, and just yesterday three of them were cavorting opposite the station. Today they are staying below and I can't say I blame them. It's a blustery morning, threatening to drench us with rain and any sensible creature is snug in its home.

True, the sight of whales would have provided a perfect ending to our trip. But without them we have still had a super week,

exploring the St Lawrence River's north shore. For this is Charlevoix country, stretching 135 miles east of Quebec City to Baie Ste
Catherine, enriched by some 400 years of history and scenes of
rare beauty.

Here green-capped cliffs tower above the river so wide (and
salty) in places that it is referred to as the sea. Mountains of the
ancient Laurentian chain are clothed in the deepest of forest
greens. Wild lupins decorate the meadows with dusty pinks and
blues. Sturdy wooden houses with verandas across the front and
huge wood piles at the back often have three or four foot copies
beside them, apparently the handiwork of winter-idled wood
carvers.

Laurentides Park

From a distance, valley communities tend to resemble toy towns. Always there is a silver-roofed church or two glistening in the sun. Historic mills and dwellings are converted for use by artists. Former summer homes of the wealthy have been transformed into adorable inns and restaurants. Pottery, handwoven and knitted clothes, wood carvings and paintings of local scenes cram the ubiquitous boutiques. Some of the first European settlers in these hills were 17th century artisans and craftsmen, farmers too, who worked the rich St Lawrence Valley soil as Indians did before them.

A century later Americans discovered this coast as a summer playground. And by the mid-19th century the British were ensconced here in holiday homes. Nowadays the Charlevoix is favored by organizers of bus tours and rail excursions. Certainly there is accommodation to suit every vacationer's taste. Touring by car, we passed attractive campgrounds, where early risers fished for breakfast in picturesque streams and rivers, attractive inns with perhaps no more than half a dozen guest rooms, each different from the rest, and traditional resorts.

I suppose it is possible to capture the flavor of Charlevoix during a long weekend, but a week allows you to stop and smell the flowers. An overnight stay in Quebec City at start and finish, two days in or around Pointe-au-Pic and two more at Tadoussac to see the whales, will give you an enjoyable fall vacation. The following highlights are bound to detain you along the way.

About 20 miles east of Quebec City, Ste Anne de Beaupré has been receiving visitors for more than 300 years, for here Ste Anne (revered as the mother of Mary who gave birth to Jesus) is believed to heal the sick of heart, mind and body. The story goes that, after surviving a horrendous storm, a grateful group of Breton sailors built a chapel here in 1658. Before it was completed, a crippled man working on the construction was miraculously cured. Other miracles followed, and in 1667 the first shrine to Ste Anne was erected. Such was her fame that 42,000 pilgrims had come here by 1700. Now the total number of pilgrims and visitors over the years has topped 60 million.

Ste Anne de Beaupré

Other buildings include a memorial chapel built in 1878 on the site of, and using some of the materials from, the original chapel. A mountain spring feeds Ste Anne's fountain, from which most visitors stop to drink. The Scala Santa resembles an opera house in miniature, but in fact contains a 19th-century copy of the 28 steps which Christ climbed to the judgment seat of Pontius Pilate. Stations of the Cross are marked with life-size bronze sculptures. A museum contains religious artifacts, some of them dating to the early 18th century. There is a hospital for pilgrims requiring medical care and an inn with 107 rooms, each with toilet and shower ensuite.

Another four miles will take you past Mont Ste Anne with its ski-runs and chalets, to Les Chutes Ste Anne—pretty enough in summer and said to be spectacular in fall. A half-mile circular walking route has been cut through the forested hillside, around a waterfall which pounds into a rocky canyon 240 feet below.

Baie St Paul is a magical riverfront town settled 300 years ago. Surrounded by the Laurentians' highest peaks and decorated by the prettiest waterfalls and streams, it has understandably attracted some of Quebec's finest artists over the years. The Cesar Mill (1772) houses a sculpture gallery and several artists' studios. There are craft boutiques and more studios in historical dwellings, as well as local inns and restaurants. By the wharf you will see an old goelette—that typical Quebecoise cargo carrier that plied the St Lawrence river in the late 19th century.

At Baie St Paul, there are choices to be made: whether to follow Highway 138 through the mountains to La Malbaie, or take the coastal road. Before doing either, you might choose to ride a ferry to everybody's favorite: Ile aux Coudres, named by Jacques Cartier in 1535 for its abundance of hazelnut trees. The island is a super showcase for traditional Quebecoise inns and restaurants. Art studios, craft boutiques and sites steeped in the history of 300 years could detain you all day.

About halfway along the coast, Pointe-au-Pic, La Malbaie and Cap à L'Aigle form one of North America's oldest vacation areas. The last two communities were named by Champlain when he passed this way in 1608: Cap à L'Aigle for the many eagles he saw nesting on the cape, and La Malbaie (Bad Bay) because he tied up there at high tide and next morning awoke to find his ship stuck in the mud.

By the mid-19th century some of this continent's most celebrated families had established summer homes at Pointe-au-Pic. More would come with a retinue of servants to settle for the season in the Manoir Richelieu. Usually they arrived in Montreal by train, then continued along the river aboard Canada Steamship Lines' "white boats."

Perched on a cliff above the St Lawrence, 15 miles wide at this point, the Manoir Richelieu was owned by Canada Steamship Lines for decades, and later by the Quebec government. The original manor was built in 1899. Destroyed by fire in 1928, it was replaced with the stone, French-style chateau a year later.

Manoir Richelieu is one of the province's finest resorts. Its leisure facilities include a heated pool, tennis courts, and an 18-hole championship golf course. Water sports are available, as is whale watching. Winter programs include down-hill and cross-country skiing, sleigh rides and ice-skating. Dinner in the Manoir Richelieu's St Laurent Room is an all-evening affair. The food is good to excellent. Service can be a little slow, but it doesn't matter since an orchestra entertains and the bread is oven-fresh.

End of the line is Baie Ste Catherine and, across the river by free ferry, Tadoussac. Dominating the town, the Hotel Tadoussac is a sprawling white building capped by a brilliant red roof and set in landscaped grounds above the harbor.

IF YOU GO: Dozens of good hotels, large and small, hug this coast. Several companies organize whale-watching expeditions. More information on the Charlevoix area and its accommodations is available from the Association touristique régionale de Charlevoix, 166 boul. de Comporte, C.P. 275, La Malbaie, Quebec G5A 1T8, telephone 418-665-4454.

QUEBEC HISTORY ON THE HOOF

Quebec City: Queen Beatrix loved it. So did the convention delegates and cruise ship passengers, heads of state and corporations.

Now I too can be added to the list of visitors who last year enjoyed a walking tour of this city's historic area, escorted by Barry Lane of Baillairge Cultural Tours Inc.

In other countries I always try to join such walks. It was with pleasure then that I learned of two young men from Ontario who conduct walking tours in one of my favorite Canadian cities. Barry developed his love for Quebec City as a soldier here, following graduation from Kingston's military college. His partner, David Mendel, is from Ottawa. Seven years ago they formed their company, realizing a need for customized tours. Now they have ten guides, taking groups and visiting dignitaries around the historic areas at any time of the year. In winter they work with school children through a program called Interface. Between June and October they do public walks, twice a day, for a fee of about $10 per person.

On the hottest day of summer, we tramped the narrow streets of this city's Upper and Lower Towns for well beyond the allotted two and a quarter hours. Our group of 10 became so involved, at the tour's conclusion we were loathe to let Barry go home.

Mind you, it is very easy to lose track of time in the city Charles Dickens described as "a place not to be forgotten, or mixed up in the mind with other places." What makes it unique? Well, for one thing it is the only walled city north of Mexico. For another it boasts the continent's largest aggregation of 17th- and 18th-century buildings. Its French culture and language have survived 400 years. History, as colorful as anything in popular fiction, is skillfully preserved. The location above and below the 200-foot cliff is unequalled. Moreover, the entire historic area has now been designated a UNESCO World Heritage treasure.

Our first stop this day is in the Upper Town, before a statue of Samuel de Champlain who started it all in 1608. Jacques Cartier had come ashore and wintered below the cliff in 1534, but it was Champlain who built the first permanent settlement here beside the St Lawrence River. The square around it became a marketplace lined with merchants' homes, while on the cliff's plateau, military, government and religious institutions were established. Now, much of the Lower Town is restored or rebuilt, and for almost a century the Upper Town has been dominated by the ponderous Château Frontenac hotel.

On a 2,200-foot boardwalk in front of Le Château we scan the river, 400 miles and more from the sea at this point, and yet so vital to us. For this is the river that brought 17th-century explorers and fur traders, and priests bent on spreading Christianity to the interior wilderness. It brought hard working pioneers in the 19th century, immigrants filled with hope of a better life in the 20th. But none were more important than James Wolfe and his men, who paddled silently along the river one September morning in 1759.

On another early morning, long before tourists and musicians and school groups crowded the boardwalk, I sought out the site where Britain's General Wolfe and France's Marquis de Montcalm met in battle that autumn day. Beyond the terrace, along the Promenade des Gouverneurs clinging to the cliff's edge 360 feet above the river, past the citadel's outer walls, I came to the Plains of Abraham in a dew-soaked Battlefield Park. History tells us that British troops had shelled the city for two months before they found a spot where they could scale the cliff's face. At the top, they waited for the French to advance. Volleys were fired. In a matter of 20 minutes it was all over, leaving both leaders mortally wounded and Canada in British hands. Following markers on the ground, one can trace events of the decisive battle. A monument pays tribute to the valor of both Wolfe and Montcalm.

At the mighty citadel built by the British, a powder magazine dating from the French regime houses a small museum of military history. Changing of the Guard ceremonies (10 a.m. daily in summer, weather permitting) are as flamboyant as any in Britain, with soldiers wearing scarlet tunics and bearskin hats, and answering to orders given in French.

For the officers at least, military life in early Quebec had its moments. There was Champlain's club called L'Ordre de Bon Temps where members held monthly feasts for fellow officers. (At one such dinner, Champlain suffered a stroke, from which he later died.) And grand balls held at the fort in 1667 are said to have been every bit as glamorous as those at Louis XIV's palace.

When the British took over, invitations to Friday night dances at the governor's residence were greatly sought after by the local girls, keen to meet and eventually marry well-heeled British officers. Even now the 1893 Château Frontenac, first link in a chain of castle-like hotels strung across Canada, continues to host glittering galas enhanced by the dramatic and historic setting.

There were no such hi-jinks in the Upper Town's religious community, founded soon after Champlain's settlers planted their roots in New France. Our walking tour takes us along skinny back streets to the Ursuline Convent's Mary of the Incarnation Center, where in 1639 the intrepid Mary started a school for French and Indian girls. Her work was not entirely successful in that Indian students, pining for their families, climbed out of the windows and ran off home. In the adjoining museum relics of the early years are many, among them the yellowing skull of the Marquis de Montcalm.

Monseigneur Francois de Montmorency Laval, first Bishop of Quebec, founded a seminary here in the 1660s to train priests for the new colony. Leaving the life of a nobleman in France to join the church, he shunned even the meager comforts offered him here and eventually died of gangrene caused by frostbite. The seminary's chapel and courtyard are open to all, its museum for guided tours only.

I could happily spend a day or more studying the rich tapestry woven by early Quebec's religious community. Of several churches, the Holy Trinity Anglican Cathedral is not the oldest or even the most dazzling, but has special appeal for surviving in a predominantly Catholic environment. Built in 1804, this first Anglican cathedral outside Britain is fashioned after St. Martin's-in-the-Fields in London's Trafalgar Square. Oak for its pews was cut from woods behind Windsor Castle, stained glass windows created in England by a Mr Clutterbuck, and its bishop's throne is carved from a giant elm tree that once shaded cathedral grounds.

The tortuously steep Coté de la Montagne leads us down to the Lower Town where in Place Royale the church of Nôtre Dame des Victoires replicates an original built in 1688. With its new-old houses lining tiny streets the Lower Town is one colorful outdoors museum and tourists love it. They crowd the shops and galleries those historic homes have become, and pour into restaurants serving traditional French-Canadian cuisine. And when they are through, they ride excursion boats and ferries to Lévis, to photograph the impressive river view.

A lengthy restoration program will eventually see 10 blocks around the square rebuilt or restored to 17th and 18th century appearance. Using plans from archives in France, exterior elevations are carefully copied, while inside the buildings are as functional as any in modern Quebec. Apartments and condominiums with 18th-century facades have increased the residential population, giving the community a realistic air as children skip rope and play ball games and chant their rhymes in French.

Our walking tour ends here in Place Royale, next to an archaeological dig which has already provided proof of habitation dating to 300 B.C.

IF YOU GO: To see all of the historic areas you require two to three days, which would allow time at the citadel, Plains of Abraham and old port restorations as well as leisurely walks through the Upper and Lower Towns. Baillairge Cultural Tours start at the Musée du Fort across from the Château Frontenac, 9:30 and 2 p.m. daily in summer. Telephone 418-658-4799 for reservations. For more information on Quebec City, contact the Quebec City Region Tourism and Convention Bureau, 60 rue D'Auteuil, Quebec, PQ, G1R 4C4. Telephone 418-651-2882.

KINGDOM OF THE SAGUENAY

Tadoussac, Quebec: Most wildlife enthusiasts plan their visit to Tadoussac for August or later, to watch the great whales frolicking here where the St Lawrence and Saguenay rivers meet. Scheduling my trip around visiting Tall Ships, I arrived in Tadoussac the first week of July and, although assured the belugas were about, I didn't see so much as a whale's tail.

It was a good trip anyway, for this is the splendidly wild terrain of Northern Quebec, dressed with pine covered mountains and rocky crags of an ancient fjord, giddy streams and pounding waterfalls, and communities that appear as remote today as they did a century ago. It is a region of special appeal to hunters and fishermen, and anyone with an eye for scenic beauty enhanced by shades of early Quebec.

Hotel Tadoussac

Our 10-day tour by car took us from Toronto to Quebec City, along the northern shore of the St Lawrence River to Baie Ste Catherine, and across the mouth of the Saguenay to Tadoussac. From here we followed the Saguenay to Chicoutimi, circled Lac Saint-Jean, and arrived home after racking up close to 2,000 miles. I have already written about the Charlevoix coast between Quebec City and Baie Ste Catherine. The following are highlights of the Tadoussac–Lac Saint-Jean segments of our trip.

Focal point of Tadoussac is the Hotel Tadoussac, a familiar sight to movie-goers who saw it as The Hotel New Hampshire. Set in colorful gardens above a nice stretch of beach, its leisure facilities include a heated pool, tennis courts, golf course and nearby hunting and fishing club. In summer, Saguenay river cruises leave from the hotel. From mid-July through fall, there are whale-watching excursions.

Vacationers have been coming here for well over a hundred years. The Tadoussac Hotel, predecessor of today's Hotel Tadoussac, opened in 1864. Canada's new governor-general and his wife stayed here while their own summer home was under construction nearby. In her diary of 1872, the Marchioness of Dufferin wrote "the inn is situated in the curve of a lovely bay, with a nice sandy beach all round it. There are rocky walks of a most amusing description for the walker, a good anchorage for the yachtsman and, as all fishing is up the Saguenay and this place is at its mouth, there is sport for the sportsman. There are white porpoises and seals and occasional whales to be seen rolling and jumping about. Altogether we thought the place most attractive."

Had her diary been dated a century later, it could have read the same. Except that the present hotel was built by the Canada Steamship Lines in 1942.

Jacques Cartier referred to Tadoussac as the "Gateway to the Kingdom of Saguenay" when he came this way in 1535. French explorer and trader Pierre Chauvin established the continent's first trading post here in 1599. And by the time Samuel de Champlain arrived four years later, it was a supply port for European ships. Reminders of these times are to be found in a replica of Chauvin's little house beside the Hotel Tadoussac. Across from it an Indian chapel was built in 1747 to replace another that stood here a hundred years before.

Cut through the forested mountains, Highway 172 to Chicoutimi took us past fast-flowing rivers with a fisherman or two hip deep in the water, and small communities seemingly all shaped from the same mold. There are two beauty spots along the way: some 43 miles from Tadoussac, a side road leads to Ste Rose-du-Nord, nestled pictorially on the river bank; and 30 miles further on the village of St Fulgence offers a dramatic view of the fjord from the peak of Mont Valin.

Today, Chicoutimi is a modern metropolis sprawled along both banks of the Saguenay. Its museum of Saguenay–Lac Saint-Jean will fill you in on regional and cultural history. And, as some cities convert waterfront warehouses to lively people places, Chicoutimi and its neighbors are putting abandoned pulp mills to similar good use.

Such is the two and a half acre site of the former Chicoutimi Pulp Company, founded in 1897 on the banks of the Chicoutimi river and operational until 1930. This is where you come to see good summer theatre, movies (including one of Canada's earliest, shot in Chicoutimi in 1915), concerts, children's entertainment and cultural events. The original 19th-century mill is converted to a terrace cafe. Agricultural and mill equipment, and interesting household bric-a-brac from the early 1900s are shown by a cheerful, English-speaking, curator.

In summer, keen tourists are known to drive from Quebec City to Chicoutimi for the day to take a Saguenay cruise. On a calm sunny morning, we came in from Jonquière, for the 8:30 departure of *Marjolaine II*. Travelling at a steady 11 knots, she took her 150 passengers on a 35-mile cruise to Cape Trinity, turned back to Ste Rose-du-Nord for lunch and had us home in time for tea.

The outbound journey was not encouraging. Within half an hour of leaving Chicoutimi, ruthless winds began sweeping the deck, as heavy looking clouds scudded across a leaden sky. Cigarette smoke filled the lounge, windows steamed up and obliter-

Ste Rose-du-Nord

ated the view, and on-board commentary about the river was inaudible above the din.

At the fjord, some of us braved the wind's wrath for a better look at the two highest capes: Trinity at 1,500 feet and Eternity at 1,670. At Cape Trinity, the engine was stopped, and to the strains of Ave Maria, we stared up at Nôtre Dame du Saguenay, 590 feet above the river. As Protector of the Kingdom, she has watched over her realm for more than a century—since 1871 actually, when Quebec sculptor Louis Jobin created her.

Pleasant though it was, our 90-minute lunch stop at Ste Rose-du-Nord would have been even more enjoyable had we thought to bring a picnic. Instead, we joined a queue for take-out fare at a café beside the dock, and sat with it on a rock beside the river. This Pearl of the Saguenay, as it is known, Ste Rose-du-Nord is indeed a diamond in the rough, far removed from the time and stress. There is little to see—the church with its driftwood altar, and a nature museum. A grocer's store and a handful of homes, at least two of which offer bed & breakfast. Our return journey was all too short. Favored by a warm sun now, we shed parkas and sweaters and stretched out on deck to savor the full grandeur and majesty of the mighty Saguenay.

From Jonquière we had an enjoyable day on the 140-mile drive around Lac Saint-Jean, into which the Saguenay flows. Terrain is less spectacular here, but oh so peaceful. Pretty too, with pictur-esque rivers, neat little dwellings and farm buildings, and that big beautiful lake. In the late 17th century missionaries and fur traders set up posts at former Indian relay stations. But since the Hudson's Bay Company and North West Company had conces-sions to operate in the region, clearing of the land for farming didn't get under way until the mid-1800s. A dreadful fire in 1870 razed many of the settlements around Lac Saint-Jean, leaving 250,000 acres of cleared land in its wake. Towards the end of the century sawmills had sprung up across the territory, and by the early 1900s pulp mills were established.

Regional emblem is the blueberry. Shops sell every conceiv-able souvenir decorated with imitation blueberries. August brings the long-awaited Blueberry Festival. In late summer, I am told, the countryside is glazed a hazy blue from the ripe berries waiting to be harvested. And a popular family outing is to pack a picnic lunch for a day of berry picking—as they did in the story of Maria Chapdelaine.

The Chapdelaines, (the Bedard family in real life) lived at Peribonka on Lac Saint-Jean's north shore, where the Musée Louis Hemon is dedicated to the book's author. There is no entry charge for the first building, an attractive little café, gift shop and display case containing Hemon's typewriter and worn leather hold-all. There is an admission charge for the rest, but only some of the seven stations are connected with the author.

One is the café-cum-gift shop. Another is a bust of Hemon, and a third is a wooden cabin owned by Samuel Bedard, in which Louis Hemon lived for six months while writing his story. Fourth is a barn displaying a mixed but interesting bag of memorabilia: letters from Louis, a 1913 death certificate showing he died from injuries received in a train accident in Northern Ontario. Also pictures of Le Nord, the ferry boat on which Hemon and Bedard first met, during its lake crossing from Robertval to Peribonka. Posters promote the 1934 movie based on the book, and filmed on location here. A later version, we are told, was filmed somewhere else.

Across the lake, just south of Robertval, Val-Jalbert is a former mill town, resurrected now for tourists. Here in 1902, Monsieur Damase Jalbert opened a pulp mill. A busy community soon centred around the mill and it had its own company hotel. There were modern company houses for employees, and a school staffed by four resident nuns.

When the mill closed, residents were forced to move to wherever they could find work, and an ailing Val-Jalbert took on the appearance of a ghost town. Returned to good health now, it is a 1,700-acre park with a pleasant picnic area and campsites. The handsome school is an orientation center, where young guides explain what's here now and a movie shows how it used to be. Two or three houses are studios, wherein artisans demonstrate their crafts and sell the finished work. The hotel has a snack bar and shop on its ground floor.

The sound of rushing water led us to the waterfall 235 feet high. Beside it, mill ruins contain some original machinery and an institutional type cafeteria. At the park's entrance a more intimate café has a few tables indoors and out. There, on a sun drenched patio, we enjoyed vegetable soup and hot bread, a spicy tortiere with salad, blueberry pie warm from the oven and coffee. All homemade, all delicious and all traditional Quebecoise.

IF YOU GO: The shortest route from Quebec City, Highway 175, cuts through Laurentides Provincial Park but by-passes the scenic Charlevoix coast. Tourist information on this region is available from the Association touristique du Saguenay–Lac

Saint-Jean, 198, rue Racine est, bureau 200, Chicoutimi, Quebec G7H 1R9, telephone 418-543-9778.

PERCÉ, THE GASPÉ'S FAVORITE TOURIST TOWN

Percé,Quebec: I suppose some might question whether it ranks with Niagara Falls, or one's first sight of snow capped Rockies on the drive to Banff, but certainly when you come around a bend in the road and see Percé rock at high tide, you are aware that this is a very special place. At the eastern tip of the Gaspé peninsula, on the Gulf of St Lawrence, the town of Percé was an important fishing center for years. Now it is a summer resort and highlight of everybody's tour of the Gaspé region.

Tiny Percé has two winning cards that set it apart from dozens of Gaspesian fishing communities in the same pack. One is the seabird sanctuary of Bonaventure Island, a couple of miles from shore. The other is this magnificent pierced rock, 1440 feet long with a natural arch at one end and 330 feet at its widest point. Rising 165 to 290 feet from the water, its appearance changes dramatically according to the light and angle from which it is viewed. Providing endless fascination, it will cause you to stop and stare often during your stay in Percé.

At the time Samuel de Champlain named Percé in 1603, the rock was in a single piece. Separation of a pillar at the far end occurred in 1845, when the top of a second arch collapsed. Long before that, it was part of a cape jutting out from Mont Joli, and now at low tide you can see that it is still attached to the mainland by a sandbar.

For an eye-level view, you can walk or drive part of the way up Cap Mont Joli to where a footpath leads to the summit, and steps take you down to the connecting sandbar. Do check on tide times before walking across the sand, or you might find yourself cut off from the shore as have others before you. Nobody climbs the rock any more. A few years back intrepid youngsters would scale it

Percé rock, from Bonaventure Island

it simply because it was there or to gather hay from the top. But in recent years crumbling has deterred would-be alpinists, and so its crown is left to the seabirds.

As for the town itself, popularity has changed but not necessarily spoiled its character. For years, summer artists have flocked here with the same regularity as Bonaventure's gannets. In consequence many little shops and studios specialize in artwork and crafts. More is displayed at the Centre d'Art in an enormous Norman style barn where Sonia tells fortunes twice a week and musicians give impromptu concerts outside. Its second floor is an art gallery containing mostly local scenes, while at ground level carvings and sculptures, ceramics, pottery made from Gaspé clay and jewelry from semi-precious stones washed ashore, are displayed for sale.

To familiarize ourselves with regional history, we drove one day to Gaspé, a rather unlovely town with a modern museum above the bay where Jacques Cartier landed in 1534. In an adjoining park, a monument to this historical landmark deserves far more time than I was prepared to give it in pelting rain. Work of the talented Bourgault-Legros family, sculptors from Saint Jean Port Joli, the memorial consists of six large cast-iron steles in the shape of dolmens, with bas-reliefs depicting events surrounding Cartier's landing.

Inside the Musée de la Gaspesie, sculptures are less easy to understand. A fox on a pole hung from the ceiling, and plaster body parts protruding from black sand hold no attraction for me. Far more interesting is regional history, documented with aged photographs and records.

Some historians believe that the first Europeans to reach these shores were Vikings, around the year 1,000. They were followed by Basque, Norman and Breton fishermen. And then in 1534 Jacques Cartier planted a wooden cross here at Gaspé, claiming the land for France. In the 17th century there were as many as 500 fishing boats anchored alongside the pierced rock. A hundred years later Charles Robin came from Jersey in the Channel Islands to found a permanent settlement. His and other companies from Europe brought their countrymen to work in the growing fishing industry. From one generation to the next, these fishermen were indebted to their employers, profiting little from the wealth of the cod they harvested.

In the museum, photographs show solemn looking women drying cod on flakes—wooden racks such as you'll see around the coast still. And tourists who, in the early 1900s, would arrive aboard rickety motor coaches at the "romantic Gaspé" from Montreal and New York.

Coach companies still include the Gaspé in their Quebec tours. These days they come to comfortable hotels with rooms overlooking the famous rock, and a surprisingly good selection of restaurants. To name some that linger in memory: Restaurante Pecherie, located beside the wharf, had opened only three weeks before I dropped in for a restful meal. Here my lunch was enhanced by classical tapes playing softly in the background, and a super view of the rock.

Also on the waterfront, Au Pirate has several stylish dining rooms in a weathered grey house where elegance is the order of the day. At half the price, and every bit as enjoyable, was my evening in the Centre d'Art's unpretentious café. Here, wild flowers decorate wooden tables, service is relaxed and friendly, the food wholesome. Our dinner included thick vegetable soup, woked shrimps and vegetables, homemade bread and ice cream.

Finally, La Normandie's dining room is perhaps the most popular in town, and advance reservations are definitely advisable. Seafood specialties include poached sole in apple butter sauce, and scallops in leek sauce. Appetizers are as interesting as marinated cod livers, crabmeat crepes and fisherman's quiche. Service is impeccable, and you are invited to take your coffee onto the terrace which overlooks attractive gardens, the boardwalk, and beyond it The Rock.

Evening entertainment in Percé is pretty much confined to dining out, theatrical performances at the Centre d'Art and interpretive talks on the Gaspé region. Also walks around town. Regardless of weather, every summer's day sees Percé's main street clogged with people shuffling from one shop to another. From there one wanders along the boardwalk and wharf, where youngsters scramble for crabs and sea urchins, excursion boats leave for Bonaventure Island, and in late afternoon seabirds swirl and screech above fishermen cleaning their catch.

For a quiet walk, you might leave your car at the highway parking lot and follow a footpath to the Wildlife Interpretive Center. The walk is pleasant and the view from the hilltop dazzling.

Following the peninsula's southern rim back to New Brunswick, we came on one lovely seascape after another. Alongside the highway, housewives offered bread still warm from their outdoor ovens, and children held wooden bateaux out to every passing motorist. Fishermen sat working on their nets, beside cod drying in the sun on trestles such as were used here 300 years ago. The drive took us most of a day. Actually, if we had planned it right we would have allowed for two.

IF YOU GO: Percé is 480 miles from Quebec City, via Autoroute 20 to Rivière du Loup, thence Route 132, which circles the Gaspé peninsula.

BONAVENTURE ISN'T STRICTLY FOR THE BIRDS

Percé,Quebec: It was a most endearing meeting, in this cramped and noisy place. From a thousand or more who looked pretty much the same to me, he spotted her without hesitation. Striding purposefully through the crowds, nudging aside his neighbors, he stood before her—his mate for life, mother of his children. With wings spread wide they stood face to face, rubbing beaks and emitting what I interpreted as joyous squawks, performing the spectacular ritual of adult gannets reunited after one of the pair had been away. Their greeting finished, she sank back onto her nest, while he went off to mingle with the hoards of gannets inhabiting these cliffs of Bonaventure Island off the coast of Percé in the rugged Gaspé region of Quebec.

The gannetry, believed to be the world's largest, is just one reason to come to this pleasant island, with a surface area of little over two and a half square miles, quiet beaches, and derelict houses that prompt thoughts of hardy individuals who lived here two or three hundred years ago.

In summer months, boats leave Percé wharf every 20 minutes for a ride around the famed arched rock, and on to Bonaventure. Three quarters of an hour after leaving the mainland, they stop at this tiny island, where passengers are invited to go ashore or return directly to Percé. My advice is that you come in early morning, wear good walking shoes and bring a picnic lunch. In fine weather, you will want to spend the best part of the day here.

Soaked in summer sunshine, Bonaventure is a picturesque island, its grey weathered wood buildings contrasting with a deep blue sky, and cliff top meadows smothered in daisies. Limestone cliffs are skirted by beaches, often deserted in spite of the countless tourists off-loaded here throughout each day. Guided walks are conducted with commentary in French and English.

Heading for the north shore gannetry, we were accompanied part of the way by an enthusiastic young naturalist. He named the magenta fireweeds and caraway plants for us, and explained that the island has no mosquitoes because its rocks are porous, soaking up rainwater which might otherwise attract insects. Wild raspberries grow prettily beside the paths, as do strange looking mushrooms. Or are they toadstools? Some are like omelettes—large, flat, yellow and orange in color. Others are tall and slim, such as those used to illustrate fairy tales. On our escorted walk we learned that the ancestors of island mice travelled here as stowaways on fishing vessels, while hares and foxes walk over from the mainland on the winter's ice. And that fishermen from the Channel Islands brought cows and plants, and cleared patches of land so they could lay out their cod to dry in the sun.

Gannets on Bonaventure Island

During our walk, we could smell, and then hear, the gannets long before reaching their cliff-top colony. Our first sight of them in great numbers had been from the boat, which took us to within a few feet of cliffs where they sat on every conceivable ledge. The whirring of wings and vociferous squawking drowned out most of the captain's narrative. Still I heard enough to learn that most of the birds are gannets, joined by numerous black cormorants and penguin-like murres. Over 100,000 seabirds make their homes here each summer. In October they fly south to warmer climes, returning each April to Bonaventure and the exact site they occupied the year before.

Traditionally, a gannet lays only one egg each spring. However, during the years when nests were systematically robbed, they would lay a second, and even a third if it was stolen. It didn't help the ever decreasing population. Babies born in summer weren't strong enough to reach the sea unharmed, or to fly on the long journey south before winter set in. And so in 1919, the north shore cliffs became a protected refuge. Twelve years ago, when the last of the human populace moved to the mainland, the entire island became a seabird sanctuary.

Now the gannetry is fenced off from visitors. This means that while you can no longer walk knee-deep in birds, you have the unusual opportunity of watching them at close range.

In early August we found young gannets in various stages of growth—some covered in tawny down, others with spotted coats. Several rather large birds were still cosily ensconced in the nests, which are little more than mounds of grass, feathers and seaweed with an indentation on the top to hold an egg. An on-site natural-ist will tell you everything you want to know: how gannets ap-pear to mate for life, take turns sitting on the egg and feeding the chick with regurgitated fish for the first three months of its life. After that period, junior must exercise his wings preparatory to leaving the cliff. If he is disinclined to make the 300-foot jump on his own accord, he will be pushed over the edge by a parent. Hopefully he survives the fall, lives at sea, and during his third year returns to find a mate and live happily ever after on the ancestral cliff.

Notices attached to the fence describe the various rituals you will see performed. One, for example, tells you that a gannet stretches his neck and opens his wings to declare territorial own-ership. (This is quite a sight, since a full grown adult is three feet tall and has a wing spread of six feet.) Another describes how a gannet will skypoint before taking off, pointing its beak up-wards, filling large air bags located in the neck, and so lessening the shock when he hits the water.

Hiking time from the dock to the gannetry is 45 minutes. Other trails will lead you around or across the island, but before setting off I suggest you visit the interpretive center and mu-seum in a cleared area by the wharf.

Exhibits here tell you that Bonaventure Island has been around for some 30 million years. Long before the arrival of Jacques Cartier, it was used as a stopover for European fisher-men who would dry and barrel their cod on shore before return-ing to their homelands. Settlers came as early as the 1600s, and in 1845 the Le Bouthillier Company of Jersey established a base here, which continued operation until 1926. In the mid-1800s, as many as 200 people lived on this tiny island. A century later the population was down to 85. Now it is nil.

The small museum traces island population growth and decline, a tiny house illustrates how settlers lived here a hundred or so years ago. And while a snack-bar nearby sells hot dogs and coffee and such, a good idea is to bring a packed lunch from one of Percé's restaurants and have a picnic at some quiet spot around the coast.

IF YOU GO: Boats ply frequently during the summer season between Percé and Bonaventure Island and you may catch any boat back. The last departure for Percé is 4:30 p.m. and no overnight camping is allowed.

IN THE MAGDALENS YOU REALLY CAN GET AWAY FROM IT ALL

Havre-Aubert,Quebec: At the Café de la Grave—with its unmatched furnishings, recorded violin music and mid-afternoon temptations such as home-made carrot cake and seal pâté—I was asked if I had the right time. At my reply the young man shook his head, studied the sun's position in the sky, discussed it with the waitress and then informed me I was running on Montreal time which is one hour behind that of the islands. Not too surprising since I was from the mainland? Well, no. It's just that it took me two and a half days to find out.

But that's what a visit to the Magdalen Islands is all about. Life here, you see, is ruled by the elements rather than the clock. This is where city pressures are blown away by strong ocean breezes. Late afternoon rush hour is a string of lobster boats returning to the port. An important decision is your selection of bouillabaisse over the fresh seafood platter. Fatigue is when you walk for miles on a beach, forgetting it's the same distance back. Hurry? Maybe, if you suddenly decide to watch the sun set beyond nature's rock sculptures at Etang du Nord or Belle Anse. On the other hand, there is always tomorrow. . . .

On your first visit, it may take a day or two to adjust your pace, to realize that Madeleinots have successively wedded modern creature comforts and technology to a lifestyle 30 or 40 years behind the times. That they live in an era when there was time to stop and talk with strangers, to welcome them to the community, and even invite one home for supper. So leave your suspicions on the mainland, along with mortgage payments, worries and eight-lane highways. They will be there when you return. Meantime you can experience a unique vacation in these hospitable islands.

If you are only vaguely aware of what and where the Magdalens are, it is understandable. You may have heard about them in early spring when protesters used to arrive at the baby seal hunt. And the lobster you ate last week could well have come from these waters. As a tourist destination for anyone living outside Quebec, however, they seem to be Canada's best kept secret.

There are a dozen islands in the archipelago known as Iles de la Madeleine, The Magdalens. Seven are inhabited, and six have been connected by road over the past 60 years. Combined population is approximately 14,000 people whose day-to-day lives are very much molded by the area's history, geography and climate.

The Magdalens have changed hands several times since Jacques Cartier came upon them in 1534. Annexed to Newfoundland in 1753 and then Quebec in 1774, they were given by King George III to Sir Isaac Coffin in 1798 as a reward for his services during the American Revolution. In 1902 a third generation Isaac Coffin sold the Magdalens to Quebec for $100,000. And, in case you are wondering, they were named for Madeleine Fontaine, wife of Francois Doublet who was their first governor.

In the late 1700s Acadians and Scottish immigrants largely contributed to the 50–50 French and English speaking population. Something of a puzzle to strangers, but accepted by the Madeleinots, is that some 13,500 are French speaking while approximately 700 people, in two small, self-contained communities speak only English.

Geographically, the Magdalens' closest neighbor is Cape Breton, 60 miles to the east, though stronger commercial ties are with Prince Edward Island, a further 15 miles south. The nearest provincial connection is Gaspé, some 180 miles distant. As for the islands themselves, they stretch for 70 miles, shaped somewhat like a letter C with the tiny Entree Island a punctuation mark 12 miles from Havre-Aubert in the south.

For so small an area, the scenery is remarkably varied, ranging from pastoral hills to windswept sand dunes, magnificent cliffs and more than 100 miles of wide sand beaches which rival any I have ever seen.

The major industry here is commercial fishing. Plaice, mackerel, cod, scallops and herrings are all brought home in abundance at some time during the year. Buy them from retail outlets near the wharfs and they will be fresh enough to jump into your pan. Lobsters trapped five miles offshore are claimed to be among the world's finest. In the two-month season a single boat may catch 10,000 pounds, sold locally or shipped to other parts of Canada. Wander along the docks around 11:30 a.m. or late afternoon and you can watch the fishermen as they measure, sort and box their lobsters.

Tourism is becoming increasingly important to the islands. Prior to 1972 a few perennial vacationers found their way here. Then, following introduction of a daily ferry service from Prince Edward Island, the trickle swelled to a steady stream, and now some 18,000 visitors a year come to the Magdalens between July 1 and August 15. The aim at this time is not to increase the number of mid-summer tourists, but to expand the season to June through September.

Because the season is short, big resort investors aren't eyeing those gorgeous beaches, and for this we can be grateful because

Madaleinot hospitality is an important aspect of a vacation here. There are some inexpensive small hotels and motels, cottages and lots of bed and breakfast type accommodation. In a private home, I had a large, bright room (shared bath) with breakfast—and a cooked dinner for a modest extra charge. What my landlady lacked in knowledge of English, she made up for 10 times over with patience trying to understand my rusty French. I found this to be so throughout the islands. Limited French is matched with a response in halting English, followed by a careful French translation. After a week, my French vocabulary increased noticeably.

So what exactly is here, now you are settled in and slowed down? Knowing that the total experience will linger in memory, it is difficult to pin-point a single major attraction. Of the wealth of natural endowments, island beaches are perhaps the most outstanding. Scramble over a dune and you will come upon miles of wide, pale sand where litter is unclaimed sand dollars and noise the screeching of gulls. And quite possibly, yours will be the only human footprints to mark it that day. In mid-June local boys splashed happily in the ocean. By now it should have warmed sufficiently to lure less hardy visitors in.

High, rust colored cliffs gouged by persistent pounding of the sea present quite a spectacle. Columns, multi-storied caves and walls provide natural shelter for your beach cook-outs when winds above are chilly. Even without a picnic along, you can spend a few happy hours exploring the sculptures.

Pointe-à-Loup is the place to dig for clams, or buy from youngsters who stand by the road with their buckets brimming over. Commercial fishermen sometimes carry passengers who can manage to be on board by 4 a.m. At Cap-aux-Meules, a 42-foot excursion boat offers three-hour fishing trips to a minimum of five and maximum of 22 passengers. For a little more than the ferry fare, you can have an interesting day on Entree Island, the English speaking community 12 miles from Havre-Aubert.

Best of all are the unplanned days. Stop at a fishing village and discover things to detain you for several hours. Climb a velvety hill to sit among wild violets or strawberries at the top. Likely as not its other side is sheered off, a sculptured cliff slapped by a boisterous sea below. Pause to admire the landscape dotted with tiny wooden houses. Brightly painted in solid reds and yellows and blues, they seem to have been tossed by some giant hand and left to settle wherever they landed.

Come evening there are French movies, and the splendid sunsets, and sitting in little cafés listening to music. Also a surprising number of quality dining places, usually in converted houses owned and operated by restaurateurs who have moved from the mainland. Such is La Table des Roy at Lavernière, where an enormous bouillabaisse contains six kinds of fish, including a couple of lobsters, while the seafood platter is a work of art. Auberge à la Jetée in a recently refurbished house at Cap aux Meules is open for breakfast, lunch and dinner and has a bar and 10 rooms for rent. Another restaurant of good repute is Maison de la Couline at Bassin. Specializing in Madaleinot dishes, its herring appetizers, whatever fish is in season, and berry pie will give you a tasty sample of island fare.

Lunch at the Café de la Grave and you will probably potter about the area for the rest of the day. Fishing huts here have become craft studios where visitors can do nice things with sea shells. In summer photographic safaris are conducted daily. Then, up the hill a bit, the Musée de la Mer has exhibits from island waters including a full-size replica of le ponchon. Le ponchon, something of a symbol in the Magdalens, is a barrel which carried the winter mail in 1910 when contact with the outside world was cut off. Sealed in metal cans and set adrift in the barrel were some 27 letters to friends and Members of Parliament urging that the broken telegraph cable be repaired—as it was a year later. The museum contains some of the original letters, including one proposing marriage. Between the museum and La Grave, a low pink building houses La Saline restaurant, and an adjoining crafts shop well stocked with woven goods, carvings, pottery, knitted and hand sewn goods produced by dextrous hands during winter's long evenings.

Many natural materials found on the islands are put to good use by the local artisans. One colorful character I met was Jean Boyer, who works with rocks gathered from the seashore. Using tools he made himself he turns and polishes the stone, creating lamp bases and vases, ash trays, plates and bowls all delicately patterned with natural colors which come to the surface with polishing. Boyer's passion is not to sell stone souvenirs, or make them, but to teach Madeleinots his skills. Ultimately he sees Iles de la Madeleine art pieces as fashionable as Eskimo soapstone carvings, but when I was there he wasn't having much luck in generating local interest.

IF YOU GO: Iles de la Madeleine are 780 miles from Montreal. There are daily air services from Montreal, Quebec, Gaspé and Charlottetown. The daily ferry service between the islands and Prince Edward Island carries cars, but rental cars are available on the islands. A freight/passenger vessel sails between Montreal and the islands and the return journey takes five days. More information is available from the Association touristique régionale des Isles-de-la-Madeleine, 128 rue Principale, C.P. 1028 Cap-aux-Meules, Iles de la Madeleine, Que., GOB 1BO, telephone 418-986-2245.

GOOD OLD ENTREE ISLAND HOSPITALITY

Entree,Quebec: It's not every day that a mayor sits on a lard bucket in front of the canned beets and raspberry jam, serenading me with western ballads—and I can't promise he will do the same for you. Upon reflection though, I'd say an impromptu concert in the grocery store is one of the more predictable things that can happen when you visit the tiny island of Entree, 12 miles from the other Magdalens.

From a distance, Entree resembles a green furry dragon, partly submerged in the ocean, some of its humps distinguished as the highest in the Magdalen archipelago. Access, unless you own or can hitch a ride on a private boat, is by ferry which operates daily from Havre-Aubert weather permitting. In mid-winter a natural ice bridge permits vehicular traffic from the same harbor.

At first glance there seems to be nothing here for tourists that they can't get several times over in Gross Iles or Grand Entree, Havre-Aubert or any of the Magdalens so conveniently strung together by a paved highway. Like the others, Entree is a landscape painted in vivid technicolor. Deep red cliffs are green capped, with a base fringe of pale gold sand. Lush, grass-covered hills are dotted with brightly painted frame houses—and a handful of cows, never milked I was told, because people here prefer the canned stuff.

Busiest place is the wharf, where fishermen come and go and sit around sorting their catch. Social center, on a weekday at least, seems to be the general store. Entree also has its own school, church and snack bar. The population, of Scottish and English ancestry, numbers 143. And let us not forget the dogs.

It may be an exaggeration to say the dogs outnumber people here. Could be that it merely looks that way, since the canines have formed a meeting and greeting committee. From almost every house I passed, a dog came to join my four-legged escort. Some dropped out as others fell into line, and throughout my island walk I never had fewer than six friendly mutts trotting beside me.

I knew Entree to be one of the two English speaking communities in the Magdalens. Still it was a surprise when stepping ashore to hear fishermen conversing without so much as a hint of French accent. This in spite of their closest neighbors being 13,500 French speaking Madeleinots just across the water. Entree residents, I was given to understand, have no knowledge of French and no desire to learn the language. Their children are taught in English. Any business they may have outside the island is conducted in English. A government appointed, bilingual co-ordinator keeps them up-to-date with provincial affairs.

Before accompanying me on my day here, I suggest you get out your sturdiest shoes. The island's main road is surfaced with three- or four-inch stones which at the least can be hard on your feet. There are no road signs. Ask directions and you will be told to go "back of the hill" or "up the road two houses past the blue." Not that you need directions. Simply follow the rocky road from the wharf, uphill past the church to Joe's Grocery, owned and operated by Yvan Quinn—and let things progress naturally from there.

The inimitable Yvan wears many hats. An obvious country and western fan (his favorite hat is a cowboy's) he has entertained professionally with his own musical compositions. He runs his store and snack bar. And for the past eight years, he has been Entree's mayor. His unexpected resignation from mayoral duties the day before my visit put the island into a declared "state of emergency" which brought the co-ordinator, Leonard and his dog, over to get things sorted out. I found them, and Quinn, and two students from Montreal in the snack bar. For reasons best known to the owner, it was closed, but he invited us to make our own sandwiches and coffee from his supplies and this we did.

I felt a bit like Alice in Wonderland, sitting there munching on a thick ham sandwich while a bunch of dogs drooled in the doorway, and this chubby chap in a cowboy hat talked of internal politics and power struggles. His resignation, he assured, had nothing to do with his six councillors being women. No, he was fed up with the bickering that goes way back to another century when one or the other of two families had control of the island. Now their descendants represent two opposing groups, who argue about everything—including whose dogs are the biggest troublemakers.

For dessert we trooped into Yvan's neat little store where he served us, and Leonard's dog, with ice cream cones. Lighthouse keeper Jack Maclean dropped by to pay for two hamburgers he had bought last week, and the storekeeper meticulously entered the sale in his notebook. Detecting that I was originally from England, Maclean pumped my hand enthusiastically. He was there 22 $^1/_2$ years ago, he said. His mother was born there, for gosh sakes. Someone asked about the guitar leaning against the freezer, and before we knew it, Yvan had put his worries aside, pulled up a bucket to sit on, and begun strumming.

Several would-be customers drifted in. Some stayed to clap out the rhythm, others left. Another served himself with a case of beer. In the next 10 minutes, I received whispered invitations to the church, the school and the lighthouse. Since I had never been inside a lighthouse (and the custodian's mother came from England) I opted for a tour of it, which necessitated a bone rattling truck ride to the point.

Jack had his son lead me up four flights of narrow stairs, and as promised the view from the top of the lighthouse was grand. Below again, he showed me his rhubarb patch. And just in case the Alice in Wonderland illusion should be wearing thin, a thrush flew into her nest containing three eggs, in a clump of grass by my foot. I was given a demonstration of the automatic generator, or whatever it is that will be activated in the event of a power failure, and it was time to leave. Vigorously shaking my hand, Jack invited me to stay at his home on my next visit. I believe he meant it. Then he instructed his nephew to drive me to the dock. Carefully.

I sat in the big old automobile, my feet resting among a dozen or more empty bottles on the floor. A tardy tortoise could have overtaken us without trying. The car's undercarriage clashed with every rock in its path. The unconcerned driver prattled on about the Leafs. The dogs began to fight. It was a fitting exit, I thought, for Alice in Wonderland.

IF YOU GO: The ferry departs Havre-Aubert daily at 8 a.m. arriving at Entree 45 minutes later. it returns again at mid-afternoon. Picnic supplies from Joe's Grocery are pretty much confined to canned goods, but there is a fair selection of inexpensive French wines. The only overnight accommodation advertised for Entree is a two-bedroom house, available by the day or week. Could be fun to stay over. Further inquiries should be made to the Magdalens' tourist association (see preceding article).

ONTARIO

In Ontario you have to think big because this is a province roughly a thousand miles from east to west and the same north to south. We have some quarter of a million lakes, including four of the five Great Lakes which give us a shoreline of 2,360 miles.

We are organized, meaning you can join kindred spirits for whitewater rafting, wilderness canoeing and kyak-camping trips. You can meet with fellow enthusiasts for hiking and rock climbing on the Niagara escarpment, rock hounding in Bancroft, scuba diving off Tobermory.

Ontario has capital cities. On the northern edge of Lake Ontario, Toronto is the provincial capital and Canada's largest city. Known in its formative years as "Muddy York," then "Toronto the Good" following World War II (in the '50s we had to go to Buffalo, N.Y. to see a Sunday movie), it is now a vibrant metropolis, all the more interesting for its multicultural population.

In Toronto you will want to visit Harborfront for its year-round antique fair and flea-market, and children's activities. Take the kids to Ontario Place on man-made islands off the lakeshore, and for a ferryboat ride to Toronto Islands. They will love the Science Center, the Metro Zoo and the Royal Ontario Museum. The Art Gallery of Ontario is important for its 5,000 works by Canadian artists. Theatrical productions rank with those of London and New York. Ball games and concerts on a grand scale are held in the Skydome. C.N. Tower, the world's tallest free-standing structure, boasts a revolving restaurant and nightclub and observation decks, from which you can see Niagara on a clear day.

Toronto has shops, 300 of them in the climate-controlled Toronto Eaton Center and more in underground concourses. Trendy little shops in the Beaches, Mirvish Village and on Queen Street West invite browsing. Honest Ed's is a store like no other. Yorkville, a village in 1853 and a hippie hangout in the 1960s, is now an elegant area of fashionable shops and chic restaurants.

TransCanada Highway ═══⬤═══ Other Major Highways ─────

Getting around Toronto is simple, with the help of a safe and clean subway system.

Ottawa has been Canada's capital since Queen Victoria chose it in 1857. Most of the city's landmarks can be seen from a Rideau Canal cruise, on that historic water link with Lake Ontario. In May the Tulip Festival is a treat. Summer visitors should try to be on Parliament Hill a little before 10 a.m. for Changing of the Guard by soldiers wearing colorful red tunics and bearskin hats. Guided tours of the Parliament Buildings are free. National museums and galleries could detain you for days.

Ontario is a province with many faces. Drive around the lake from Toronto and you are into Niagara, a region of fruit farms and wineries and the world famous falls. Gentle farmlands of southwestern Ontario surround Stratford, where swans drift on the River Avon and Shakespeare is alive and well in modern theatres.

Drive east instead of west from Toronto for Kingston, once the capital of Upper Canada. Here, where Lake Ontario meets the St. Lawrence River, you will have an attractive base for exploring the Thousand Islands, and can watch the sunset retreat ceremony at Old Fort Henry.

A three-hour drive north of Toronto has you in "cottage country," a vacation area of lakes and islands, much of it in a national park. At Midland, Ste Marie Among the Hurons recreates the mission built by 17th-century Jesuit priests, then destroyed by them when Iroquois attack was imminent. Six of Canada's eight martyr saints were from this mission. They are now remembered in the twin-spired shrine nearby.

Ride the *RMS Segwun*, a restored steamship sailing the Muskoka Lakes out of Gravenhurst. Or the ferry to Manitoulin, the world's largest freshwater island. Howl at the wolves in Algonquin Park. Continue north around the rugged shores of Lake Superior to the Lake-of-the-Woods for scenery that's sheer poetry. Take a train to the end of the line on James Bay. Fly into a fishing camp, accessible only by air. If you decide our park waterways are too busy, a floatplane can take you (with your canoe, tent and supplies) to an uninhabited area for a few days or weeks. At a predetermined time, you will be returned to civilization, perhaps feeling akin to other adventurers who paddled these waterways centuries ago.

To learn more about Ontario, contact Tourism Marketing Branch, Ministry of Tourism and Recreation, 77 Bloor St. West, Toronto, Ontario M7A 2R9. Telephone toll free (all North America, except Alaska, Yukon and Northwest Territories): 1-800-ONTARIO.

UNDERGROUND TORONTO

Mississauga, Ontario: 9:35 a.m. The cabbie depositing me at the suburban railway station said I would "catch my death" if I wasn't more careful. Shivering in the station's glass shelter for the next 10 minutes I felt he could be right. But then the train arrived, comfortably heated to suit my spring attire, and I warmed to the prospect of escaping winter's icy grasp—if only for a little while.

The outside world this winter morning is grey and white, with temperatures around 15 °F, and a light but persistent snowfall. Not that I need to worry about that. Dressed for indoors, I have no intention of venturing out again today. My plans are to enjoy downtown Toronto.

Toronto—devoid of icy sidewalks and honking motorists and bone-chilling winds that whip around street corners. A city of ever-blooming trees and waterfalls, brightly lit avenues bordered with side walk cafés, park benches and flowers brightening shop doorways, and best of all a climate-controlled Toronto: warm, dry and windless.

It is of course Toronto's hidden underground city, with a network of tunnels and walkways connecting half a dozen shopping complexes, hotels, cinemas, live theater, night clubs, subway stations, Toronto's chief railway terminal, and most recently a multi-million-dollar domed stadium for sports and theatrical events.

In subterranean Toronto you can book a trip, get a tooth filled, have your shoes mended and a tennis racket restrung. You can get your hair styled, exchange foreign currency, bank by computer, and see an optometrist. You can swim, watch live theater, buy a chocolate sports car, fresh lobster, a fur coat or a live puppy. Confine yourself to walkways and you won't have to surface for seven blocks. Use the subway, with its clean underground sta-

tions and you can carry on for miles, shopping, working and playing in the warm artificial environment.

10:07 a.m.: Union Station, that cavernous monument to times
when steam trains regularly huffed and hissed into town. A
chilly, impersonal place, it has nothing to detain me today as I
hurry from the train, and exit via a tunnel to the lower level of
the Royal York Hotel. Still one of the city's largest hotels, it is
dwarfed by the banks, Toronto-Dominion, Royal, Commerce and
Montreal, whose skyscrapers dominate the downtown scene and
whose combined underground development constitutes a lion's
share of the total system.

Eaton Centre, Toronto

I could walk up to the hotel's lobby, a touch of class in red velvet, brass and chandeliers, but I don't. Today it is not upward, but onward to the Merchant's Mall and first of the bank complexes and the Royal Bank Plaza.

The Royal Bank building is that glittering gold edifice, resembling the Towering Inferno when the sun sets on its southern facade. Its interior hasn't been neglected either. In the basement we have a rain forest with Canadian evergreens, waterfalls and way above it—way, way above it—a suspended sculpture composed of yellow and white reeds. Dozens of shops radiate from this centerpiece.

10:25 a.m.: Following the ramp around those rumbling waters I come to a clutch of food emporiums, their communal seating a bright patch of color. Over a warm Danish and strong coffee I study a map of the below-ground network, and roughly chart my course—due north to the Eaton Center, with a couple of jogs here and there. A kiosk catches my eye. It sells telephones, champagne bottles, personalized greeting cards and similar novelties, all of them made from chocolate.

Streets below the Toronto-Dominion Center are lined with shops. If you want to check on the outside world, here's your chance at the tower's 54th floor Fifty Fourth Restaurant and Lounge (open for drinks, lunch and dinner; evening entertainment after 8 p.m.). A wide concourse connects the Toronto-Dominion Center with Commerce Court to the east, a complex with 35 more shops and food outlets.

North again from the Toronto-Dominion Center for First Canadian Place, its major occupant the Bank of Montreal. This one is a beauty. On three levels soft lights touch upon miles of carpeting, lots of public seating beside potted trees, an art gallery, stores and restaurants.

Eateries here run the gamut from Terrace Fast Foods, to The Savoy with a good European menu. Technically within First Canadian Place, its entrance is reached from the outside—14 paces door to door.

11:15 a.m.: Open spaces in First Canadian Place encourage wandering. Mine takes me to exchange some foreign currency, collect travel brochures and air fares for a proposed trip, and search through bargains for fashions my size.

11:50 a.m.: I like The Lanes, Toronto's oldest underground shopping concourse which leads to another beneath the Sheraton Center Hotel. Between them they house dozens of shops, cinemas, and more food outlets. My thoughts on those half-price little dresses, I buy a copy of a currently popular diet and exercise book, and duck into a hairdressing salon for a shampoo and set.

Continue north through the Sheraton Center and you will eventually reach City Hall, where brief tours are conducted daily. To the east, there is a new underground link between The Lanes and Simpson's department store. A few years ago, downtown shoppers would ask, "Is this Eaton's or Simpson's?" when reaching for their charge cards. Now there is no mistaking the two. Simpson's, designated a historic landmark, has just come through a massive overhaul. Its basement Food Halls almost match those of London's Harrods. Eaton's is part of the modern complex stretching from Queen Street to Dundas. What can I say about the Toronto Eaton Center that hasn't been said before? A shopper's wonderland in winter, when sunlight floods through a great glass roof onto trees and park benches, its summer decor is so inviting that even city sparrows have come in from the cold.

The mall has 300 stores on three levels. Cineplex houses 21 cinemas. Fashion shows, concerts, autographing sessions with authors and entertainers—there is always something going on at the Toronto Eaton Center.

1 p.m.: A mammoth sidewalk sale impedes me as I emerge from the Simpson's connection and encounter hundreds of coatless office workers browsing in the center. My lunch date is with a young friend at The Magic Pan Creperie. Two spinach salads, two crepes—one chicken-filled, the other with seafood—a glass of milk and another of wine. I think $30 a fair price for our pleasant break in the seclusion of potted plants.

There is underground life beyond the Eaton Center, three subway stops north on Yonge Street at Bloor. Dominating this section, which runs below Bloor from Bay Street and beyond in both directions, is the Hudsons Bay Company's store. An unobtrusive door in the Men's Department leads to the Plaza II Hotel, where you can find a pleasant dining room tucked away from the crowds.

2:40 p.m.: Being this close I am tempted to dash for half a block above ground to the Metropolitan Toronto Library, which is so vast that an orientation film in the lobby introduces you to its treasures. Instead I follow walkways beneath Bloor Street, lined below-ground as above with interesting shops. It must be 10 years since I've been to an afternoon movie, but I indulge myself now because something I have been wanting to see is scheduled to start in 10 minutes and my feet are screaming for a rest.

Pedestrian traffic is at its peak around 5 p.m. so I seek refuge in the quiet opulence of Holt Renfrew, and the fragile world of Ashley China. Cotton skirts on special at The Bay are my size. I buy one, then join subway crowds thronging south to Union Station. Lockers there are large enough for top-coats and boots, and ample for my bits of shopping. Back through the tunnel refreshed and empty handed, I find my husband comfortably ensconced in the Royal York's lobby.

7 p.m.: Invitation to a press reception in the hotel's Alberta Room provides an opportunity to relax with a drink and nibbles. Otherwise we would have dallied at The Black Knight while deciding where to go for dinner.

From the hotel's varied restaurants the Imperial Room was our first choice, but with Lena Horne packing them in that night we didn't have a hope.

8:30 p.m.: Through almost deserted tunnels we reach the Sheraton Center, which is busy this evening. The Pinnacle on the 43rd floor boasts a fair view of the city, and the pub has Toronto's longest bar. We settle on Café of the Redwoods for its Canadian fare: a good pâté in pastry, thick corn soup from a Six Nations Reserve recipe, buffalo meat (disappointingly bland) and dessert. Service is courteous if slow, but what's the hurry? Rhythmic old favorites played by a quartet set my tired feet tapping. We order a nightcap and raise our glasses to Underground Toronto.

IF YOU GO: Underground Toronto can be reached via the various suburban GO-Transit routes leading to Union Station, or the Toronto Transit Commission subway lines. For a map, contact the Metropolitan Toronto Convention and Travel Association, P.O. Box 126, 207 Queen's Quay West, Toronto, Ontario, M5J 1A7, toll free telephone number 1-800-363-1990.

HONEYMOON CAPITAL OF THE WORLD

Living just west of Toronto as we do, we often have house-guests with two or three days' business in that city, or passing through on a Canadian vacation. The city they can do on their own, but when it comes to Niagara we give them a full day's personal tour. This takes in the Falls, lunch in the Skylon Tower's revolving restaurant, a leisurely drive along the parkway to browse in Niagara-on-the-Lake boutiques, tea in one of the vintage hotels (or ice cream in a little café where it is made on the premises if preferred) and home.

Accordingly I have seen the famous Falls in all seasons, and all weather. I arrived one day at seven in the morning and found the main attraction marred by a film crew and its attendant gear. I have seen them in January when the spray turns roadside trees into a fairyland of frozen filigree and icicles several feet long. In April when Queen Victoria Park is carpeted with 500,000 daffodils, and a month later when frothy blossoms of fruit trees line the parkway. Once we brought a mustard-keen photographer to the Falls only to discover them turned off for repairs!

September is my favorite time. The Falls may be Niagara's power, but its glory comes in autumn when the maples turn scarlet and black squirrels outnumber people, and we buy baskets of grapes and pears from local orchards.

Seventeenth-century Jesuit missionary Father Louis Hennepin was the first white man to record seeing the Falls. Indians living in the area called it Onigra (Thunder of Water) and sacrificed some of their most beautiful maidens over them. Why honeymooners continue to flock here is anyone's guess. Perhaps Napoleon's brother started the trend when he came with his bride from New Orleans. Now couples receive a certificate signed by the mayor confirming that they honeymooned in the Honeymoon Capital of the World.

The Horseshoe Falls provide the main event. One hundred and seventy six feet high, and 2,500 feet wide at the curved crest, they pour furiously onto the rocks below at the rate of 34 million gallons a minute. If you are content to stroll or drive past them, it costs nothing to witness this phenomenon. Over the years though, adventurous alternatives have been devised. Some rides are seasonal, the exact dates and times of operation determined by weather conditions, so it may be as well to telephone ahead of your spring or autumn visit.

Most exciting by far is the *Maid of the Mist,* which operates between May and October. The original *Maid* brought passengers to the base of the Horseshoe Falls as early as 1846. Now four diesel boats make the half hour trip with departures every 15 minutes. Passengers are provided with raincoats to keep off the spray, and you might bring a plastic bag to protect your camera. From above, these boats resemble toys in a bath rocking towards a tap turned on full blast. As a passenger you feel as if you're in the Land of Giants heading towards the faucet.

Table Rock Scenic Tunnels are open all year. Entry is in Table Rock House where you are given a raincoat, this time with rubber boots. An elevator takes you to the river level from where you walk through tunnels to three viewing platforms on natural rock extending to within a few feet of the thundering Horseshoe Falls. Needless to say the noise is deafening.

Towers tend to dwarf the cataracts rather than you. Of several near the Falls, tallest at 775 feet is The Skylon with observation decks inside and out. Its Summit dining room has a buffet lunch daily in season. The revolving restaurant above it, open all year, serves good food at reasonable prices.

Heading north from the main falls you come to the Great Gorge Trip, allowing you to walk by the rushing river. A daredevil gallery here contains contraptions used by men attempting to navigate the rapids. Half a mile further on the Spanish Aero Car glides above the rapids. Both the gorge and aero car operation are open between May and October.

Nineteenth-century visitors saw the road above the Falls crowded with carnivals and side-shows, and could pay a nickel to view the cataracts through holes in a fence. Then in 1885 the Ontario Legislature showed unusual foresight in establishing our first provincial park here. Two years later the Niagara Parks Commission was formed. It does an outstanding job of landscaping and maintenance along a parkway following the river for 35 miles between Fort Erie and Niagara-on-the-Lake.

North of the Falls this parkway leads to a quieter beauty. Nature trails are cut through woods above the gorge; tree-shaded picnic spots are chosen for the view. In Niagara Glen Nature Area two and a half miles of walking paths lead into the gorge and along the banks at river level. The Niagara Parks School of Horticulture is world famous. Its students are responsible for the school's 100 acres of campus and gardens, which attract numerous wedding parties for photographs.

Around now, history takes over from the scenic attributes. Battle sites, restored buildings and a reconstructed fort all serve to ease you into the 19th century, at what used to be the capital of Upper Canada, Niagara-on-the-Lake.

Seven miles from town, Queenston Heights is marked by Brock's monument. Armed now with a walking tour pamphlet, you can follow the Battle of Queenston Heights in these parklands where General Sir Isaac Brock lost his life during the 1812 war.

Some say Ontario's prettiest little town is Niagara-on-the-Lake, reminiscent of a restored pioneer community except that citizens don't go around in gingham bonnets and there is no admission charge. Virtually destroyed during the 1812 war, most of the present town dates to the late 1800s while Fort George which served as the British army headquarters on the Niagara Frontier is rebuilt to 1813.

Theater first came to Niagara when actors performed at military forts along the river. More dramatic theatrical history was made with the first Shaw Festival presented in the old court house in 1962. Popular from the start, it became an annual event to include works of Shaw and his contemporaries, and in 1973 it opened in a new Festival Theater, attended by Her Majesty Queen Elizabeth and His Royal Highness the Duke of Edinburgh.

I don't know of another small Canadian town with so many lovely old inns. When Queen Elizabeth visited she lodged at The Pillar and Post, handsomely converted from a fruit canning plant (room 205, if you care to sleep royally). In the 1860s guests arrived by steamer or stagecoach to Long's Hotel, renamed the Prince of Wales since Edward VII stayed here. The Oban Inn was home of a lake captain from Oban, Scotland, in the early 1800s. And the Angel Inn was called the Harmonious Coach House in the late 1700s. A small portion of the original tavern is visible still. So, once in a while is Swayze, ghost of a British soldier murdered in the dining room during the 1812 war. All of these hotels are furnished to period, have good to excellent dining rooms and attractive bar lounges.

IF YOU GO: In summer parking can be a pain at both Niagara Falls and Niagara-on-the-Lake, so you may want to consider public transportation or a tour from Toronto. Driving from Toronto, take the Queen Elizabeth Way then follow signs to Niagara Falls, or take the exit at Highway 55 and follow signs to Niagara-on-the-Lake. Niagara Visitor and Convention Bureau, 4673 Ontario Avenue, Niagara Falls, Ontario L2E 3R1 (tel 416-356-6061) provides information on the area, including accommodations.

LUXURY IN THE ALGONQUIN WILDERNESS

HUNTSVILLE, ONTARIO: A loon's cry carries clear across the lake, then all is quiet. It is a noisy silence, one of forest chatter, sudden scurrying beneath path-side ferns and padding of my feet on the trail. Soon a bell will disturb the forest wildlife, summoning me to a feast most civilized in its wilderness setting. As I head for the rustic luxury of Arowhon Pines my thoughts are with the intrepid lady who came to build here in this 2,910-square-mile wilderness preserve almost 60 years ago.

She is the late Lilian Kates who, at the height of the Depression, heard of a naturalists' camp for sale in Algonquin Park. Undaunted by its isolation, she converted the bankrupt camp to a co-ed summer place for kids and renamed it Arowhon (from Samuel Butler's book Erehwon, which is Nowhere spelled backwards).

Camp Arowhon's second season brought a need to accommodate visiting parents. Two brothers with axes were hired, land cleared and the log cabin community known as Arowhon Pines started on the shore of Little Joe Lake. In 1970 Lilian Kates retired, leaving son Eugene and daughter-in-law Helen to run both camp and resort. All accommodation has been upgraded, so now 110 guests are comfortably accommodated in the one- to 12-bedroom cottages.

In the early days both guests and supplies arrived by train, then boat. That winding road cut for five miles through the woods from the park's highway came later, as did the ensuite bathrooms and carefully restored pioneer decor and furnishings. With imagination and sheer hard work, it took Helen and Eugene a decade to successfully blend stylish living and wilderness without one encroaching on the other. Winter safaris in search of Ontario antiques reaped handsome rewards. In both cottages and the dining room, the outdoors is brought in with wild flowers, pictures of park scenes and wildlife on knotty pine walls, and log burning fieldstone fireplaces. (All accommodation is electrically heated, but for added cheer you will wake up to a fire burning in your lounge's hearth on chilly or damp mornings.)

Heart of the resort is the six-sided log dining room, originally a dormitory for parents visiting their children at camp. Warmth glows from a circular stone hearth in the room's center, but it doesn't stop there. It radiates from early Canadian furniture and braided rugs, wild flowers in stone crocks and copper pots, and the Kates' genuine interest in how you enjoyed your day.

Honey-colored log walls and attractive table settings give the place style. Still it is the food that causes canoeists to paddle faster and hikers to break into a trot at the sound of the chow bell. More Canadian fare has been added to the menu in recent years. Now Arowhon chefs do lovely things with Ontario lamb and wild rice, brisket beef with potato pancakes, homemade chutneys and chilis. There are fiddleheads from New Brunswick,

Arowhon Pines

Quebec tourtières, and maple syrup desserts. Canada's different cultures are also represented in Chinese and Japanese, French, English and German foods. Weather plays an important part too. If it is wet or cool, it's no accident that a fire blazes in the dining room hearth and comfort foods are coddled in copper chafing dishes. Warm evenings bring lakefront barbecues.

Chefs work with the very best ingredients of course. "What's freshest?" is the question Helen asks of her favorite fish man in Toronto's St Lawrence market before deciding what to buy. Three times a week a car is sent 175 miles to the city, bringing back Atlantic and Pacific salmon, Florida grouper, Manitoba pickerel, and whatever else is super fresh. (Baby grouper, marinated in soya sauce, ginger and sesame seeds, is a fish lover's dream.) Order trout and it will be on your plate within four hours of leaving the local trout farm. Herbs are grown on site; vegetables and fruit bought from local farmers in season and Toronto markets at other times.

Breakfast is designed to stoke your fires for an energetic morning, although I do know someone who went back to bed to sleep it off. Juices, fruits, yogurts, homemade granola and warm-from-the-oven breads cram the buffet table. Pancakes, sausages, eggs and bacon, haddock poached in cream and Scottish kippers are cooked to order. Chances are you may get no further than the porridge. Homemade, served with nuts and raisins, brown sugar and honey, it has you going back for more.

Weekend buffets are large enough to feed an army. Homemade soup and a slice of the plaited challa bread with whipped butter should suffice for lunch. But who can pass up the 14 or 15 other dishes that include imaginative salads, hot and cold entrées.

Pastry chef Terry McKelvie, in his eleventh season at Arowhon, is used to compliments from regulars who arrive salivating at thoughts of his English trifle, ice bombes and crème caramel in syrup beds, chocolate eclairs and fresh fruit pies. Weekday lunches and dinners have the same buffet arrangements for homemade soup, salads, appetizers and desserts while entrées are cooked to order. There are always at least three main courses. Have one or have them all, and nobody will count your trips to the dessert table because unlimited food is included in your rent. For a day away, picnic hampers are provided.

The same generosity is carried over to use of leisure facilities. This means no charge for tennis courts (with rackets and balls), canoes, row boats, sailboats, windsurfing boards, sauna and videos. The only extra I know of is for motorized boats.

You will want to see more of the park. Bird watchers love it. So do canoeists. While there are over a thousand miles of waterways to be explored, 10 minutes' paddling from Arowhon docks will bring you to uninhabited islands and sand slips for your wilderness picnic. The resort has walking paths. For longer hiking trails, drive back onto the main highway where each trail has a parking lot and descriptive pamphlets at the entrance. Some lead to stunning lookouts, others to beaver dams or river and rapids views. A museum will acquaint you with Algonquin's history, and resident wildlife preserved for posterity. Although times when deer could be seen by the roadside are gone, you may well catch a glimpse of one or two on a trail. The '80s have brought an explosion in the moose population. On recent visits I have had a red fox run across my path on the road to Arowhon, and a moose outside my cottage at dawn.

Algonquin is one of the few accessible places on earth where timber wolves are to be found. In August park naturalists conduct wolf howl expeditions in which groups are taken to areas where dens have been located. There you are shown how to howl, and with a bit of luck a wolf howls back. Last summer Arowhon guests went off to howl at the wolves. They had no response, but on returning home found a female wolf sitting by the dining room's back door. Obligingly, she allowed herself to be photographed before disappearing into a starry Algonquin night.

Come evening, movies are shown in the resort's lakefront lounge, but most guests prefer to sit around their cottage fires. That's one of the nice things about this place. Because it attracts people from all walks of life, and so many different countries, there is almost always somebody interesting to talk to. Arowhon

Pines has been glowingly written up in such top-drawer publications as England's *Observer, Sunday Times* and *Daily Telegraph.* *Better Homes and Gardens* described it as a "utopia in the wilderness." *Travel-Holiday* magazine included the resort in its Fine Dining Awards. If that's not recommendation enough, I should perhaps mention that this is one of only three Ontario resorts accepted into the exclusive Relais et Chateaux membership.

Rates (accommodation and all meals, plus use of all recreational facilities) are from $135 per person per day double occupancy, or $810 for seven nights, plus 15 percent service charge and tax. There is a 10 to 25 percent reduction in spring and fall. Credit cards are not accepted.

IF YOU GO: Arowhon Pines in Algonquin Provincial Park is 175 miles north of Toronto and about the same distance west of Ottawa. It is open between mid-May and mid-October. During winter, inquiries should be directed to Arowhon Pines, 297 Balliol Street, Toronto M4S 1C7, telephone 416-483-4393. In summer contact them at Huntsville Post Office, Ontario, POA 1KO, telephone 705-633-5661.

CATCH THE RIVER SIGHTS ON A ST LAWRENCE RIVER CRUISE

Kingston, Ontario: It's fun to wake up, lift the bedroom curtain and see an island drifting by. The first one had a little cottage on it, and a canoe tied to the dock. The next was so small it supported no more than two spindly trees and patches of scrubby grass. The third, though doubtless known as The Cottage, resembled an English mansion, while flags of four nations flew out front in honor of current house guests. I enjoyed the luxury of lying in bed and watching the world drift by—even when I remembered it was I, not the island in transit.

There are about 1,800 islands in the Thousand Islands region of the St Lawrence River. Last night we anchored among them, perhaps where explorers, voyageurs and pioneers once camped en route to the interior. It is an appropriate stopover for us, because we are on a Heritage Waterway tour and our ship is reminiscent of the steamboats that plied this river a century or so ago.

She is the *Canadian Empress,* an ungainly looking vessel at first sight, but dear to us by the time we part. Travelling between Kingston and Quebec City her itineries include weekend getaways and three to five day cruises.

Summer is by far the *Empress's* busiest season. Yet in May and October, when the days are usually warm and nights pleasantly cool, cruise rates drop appreciably. By the way, October—not September—sees the riverbanks ablaze with spectacular colors. Influenced by the warming effect of the water, the riverside leaves are barely tinged with gold when others are dead and carpeting the ground inland.

Owner Bob Clark deserves success with his *Empress,* in return for the tender loving care he continues to lavish upon her. As he tells it, he was a semi-retired builder back in 1979, and a mite bored with it all. Then one golden afternoon he took a couple of beers over to a friend who was raking leaves at his cottage. Talk turned to the many cruise boats going by, and Clark calculated that 24 boats carried 14,000 passengers a day out of Kingston, but none had overnight accommodation. When steamboats carrying travellers from Quebec City at the turn of the century were recalled, the possibility of building a replica came to mind. The idea took hold and Clark's boredom was swept away with his pal's leaves.

One of the Thousand Islands, from the Canadian Empress

The all-aluminum *Empress* was 11 months in the planning and another 11 months under construction at the Algan Shipyards in Gananoque, Ontario. This marriage of steamboat authenticity with modern technology and comforts resulted in the birth of a twin-engine diesel ship, 108 feet long with a capacity for 66 passengers in 32 staterooms and a crew of 12 to 14.

Following her launching in September 1981, the *Empress* made four cruises that year, initially to iron out wrinkles in design and on-board routine. There were remarkably few: a patio door from the main lounge is now made to close by itself for the comfort of people inside; three brass hooks in each cabin (the same as on the original steamboats) proved inadequate for modern travellers, so they were replaced with rods and hangers.

Even the inexperienced eye can see that no expense was spared to achieve an authentic decor. Where possible, Canadian materials were employed, but often Clark had to shop farther afield—in Belgium for the rich velvet drapes, Sweden for stateroom doors and England for plush Axminster carpeting. Elaborately patterned tin ceilings in the public areas are particularly interesting. After months of research, Clark tracked down some abandoned molds used for ceilings in the old river boats and had them put back to use.

Staterooms are small, but elegant. Each has at least two full sized windows for river viewing, and thermostats for individual control of the air conditioning. Fixtures and furnishings are expensive, like our trundle which makes into a double bed, with its brass rail on three sides and salmon-colored velvet cover to match the curtains. We have the thick Axminster carpeting, private toilet and shower, full length mirror and marble basin with large brass taps. Our luggage fits neatly into the closet space. Then, because well rested passengers are more inclined to be happy passengers, all mattresses are of higher quality than those used in some first-class hotels.

It is this generous approach that makes it work so well. Clark says he is selling nostalgia, quality and service. The nostalgia is self-evident. So is the quality. To mention one example, he buys produce from a small wholesaler who charges more than his competitors, but will deliver on Sundays immediately prior to departure. Service? Crew members also represent the cream of the crop. The ship has two crews, allowing for a full change-over at each end of the journey so passengers are never greeted by a tired staff. All are carefully picked from hundreds of applications received each season. Deck hands and waitresses on our trip were Queen's University graduates. Of our skipper, Captain Vinton Keough, who once piloted the Royal yacht Britannia into Kingston harbor, Clark quips, "If he was good enough for *her,* I figured he'd be okay for us."

About 70 percent of our passengers are retired people, in groups from Irwin, Pennsylvania, and Strathroy, Ontario. We also had two teen-aged boys, who quickly proved there is no such thing as a generation gap. The rest included several American teachers, a well travelled couple from Philadelphia who compared this with their recent Alaskan cruise, an architect from Birmingham, an accountant from Mississauga, and a Dearborn, Mich., realtor. The Tremblays from Chicoutimi were a treat: Lu-

The Canadian Empress *at Prescott, Ontario*

cienne, who had lost weight and learned English in preparation for this week; Lorenzo who knew the intimate details of every lock we went through, every hamlet and historic site passed. During those long cold evenings in Northern Quebec, he said, they would spread their maps and brochures on the kitchen table and dream of their cruise on the St Lawrence.

Had we voted for the most popular crew member, doubtless Fred Whitney would have won hands down. Fred, who gave the older folks clues in Trivial Pursuit, struggled to get a fire going for the weiner roast, counted heads on land excursions and each night wrote, printed and delivered beneath cabin doors a newsletter detailing the day's events.

One of Fred's letters reminded me I had dallied enough watching those islands from my bed, because soon we would be stopping at one in New York State. It is Heart Island, where the poignant story of George and Louise Boldt unfolds in a castle which will never be finished, since all work ceased upon Mrs. Boldt's death in 1904. More than $2 million had been put into the building, and a further fortune was to make it one of the world's finest homes. But instead, tourists now tramp through the empty rooms, gum wrappers lie in Italian marble fireplaces and crude graffiti decorates bedroom walls.

As the *Empress* hummed on to Prescott that day, we lunched on sole with wild rice and discussed the remarkable George Boldt, who came to the United States from Prussia at the age of 13, got himself work peeling potatoes and eventually became owner of the Waldorf-Astoria Hotel in New York. Boldt loved this area. He had a farm here large enough to supply produce to his hotel. But perhaps his chef, Oscar, brought a more lasting fame to the region. He created a salad dressing which he named Thousand Islands.

Our own chef was Carmine, who produced imaginative meals from his little galley three times a day. In true cruise boat tradition, we all ate too much. Take our last evening when Carmine and Fred barbecued filet mignon steaks as we tucked into breaded mushrooms and salads. Three hours later we all turned up for a weiner roast, consuming several weiners apiece while listening to visiting musicians. Afternoon tea, with cake or hot scones and preserves, was always well attended. Tea, coffee, soft drinks and snacks left out 24 hours a day were replenished often. The bar, open from 11:30 a.m. to 1 a.m., except Sundays, when it closed at 11 p.m. was seldom without customers.

Boldt Castle was the first of our four shore excursions. Prescott was second, for a visit to Fort Wellington, built during the war of 1812 to protect British shipping between Upper and Lower Canada. Here, a costumed guide explained how the fort was garrisoned for several years after the war, then fell into ruin. The present fortress dates from 1837.

We dutifully toured officers' quarters and the blockhouse, and watched a demonstration of musket firing—good naturedly repeated for a woman whose camera malfunctioned the first time around—and met school children dressed to the period and enjoying their summer roles immensely.

With two visits to Upper Canada Village planned, we docked overnight at Crysler Park Marina about a mile and a half away. What is now Crysler Park was the site of an important battle in the War of 1812. It was November, 1813, when Upper Canada settlers joined regular British troops in the fighting at Crysler's Farm. Their victory, on the heels of another in Quebec, prevented the American capture of Montreal, which would have cut off vital supplies to British troops in the west.

On a warm and peaceful evening, horse-drawn wagons took us back in time, past the deserted battle site and into Upper Canada Village for a turkey dinner at the 19th-century Willard's Hotel.

On the river, too, we had near perfect weather. Always in sight of land, we could sit on deck for hours, watching an ever-changing view. We waved and shouted greetings back to cottagers, leisure sailors, and even the crews of foreign freighters rumbling by. I think we went through seven locks. After the first two, nothing less than a 35-foot lift caused me to stir from my chaise. Then, all too soon, the cottages had given way to neat little farms and villages, and we were passing into the suburbs of Montreal.

We docked at the foot of Old Montreal to find tour busses waiting for our groups and taxis for the rest of us. A van had brought the new crew and food supplies from Kingston. Three hours later a group of strangers boarded our *Empress.*

IF YOU GO: Current rates depend on cabin location and time of year, but range from $696 per person, double occupancy for a three-day cruise, to $1,158 for five days. *Canadian Empress's* newer and larger sister, *Victorian Empress,* cruises as far as the Saguenay. For schedules, prices and further information contact Rideau St Lawrence Cruise Ships, 253 Ontario St., Kingston, Ont., K7L 2Z4, telephone 613-549-8091, toll free 1-800-267-7868.

UPPER CANADA VILLAGE

Morrisburg, Ontario: At a glance it could have been any rural community coming alive on a new day. Horses were being brought from the barn, pigs were getting fed, and querulous geese strutted by the millpond on grass drenched in early morning dew. When villagers appeared, it was obvious I had stepped back in time. The proprietor opened up his general store, showing shelves crammed with goods essential to 19th-century pioneers. A stagecoach ambled past. Beside the canal, two young men worked the locks in readiness for passengers to board their horse-drawn bateau. And when I stopped to admire a particularly pretty garden, a costumed housewife came out of her cottage to identify 50 different blooms growing there. Soon, crowds of visitors would spoil the tranquillity, but until then, on that sunny summer's morning, life appears serene here on the banks of the St Lawrence River a century or two ago.

The scene is Upper Canada Village, a superb recreation typical of farm settlements in the St Lawrence Valley between 1784 and 1867. It came about in the late 1950s when eight villages and 35 miles of riverbank settled by Loyalists in 1784 had to be flooded during construction of the Seaway Power Project. The best of their buildings were rescued to form the nucleus of this village, opened to the public in 1961.

Today there are 40 buildings, including private homes, churches, taverns, offices and factories relocated from elsewhere in the valley. Cattle and sheep graze in the fields, residents go about their business, and craftsmen demonstrate pioneer skills. Perhaps I feel more attuned to the represented period than most, because I came here in the style of early travellers on a horse-drawn cart, from a riverboat en route from Kingston to Montreal.

The region's earliest settlers were United Empire Loyalists, who crossed the border after the American Revolution. Brave and hardy souls, they arrived with no more than a few tools, seeds, food and livestock, to settle lands given them by the British government. In the mid-19th century a new wave of immigrants came from England, Scotland and Ireland. Most were uneducated. Few had farm experience.

Theirs was a formidable task. Upon arrival, a family would set about building some sort of crude shelter. Next, land was cleared for a sturdier, one-room log cabin and whatever primitive furnishings were considered necessary. Whipsaws were supplied to every fourth family and since each saw required two pairs of strong arms, this was a co-operative venture. The bane of every settler's life were stubborn tree-trunks and enormous boulders that had to be wrenched from the ground. Stumps and left-over trees and branches were generally burned and a farmer's first cash crop would have been potash, sold for the manufacture of soap, glass and gunpowder. His first planted crops were probably corn, wheat, potatoes and peas.

Practically every building here will capture your interest for one reason or another. The comforts and appointments of some of the homes are surprising. Other homes are so spartan you wonder how people survived the winters. A group of farm dwellings demonstrate the progress of one family over the years. On arrival in 1794 their first home was a rough log cabin later taken over by the sheep. By 1820 they had acquired a roomier log house. Almost 40 years passed before a handsome stone farmhouse was completed. The second log house was given to the hired hand (probably a newly arrived immigrant from Britain). By this time certain refinements had appeared in these rural communities. There was actually time for leisure so women could tend flower gardens and embroider their household linens. There's a sewing machine and piano among imported furnishings in this 1846 home (restored to the 1860s) built by the grandson of a Loyalist settler.

Industries prospering in Upper Canada by the mid-19th century are well represented in the village. The Asseltine Factory, for example, opened in 1840, at which time there were 17 other such mills in the valley. Ten years later 90 full-scale mills were operating. Sawmills helped eliminate the use of those back-breaking whipsaws. The sawmill here, containing a water-driven vertical saw, dates from 1846. However, the region's first community mill was constructed by the British government at Cataraqui (later to become Kingston) for the first Loyalist settlers. A more recent acquisition is Bellamy's Flour and Grist Mill from Augusta Township. In 1848 its annual production was listed as 1,000 barrels of flour. By 1876 production for the year was up to 5,200 barrels of flour and almost 7,000 of feed.

At first, travellers were invited to stay overnight in private homes, partly because they brought news from the outside world. Then, with the increase of traffic, licensed taverns were established. Michael Cook was given his first license in 1804 and operated a tavern convenient for both river and highway travellers between Kingston and Montreal. It was taken over by the military during the War of 1812 and left in such disrepair that Cook was compensated for it by the British government. With this money he opened Cook's Tavern, now of Upper Canada Village. In addition to providing clean lodgings and a hot meal for travellers, such inns were social centers for area residents. Typically, the ballroom here was used largely for public meetings, and as an overflow dormitory for guests. In the barn next door is the village stagecoach, reminding us of times when a fairly efficient passenger and mail service linked Upper and Lower Canada.

If you can be here soon after opening time, you will be able to talk to residents without much interruption. As the day's first visitor at the Doctor's House, I was told how early settlers had to rely on remedies and potions passed among themselves. I learned that the country doctor doubled as a pharmacist and, until the mid-19th century, had to perform amputations (usually resulting from farm accidents) without use of anesthetics.

The lockmaster is a cheerful soul who said he fares very well. His house is provided rent free. If he wants, he may farm canal lands. And he is paid a wage. In return he must be an educated man, capable of keeping books, making reports and accounting for toll fees collected. As long ago as 1783, a canal and lock system existed about 50 miles east of here. It was rebuilt in 1804, and those plans were followed in constructing the village canal system. A Museum of the River will acquaint you with the St Lawrence River story, dwelling on its importance as a highway long after road and rail facilities were introduced to the region. At the neighboring blockhouse you will learn how flags were used to send messages from one station to the next.

Walking on the uneven roads is tiring so try to hitch a ride on a wagon or the bateau *Marguerite* where possible. First-time visitors will want a full day here with time out to watch demonstrations of pioneer skills. Picnic facilities are provided by the millpond. There is a modern restaurant outside the village entrance, while dining rooms in the 19th-century Willard's Hotel serve lunch, tea and dinner. Village cheese was selling here last summer; orders for freshly baked bread were being taken for pick-up later in the day.

The village is located in Crysler Farm Battlefield Park, containing, amongst other things, headstones from early cemeteries flooded by the Seaway project and a Loyalist tribute to settlement of the area in 1784. A battle memorial building is devoted to the decisive battle fought here on November 11, 1813. For recreational diversions, Crysler Beach has a supervised swimming area and playground. The marina has docking facilities for up to 60 pleasure craft. The Upper Canada Golf Course has a pro shop, equipment rentals and a licensed restaurant. With all this, plus excellent campgrounds, motels and picnic facilities by the river, a visitor could happily stay in the area for several days.

IF YOU GO: Upper Canada Village, near Morrisburg, is about 275 miles east of Toronto or 60 miles west of Montreal, via Highway 401. It opens daily at 9:30 a.m. between mid-May and mid-October. There is a modest admission charge.

KINGSTON, A CAPITAL GATEWAY TO THE PAST

Kingston, Ontario: Like most of us, I suppose, I knew that Kingston is Ontario's oldest community and one-time capital of Canada, site of a world-renowned university, military college and six federal prisons. In times before superhighways, I found it a nice lunch stop on the drive from Toronto to Montreal. Now, arriving two days early for departure on a river cruise, I discover it to be a city deserving much more than a casual glance.

For starters, Lake Ontario waters flow into the St Lawrence River at this point. It is the southern terminus of the Rideau Canal, and gateway to the spectacular Thousand Islands region—making it an ideal base for leisure sailors. For the rest of us there are boat excursions lasting several hours or days.

All over town, 19th-century buildings have been carefully restored, some as living museums and others to house interesting shops and restaurants. In summer, no less than a dozen theatrical groups offer presentations on subjects as Canadian as Sir John A. MacDonald and Anne of Green Gables. There are open air markets, waterfront parks, and delightful areas that have changed little in appearance these past hundred years.

When in 1673, Louis de Buade, Comte de Palluau et de Fronte-nac, began trading with Indians who arrived via the various water routes, he established a trading post here. A century or so later the community had grown into an important British army garrison, port, and the commercial center of Upper Canada. By the mid-19th century, it was home to Queen's University, a mighty stone fortress—and a promising young lawyer, destined to be Canada's first prime minister. For three years, from 1841, Kingston was capital of the province of Canada.

These days, anyone the least bit interested in the country's past can have a great time touring the handsomely restored buildings. The most impressive by far is Old Fort Henry on the outskirts of the city. As the connecting link between Upper and Lower Canada, with an important dockyard on Lake Ontario, the city was vulnerable to U.S. attack. In the War of 1812, with the enemy alarmingly close, original wood and earth fortifications at Point Henry provided little defense. And so, plans were drawn up for a massive stone fortress to be fitted with 37 guns and manned by close to 500 officers and men.

Construction was started in 1832. When completed, it was considered to be Canada's strongest military fort. Now a major visitor attraction, Old Fort Henry is furnished to period and staffed by student "soldiers" between May and October. The famed Fort Henry Guard is the only Canadian unit to have performed twice at Britain's Royal Tournament. Their ceremonial retreat, performed during July and August, is a military spectacle to rival any in the world.

After the War of 1812, this gateway to Upper Canada continued to prosper. Presence of the military and naval shipyards generated a steady commercial growth, which accelerated considerably in 1841 when Kingston was chosen as the capital of Upper and Lower Canada.

Merchant and entrepreneur Charles Hales profited from the resultant real estate boom. Some of his new-found wealth went into construction of a grand Italian-style villa in the best part of town. Because of its frivolous architecture and Hales' background, it was immediately nicknamed Pekoe Pagoda. When the government moved to Montreal, Hales' business ventures declined and he rented the villa. His most illustrious tenant was a local lawyer and member of the legislative assembly, John A. MacDonald. In a letter to his sister-in-law, MacDonald described his new home as "a house built for a retired grocer who was resolved to have an 'Eyetalian Willar' and who has built the most fantastic concern imaginable." MacDonald named the property Belleview.

It is recommended that visitors call at the museum beside Belleview, before touring the home. There you will see bits and pieces found in and around the estate during its restoration as a national historic park. And you will learn about the Scottish lad who arrived in Kingston at the age of five, and in 1867 became Canada's first prime minister.

Like so many of our living museums, Belleview is enhanced by costumed employees who are quick to describe the functions of various rooms and furnishings as well as the lifestyle of the Mac-Donalds during the year they lived here. These young women go one step further, acting out little skits and giving musical performances with violin and flute in the parlor.

Quite different from the traditional buff stone houses of the wealthy 19th-century Kingstonians, Belleview is white with a dark green trim, has a central tower and ornate little balconies suspended from upper windows. The main door has no handle. Residents either carried a key or rang for someone to let them in. By all accounts this was a comfortable, though not particularly happy home for the MacDonalds. Isabella was so ill she seldom left her ground-floor bedroom, and the couple's infant son died here. While the house is beautifully furnished to period, only a red velvet couch in the sick room and a baby's rocking crib belonged to the MacDonalds.

Take time to tour the estate, attractively laid out with pleasant walkways, an orchard and formal gardens. Gardeners dressed in 19th-century style work on the kitchen garden where, when I was there, cabbages, onions, tobacco and poppies flourished.

As Canada's capital, the already well-established community enjoyed a flurry of building activity. Houses were constructed for government officials. The new general hospital was converted to legislative chambers, and foundations were laid for a magnificent city hall, from which John A. MacDonald conducted his business as alderman on Kingston's first city council. Completely refurbished 10 years ago, the city hall now has guided tours conducted daily (except Sundays) during summer months.

For tourists, this is a most interesting area. In front of the city hall Confederation Park was established on the waterfront to commemorate Canada's centennial. Excursion boats come and go from the docks, while Chamber of Commerce sightseeing trains depart from the Information Center. Behind it, Market Square is the site of a farmer's market three days a week and an antique fair on Sundays. A short walk brings you to more museums, craft and specialty shops, and restaurants in 19th-century buildings.

Sightseeing guides of Kingston list dozens of restaurants. Best known are probably Chez Piggy in what was a livery stable in 1810, and the Firehall Dining Room in a 19th-century fire station. I particularly enjoyed the General Wolfe Hotel's dining room, and the free 20-minute Wolfe Island ferry ride that took me there from Kingston's harbor.

When we docked at the island, some passengers stayed on board for the return journey, treating it as a tour boat. A fine alternative is to join the thousands of passengers who daily tour the Thousand Island region out of Kingston. Two that I watched leave, packed on all decks, are the replica side-wheelers *Island Queen* and *Princess*. Their two- and four-hour cruises into the Thousand Islands operate from May to October. In spring and fall, the *Princess*'s itinerary takes her along the Rideau Canal. The bars are open during all but the early morning departures.

As far as I know, the only passenger boats from Kingston having overnight accommodation are the *Canadian Empress,* which is the subject of my previous story, and her larger sister, the *Victorian Empress.*

IF YOU GO: Kingston is 160 miles east of Toronto. Belleview is open all year, but closed on statutory holidays between October and May, and admission is free. Old Fort Henry is open to the public between May and October. There is a small admission charge for adults. More information is available from Kingston Tourist and Visitors Bureau, 209 Ontario St., Kingston, K7L 2Z1. Telephone 613-548-4415.

FRENCH RIVER FISH TALES

French River, Ontario: Our guide Ed Smith made no bones about it. We were, beyond all doubt, the funniest people he had ever taken fishing. Most of his customers find this a quiet and serious sport. Yet here we were laughing our fool heads off, and before long had him doing the same. I had the feeling he could hardly wait to tell his friends about us, the funny ones who didn't know how to cast, or bait the hooks, and allowed their lines to unreel till they touched bottom.

It was a great day anyway. Michael and I stopped off at Sand Beach Lodge for a brief rest on our way to the prairies. Daphne, vacationing from England, had been sent here by friends to enjoy a typically Canadian experience. And so at eight on a warm sunny morning, the three of us met on the dock, where Ed welcomed us aboard a 16-foot boat equipped with everything we needed for an outing on the river.

At our first stop he showed us how to bait hooks and cast them into the water, his patience never flagging as he extricated our lines that constantly drifted and tangled with each other. Within minutes a glittering yellow sunfish, all of four inches long, dangled from my rod. Things were going so well, I asked the obvious.

"If I require the services of a taxidermist at the end of all this, how much would he charge?" Chortling at my optimism, he said $150.

Next Mike caught a walleye estimated to weigh four pounds, and Daphne hooked a slightly smaller bass. Their success proved so heady they began using phrases like "natural talents" and "gifted amateurs," and even talked of becoming guides. Several times I had something quite monstrous flailing at the end of my line, but I couldn't bring myself to jerk the hook into its flesh as urged by Ed. And so the rod would eventually bounce back (usually hitting me in the face), while a huge black shadow could be seen gliding to safety. In spite of ourselves we caught more than enough for lunch. Nothing gigantic though, like the 97-pound sturgeon Ed had recently caught in this part of the river.

Unquestionably we are in God's Country, here on the waterways of Northern Ontario where noise is a loon's call and the air is pure. This is the French, an historic river connecting Lake Nipissing to Georgian Bay, once the route of voyageurs and fur traders. Dotted with islands, its shores thick with trees and balding rock of the Cambrian Shield, it is a northern scene painted by the most gifted of landscape artists.

At noon we pulled into a rocky cove for lunch. Ed and Daphne gathered twigs, and soon we had a crackling fire. From his box of tricks, he brought out a heavy black pan, greased it liberally and tossed in several pounds of bacon, then sliced potatoes and onions, stirring so they would all sizzle merrily together. To the delight of hovering gulls who received the leftovers, four or five of our fish were deftly filleted and fried in the second pan. At the last minute, baked beans were added to the general fry-up; homemade bread was buttered. Homemade cookies, peaches and pears, with coffee brewed in a can suspended over the fire, completed our meal. It was all absolutely delicious, and I'm ashamed to say we ate the lot.

The owners of Sand Beach Lodge, Dean and Erla Wenborne, were away for the day when we arrived. I assumed them to be enjoying the bright lights of Sudbury, but no. Time out for them is a picnic for two on the river bank some miles from the lodge.

That says a lot, I think, for the appeal of this region, and of the Wenbornes, who love it so well. The lodge has been home to Dean, on and off, for 40 years. When his parents bought the property in 1947, things were a little primitive. Nowadays guests demand comforts with their wilderness. Our hosts sensibly comply with clean and comfortable lodgings, good home cooking, and up-to-date amenities for fishermen.

Many guests are regulars who return once or twice a year. Some who bring their own children now, used to accompany parents on vacations at Sand Beach 20 or 30 years ago. Most people are here to fish. At an evening marshmallow roast I met only one who wasn't. She was a Chicago woman on her fifth visit with her husband and son. At first she says she spent a lot of time checking out other resorts. Finding nothing to match Sand Beach Lodge, she now relaxes on the beach with a pile of books and takes trips to Sudbury and North Bay.

Some 55 guests can be accommodated in one- to four-bedroom cottages. Almost every bedroom has an ensuite bath. Ours, with a family-sized living room and screened porch overlooking the river, was nestled among lofty pines.

Built in 1928 as a summer home for the Seagram family, the central lodge has been added to and modernized for current tastes. Still the original character remains, through lustrous pine walls and floors in the dining room and library.

According to Dean, "if the dining room is empty at lunch time, we're all having a good time." It's true. Arriving here around noon, we were the only diners "home" for lunch. Everyone else was out on the river. Meals here are, shall we say "hearty?" Breakfasts are sized to fuel you for a day in the outdoors. Eggs, bacon, sausages, home-fries with home-made bread and rolls will keep you going till you've hooked your shore lunch. For dinner we had excellent soup, a choice of steak, lamb or ratatouille with fresh vegetables, and locally picked blueberries in a perfect pastry for dessert.

As experienced fishermen know, there are seasons for fishing certain species. The third Saturday in May opens the walleye and northern pike season. Muskies can be caught from the third Saturday in June, and a week later small and large mouth bass become fair game. Fishing licenses are available at the lodge. Staff members will freeze and pack your catch so that you can take it home at the end of your stay. As for the friendly neighborhood taxidermist, a visit can be easily arranged. I'll probably get to meet him next time.

IF YOU GO: Sand Beach Lodge is open from mid-May until the end of October. A guide and boat (up to four passengers) costs $144 per day. Accommodation and three meals cost $79 each per day double occupancy, or $473 per week. The nearest major airport is Sudbury, where you can be met by a car from the lodge. By road from Toronto it is 200 miles north on Highway 400 to 69, then 607, and east on Dry Pine Road after which you can follow the signs. For more information write Dean and Erla Wenborne, Sand Beach Lodge, RR 1, Alban, Ont., POM 1AO. Telephone 705-857-2098.

TENNIS, AND A TASTE OF PERFECTION, AT THE INN AT MANITOU

McKellar, Ontario: Bent over her latest creation, Michele is so intensely involved with the task at hand it takes her four or five minutes to notice that she has a visitor. Putting aside one color, she introduces another to the creamy background—this time deep orange for the roses, each as delicate a creation as the real thing. When she is done she stands back, lips pursed, staring with the critical eye of an artist. One last squiggle before it meets with her approval. And another scrumptious dessert is ready for guests at the Inn and Tennis Club at Manitou.

A member of the prestigious Relais et Chateaux group, the inn is both the pride and pleasure of owners Ben and Sheila Wise, who go to untold lengths to provide the best of everything for their guests. This has not gone unnoticed. At the R & C World Congress in Brussels last year, the Inn at Manitou was awarded the 'gold' first prize as premier hotel of all 225 Relais et Chateaux members outside France.

Since 1958, the Wises have operated a summer sports, art and theater camp for young people here on the shores of Lake Manitouwabing. Nineteen years ago, these facilities were used for an adult tennis clinic. It was so successful a second clinic was held, and then a third. By that time Ben realized that some pretty important people were sleeping on bunk beds in order to take part in his tennis program. So he set about designing an elegant little inn where they could relax in comfort after a day on the courts. Now there are spacious rooms and suites, eye-catching decor enhanced by antiques and objets d'art from around the world, and international cuisine prepared by European chefs. The Inn at Manitou could easily serve as a model for gracious hospitality, and the staff outnumbers guests—yet still the Wises strive for improvement.

Until now most guests have come for the tennis clinics of three, four and seven days. For them there are 13 tennis courts, and a ratio of three players to one pro. Last year, however, a new spa facility has opened, offering wondrous therapies and treatments and pampering by experts. Exercise classes and water aerobics will tone your body, woodland hikes and picnic excursions lift the spirits and soothe the soul.

Use of recreational facilities without instruction is complimentary, except for horseback riding. This means you can windsurf, sail or take a canoe into the ever-beautiful waters of Georgian Bay. Ride a mountain bike through surrounding countryside, go fishing or lake swimming, or relax poolside. Personally I could pass some happy time on my deck above the lake, or simply watching the clever little martins busy with their young in houses Sheila has placed around the grounds. Actually, it wouldn't be difficult to do no more than sit in the sun contemplating your next meal.

Cuisine at the Inn is excellent. Thoughtful presentation plays an important part. Three different table settings are used in the course of the day, plates are selected to enhance the food. Waiters and waitresses—bubbly students from Ontario colleges and universities—wear tennis whites for breakfast and lunch, formal attire at night. Dinner is accompanied by melodies from the resident pianist playing on an 80-year-old rosewood piano.

The new spa menu is available to all guests. Low in sodium, fat, cholesterol, and calories, a typical lunch might be a consommé of vegetable infused with lemon balm, wild mushrooms with truffle juice, a green beans and flower salad with oil of rose, crusty cobbler of salmon spiced with mango chutney and assorted fruits. Eat all that, and you have consumed well under 600 calories. Regular fare? Well you can't go wrong when your day starts with coffee and oranges brought to your front door. In the sun-drenched dining room, a breakfast buffet table is packed with juices, cereals, yogurts, breads, pastries and fruit. Eggs and bacon are cooked to order. Mid-morning and afternoon snacks of fruit and juice are brought to the tennis courts. (During Wimbledon, strawberries and cream, with champagne, are served from silver trays.)

Lunch is a lavish buffet, involving salads, hot and cold entrées and soup and juice. The five course dinner menus are changed every few days. This way if you can't quite make up your mind, you have a second chance next evening.

Ben and Sheila Wise travel extensively in Europe and beyond, always on the lookout for unusual furniture and art pieces. Their success is seen in a single glance around the entrance lounge, where a century-old table from Britain has been restored to act as a reception desk. The three-seated chaperone chair is from Italy, a screen and several sculptures were brought from the Orient. Guest accommodation isn't exactly neglected either. Among other antiques in my split-level suite is a century-old French marble fireplace. Flooded with natural light through roof bubbles, the bathroom contains more than the usual goodies. I chose to ignore the magnifying mirror and scales but the hair dryer, whirlpool, sauna, goat's milk soap and other amenities could have kept me busy for the best part of the day. There are other nice touches, such as the welcome basket of fruit, champagne and mineral water on ice, and the fireplace laid ready for a match should the weather cool. Thick terry robes are provided, and in case of showers an umbrella for two stands in the corner. Also, this is one place where you don't have to sneak your bath towel to the pool, or ask for one when you get there. Every chaise has a large towel tucked into its struts—replaced of course after use.

The Inn accommodates 64 guests from mid-May through the third week of October. 1990 rates start at $173 per person daily (plus taxes and 15 percent service charge) double occupancy in a standard room, $232 with lake view, Jacuzzi and whirlpool. A junior suite costs $255 to $264. All meals and snacks are included. Tennis clinics cost $255 for three days. Spa programs are $85 for one day, to $510 for a seven-day package. Discounts are given in Spring and Fall.

IF YOU GO: McKellar is 160 miles north of Toronto, two and a half hours by car, one hour by float plane. For more information, contact the Inn and Tennis Club at Manitou, McKellar, Ont., P0G 1C0, telephone 705-389-2171 in summer or 416-967-3466 in winter.

ADVENTURE BY RAIL IN ONTARIO'S NORTHLANDS

Adventure vacations can be pretty expensive these days, especially with youngsters along, but not all of them are out of reach. Sure, given the choice of a free trip to the Amazon or a train ride to Moosonee, we'd all be off for our typhoid shots within the hour. But as fare-paying passengers with limited funds, we might settle for the untamed frontier spirit that still pervades lands beyond the highways of Northern Ontario.

Trains to Moosonee and the Agawa Canyon are packed all summer, such is the popularity of these one-day excursions. Most participants make the trip as part of a tour of Northern Ontario. Others are up from Toronto or Detroit especially for the train ride. Either way, you need a minimum of two nights in the departure towns of Cochrane (450 miles from Toronto) for Moosonee, and Sault Ste. Marie (425 miles from Toronto) for the Agawa Canyon.

MOOSONEE VIA THE POLAR BEAR EXPRESS. Children love this one, for the entertaining ride, the frontier town atmosphere, the patience of Indian women selling affordable souvenirs, a canoe ride across the Moose River and the presence of seaplanes buzzing importantly about. Parents love it for Ontario Northland Railway's family plan, allowing them and their dependents up to 22 years old to travel for $90 return fare.

Freight/passenger trains make the Cochrane–Moosonee run three times a week, while the excursion train operates every day except Fridays between late June and late September. Today we are on the one-day excursion departing Cochrane at 8:30 a.m. That's if the overnight from Toronto has arrived on time for its passengers to make the connection.

While scenery along the 186-mile track is not spectacular, the sense of adventure lies in just knowing this ribbon of steel is the only surface route between us and the outside world. At first the terrain is agricultural. Forty-three miles along the route brings us to an Ontario Paper Company logging operation. Halfway and we are into the Hudson Bay lowlands. Childrens' hour with the train's resident pianist begins in the entertainment car; snacks and beverages are served. Occasionally, Indian children wave at the train from the steps of tiny cabins, surrounded by forests of tall pines. More children are at Moosonee's little green and white station. "Gateway to the Arctic," the sign says.

A street leading from the station to the river is literally clogged with tourists on excursion days. In spite of the traffic, this is still very much a frontier town. Modern-day pioneers with nylon knapsacks, Kodiak boots and an aluminum canoe set off for a prolonged wilderness experience. Two nuns from our train climb into a seaplane to continue their journey to a remote mission.

The rest of us have 4 1/2 brief hours to explore. Don't expect much in the way of paved roads or sidewalks or nicely kept lawns at Moosonee. The dust can be fierce, the mud even worse and, if mosquitoes bother you, remember to bring insect repellant.

This is it—a rough and tumble settlement cut off from the rest of Ontario until the railway tracks were completed in 1932, uninhabited prior to 1900 when a Mrs Annie Hardy decided to pitch her tent by the river. A few years later, the Revillon Brothers opened a fur trading company and sawmill here. The Revillon Frères Museum now lets you in on those pioneering times.

The region is populated mostly by Cree Indians. Their crafts and art are displayed and sold in the James Bay Education Center, and at the Weneebaykook Gallery, where talented artists are at work.

Buffet lunches are catered in licensed dining rooms of the town's two hotels on excursion days. There's Chilly Willy's Variety and a Hudson's Bay Company store which looks like any other supermarket until a customer arrives by canoe. And that's about it.

Cree boatmen wait with motorized canoes to transport tourists across the river. Current one-way fare is $3. The Hudson's Bay Company established a fort on this island in 1673. For generations before that, the Crees camped here during spring and fall goose hunts. Now we are greeted by Indian women and girls selling native souvenirs. More are at the Anglican Church Parish Hall offering light lunches and snacks, and in the bannock tent someone cooks the unleaven bread over a fire.

St Thomas Anglican Church is a little beauty, built in 1860 and open now so we may see its moosehide altar cloth and lectern hangings, embroidered by parish women. Plugs in the floor are interesting—if necessary, they are removed in spring to allow flooding of the church. A messy business for sure, but preferable to the building's being swept away with the ice flow when winter is over. Once it did just that and had to be towed back home.

Moose Factory's Centennial Park Museum traces the Hudson's Bay Company's activities in the area. It contains an old blacksmith's shop, cannon, a fur press, usually a few dogs, and a powder magazine that has the distinction of being Moose Factory's only stone building.

Passengers for the excursion train leaving at 5:15 should be at Moose Factory's dock soon after 4 p.m. That allows for possible delay in crossing the river, and time to buy a quality souvenir from the gallery. During the return train journey, dinner is served on board and entertainment is for adults.

There is plenty of free parking at Cochrane's railway terminus. Overnight accommodation in Moosonee is available at two moderately priced motel-type lodges. Escorted tours of Moosonee and Moose Factory include pick-up at the station, and motor boat ride across the river, all within allotted excursion times. With two or three days in Moosonee you will have the opportunity for longer excursions to Shipsands and Fossil Island. Campsites at Tidewater Provincial Park can be reached by water taxi from Moosonee.

AGAWA CANYON VIA ALGOMA CENTRAL RAILWAY. This excursion train operates out of Sault Ste Marie, Ontario, between early June and mid-October. At 8 every morning, it's off on a 114-mile journey through wilderness territory. It unloads passengers onto the canyon floor for two hours and has them back in "The Soo" by 5 p.m. Regrettably there is no advance booking of individual tickets, except on the day before your trip. Then, or on the excursion day, they must be purchased from the Sault Ste Marie station ticket office.

Construction of this railway began in 1899 and was completed 15 years later. Its purpose was to carry pulpwood, lumber, and ore from the mines to the furnaces of Algoma Steel Corporation. A challenge even to modern engineers and equipment, I would think, its tracks are laid over waterfalls and ravines, through dense bush and on trestles so high and so long I wonder why they don't collapse.

Coaches on the excursion train are allocated, but not specific seats, so if you want a window seat you should be on board by 7:30 a.m. Particularly scenic spots are marked on mile-posts along the track; matching descriptions are on pamphlets handed to passengers as they board the train. Once you're on your way, a hostess announces upcoming landmarks, meal times and other important happenings, over a public address system.

At first there's nothing very inspiring. We pass Abitibi's paper mill and the main entrance of Algoma Steel, cross over the Trans-Canada Highway, then move into the jungle-like interior. There must be 30 or more shades of green out there; even more reflecting in a lake with tiny cabins fastened to its shoreline.

The village of Searchmount shows no sign of life as we amble through. Its lumber piles are veneer logs, glistening beneath a spray applied to prevent staining. By 10 a.m. we are into the promised land, witnessing those panoramas that look so unreal on calendars and postcards. A giant metallic snake, the train slithers along at an average 40 miles per hour. From the outset, breakfast is served in the diner. Pancakes and sausages with syrup and eggs. Children's orders half-price. Box lunches are distributed for picnics in Canyon Park.

At 11:10 we begin our descent of some 500 feet in 12 miles, to the canyon's floor. The view is fabulous, even in the blur of rain splashing our window. Lunch is served in the diner—edible and moderately priced. We eat meat pie, potatoes and corn and a cardboard pie, and watch for waterfalls on either side of the track.

In fine weather, I have no doubt that the Agawa Canyon Park is a scenic gift from heaven. There are footpaths beside the river, picnic tables, swings and slides for children and a look-out trail. We walk to Bridal Veil Falls, just seen from the train, and climb to an intermediate lookout, its steps slippery because of recent showers. The upper lookout, reached in roughly 35 minutes, is said to afford fantastic views. With more than 500 tourists ahead of us, we give it a miss. Several passengers have come with fishing rods and high hopes, and plastic bags to keep hairdos intact. At 1:20 p.m. we start the return journey. By 2 o'clock almost everyone in sight is asleep.

I turn my attention to the railway's souvenir newspaper and guess only eight things wrong in a picture containing 16 mistakes. I learn that in 1914, tracks were extended to Hearst, 296 miles from Sault Ste Marie, and that a two-day excursion to this French Canadian frontier town is recommended for the true railway buff. An alternative is to leave the train somewhere along the line to stay at one of the lodges accessible from the tracks. The ultimate wilderness experience, I suppose, is to bring your own canoe, tent and spirit of adventure, and ask the conductor to let you off at the lake or river of your choice. Tell him what day you plan to return to civilization, and he will pick you up at the spot where he dropped you a week or a month before.

It is advisable to be in Sault Ste Marie the day before your excursion because sometimes very few tickets are left on the departure day. Busiest period is the last week of September and the first of October when autumn leaves are at their best. Groups of 20 or more, organized by tour wholesalers or travel agents, can be booked in advance. Sault Ste Marie has numerous hotels and motels, some within easy walking distance of the train. There is plenty of free parking at the station.

IF YOU GO: The Polar Bear Express to Moosonee. Current return fare on the excursion or passenger/freight train is $36 for adults, $18 for children and seniors. A family ticket is $90 (two parents and dependents). The Ontario Northland Railway, Union Station, 65 Front Street West, Toronto, Ont., M5J 1E6 (telephone 416-965-4268 or toll free in Ontario: 1-800-268-9281), will provide schedules, as well as information on area accommodation and its tour packages from Toronto.

Up the Agawa Canyon. Current ticket prices are $35 for adults, and half price for youngsters. For brochures and further information, contact Passenger Sales, Algoma Central Railway, 129 Bay Street, Sault Ste Marie, Ont. P6A 5P6, telephone 705-254-4331.

FUR TRADING YEARS AT FORT WILLIAM

Thunder Bay, Ontario: They would come, these incredible men of the north, some from as far away as the Rocky Mountains to attend the Great Rendezvous at Fort William on the northwest rim of Lake Superior. As soon as the ice melted in northern rivers they set off, their 25-foot canoes weighed down with furs, to reach the fort by early July.

In Quebec meanwhile more canoes were loaded, this time with trade goods from across the Atlantic. Thirty-six footers, they were manned by stocky Montrealers whose journey to the Rendezvous took six to eight weeks. In all about 2,000 people—voyageurs, Indians and North West Company officials—converged on the fort for those three weeks in July. A time for discussions between company big-wigs, and trading with the Indians, it was by all accounts a three-week party for the exuberant voyageurs.

Inland headquarters of the North West Company from 1803 to 1821, taken over by the Hudson's Bay Company until it closed in 1881, Fort William stood then as its re-creation does now on the banks of the Kaministikwia River. Fewer than two dozen employees lived here most of the year. For them there were maintenance and farm chores, and occasional trading. Then came the big Rendezvous and the fort sprang into action. Much more than an average trading post, it was an enormous warehouse and shipment center from where trade goods and provisions were distributed to smaller outposts. So July was time for frenzied activity including the important business of swapping imports for skins.

William MacGillivray, a Montreal agent and the company's chief director (after whom the fort was named) had comfortable quarters in the Great Hall during the Rendezvous. Company partners and clerks were also lodged within the fort. Voyageurs lived outside in two camps; one for the winterers and the other for those from Lachine. The northerners considered themselves a

Old Fort William, Thunder Bay

cut above the "pork eaters" from Montreal. Maybe they were, for who could argue with men who spent their winters tramping from one lonely outpost to the next. Hostility may have prevailed between the voyageur camps, but neither lot frowned upon the favors of Indian women from the third encampment outside the palisades. Today Fort William is a magnificent reconstruction, on the same river banks but nine miles from the original site, in the city of Thunder Bay. Reminiscent of Williamsburg, Va., perhaps because of the company partners strutting about in their elegant European clothes, and with a strong flavor of Winnipeg's Lower Fort Garry, its construction has so far cost the Ontario Government $12 million.

Introduction is by way of a slide show in a theater beside the gift shop. If that doesn't whet the appetite for a first-hand adventure into the past you can leave with an easy conscience because the ticket box is beyond this point. A walk along a forest path sets the mood. The Indian encampment, where a family diligently works on birch bark delays us momentarily, then we turn the corner to see docks and massive gates of the fort itself.

The buildings are attractive, no doubt closely matching the originals, but it is the fort's "residents" who draw you into the past and set you down in an average day here—in the year 1816. As well as being dressed for the part they perform chores, perfect skills and always answer visitors' questions in the present tense. It is no hard task to believe that they, and you, are really there.

Take the company store. Step inside and the clerk tries to interest you in buying. What will it be now, he wants to know. A dozen buttons, a check shirt or an earring are each valued at one beaver skin. (First you change your pelts for tokens, company currency used in the store.) A pistol is worth four, a gun 12 and a striped blanket six beaver furs.

The fort doctor shows us his medications. Biggest killer and occupational hazard of the voyageurs, he says, is hernia. "And we can't do a damn thing about that." Voyageurs, we learn, must carry 180-pound loads on their backs, and so develop strong arms but weak legs from constant crouching. Next door an orderly is apologetic. He would introduce us to his patient, had he not died minutes before. And so it goes. The shoemaker, tinsmith, cooper and tailor demonstrate and explain their trades. A giant birch-bark canoe is under construction in the Canoe Shed. At the Council House a meeting of company partners is in progress. Members wearing ruffled shirts and cutaway coats earnestly discuss company policies. At one point a junior is rebuked for permitting his eyes to wander when two 20th-century girls arrive wearing rather brief attire.

Sounds and smells as well as sights enhance the picture. Odors are of hides and herbs, wood fires and newly baked bread. Sounds are from a smithy's hammer, a flock of sheep, bagpipe practice and the fort's fiddler.

For reasons of authenticity, buildings are not named or numbered. With main dwellings built around a square and a detailed map handed to you at the ticket office, you'll have no trouble finding your way around. Or you can join a 90-minute guided tour, which is available after Labor Day when the "residents" return to school, leaving tour guides as your chief information source.

The cruise boat *"Welcome"* travels the Kaministikwia River these days on a 90-minute journey from Thunder Bay Marina to Old Fort William and passengers return to town by bus. Landlubbers find plenty of signs directing them to the fort.

Thunder Bay is a modern city with good shopping plazas and hotels and excellent campgrounds. We stayed at Kakabeka Falls Provincial Park, 18 miles west of town. It has limited camping facilities, but gorgeous waterfalls and wooded sites. On the shores of the Kaministikwia River here we sat around our campfire that night, choosing to believe that Indians and voyageurs had done so a century and a half before.

IF YOU GO: Thunder Bay is 875 miles northwest of Toronto via the Trans-Canada Highway. Old Fort William's summer season is between late June and Labor Day, 10 a.m. to 9 p.m. but on a more limited basis is open year round. Admission is $6.50 for adults, $4.25 for students, under fives free.

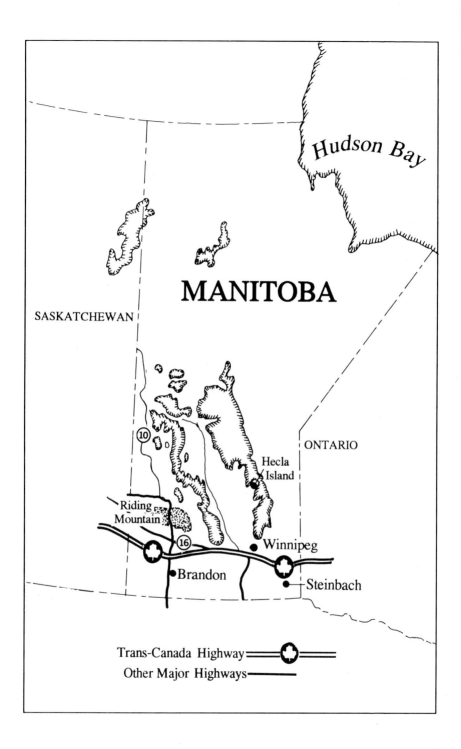

Hudson Bay

MANITOBA

SASKATCHEWAN

ONTARIO

10

Hecla
Island

Riding
Mountain

16

Winnipeg

Brandon

Steinbach

Trans-Canada Highway 🛡

Other Major Highways

MANITOBA

This is Canada's heartland, a prairie province with so many lakes (100,000 at last count), some have never been fished. Terrain is not quite what you expect either, including as it does great forests and plains, a desert where cacti bloom and powdery sand beaches that are more readily associated with the Atlantic provinces. Over half Manitoba's population lives in Winnipeg, the provincial capital changing so rapidly we can hardly keep up with it. Culturally rich, the city is the home of an internationally acclaimed symphony orchestra and ballet company, top notch art galleries and museums. Last year saw the opening of a gambling casino in one of its best hotels. Restaurants, museums and annual events benefit from the city's ethnic diversity.

It all began here at the junction of the Red and Assiniboine Rivers, where the hub of a 19th-century settlement was a Hudson's Bay Company trading post. Now this area is undergoing a $100 million redevelopment program providing the city with more parks, an amphitheater and farmers' market.

That futuristic looking structure on Winnipeg's eastern outskirts is the Royal Canadian Mint, designed to accommodate public tours and capable of producing two billion coins a year. Displays include commemorative coins such as a silver dollar minted in 1981 featuring a steam train on a map of Canada. It reminds us of the first train to chug into Winnipeg a hundred years before, opening the prairies to European immigrants via eastern Canada and the United States.

Few grandchildren of those immigrants have forgotten their heritage. Some of the first settlers were brought here from the Scottish highlands by Lord Selkirk. Now the town named for him hosts the Manitoba Highland Gathering each July, and goes western in August with a rodeo and agricultural fair. At Steinbach, Mennonites celebrate their culture with Pioneer Days. A Festival du Voyageur recreates the spirit of French explorers, while a great Rendezvous at Lower Fort Garry relives times when this was headquarters for the Hudson's Bay Company's vast fur trading empire. South of Dauphin, the Selo Ukraina (Ukrainian village) has a 5,000-seat amphitheater that provides a grand stage for August's National Ukrainian Festival. Gimli remembers its beginnings during a summer Icelandic Festival.

Manitoba has outstanding national and provincial parks. One of the finest is Whiteshell, with campgrounds, resorts, beaches, lake swimming, fishing and a golf course attracting Winnipeggers on summer weekends. Bird watchers flock to Birds Hill Provincial Park, also within commuting distance of Winnipeg. For creature comforts in wilderness country, you will go a long way to beat Riding Mountain National Park. Grand Beach has been voted one of North America's most beautiful and if you are hoping for a trophy-sized trout try Clear Lake, so named because you can see the lake bottom at 35 feet.

A train journey from Winnipeg to Churchill (1,000 miles) is one of North America's last great rail adventures. This is Canada's only arctic seaport, also known as the Polar Bear capital of the world. Beyond the tree line but carpeted with wild flowers in summer, Churchill's greatest fascination is its polar bears that come south with the ice flow in summer and beluga whales swimming in the bay. Nature safaris include half and full day expeditions in tundra vehicles to look for the bears and by boat to see the whales. An Eskimo Museum contains Inuit carvings dating to 1,700 B.C. Fort Prince of Wales, built in the 1700s by the Hudson's Bay Company is now a National Historic Park, reached by boat between June and September and dog team in winter. Here on Hudson Bay you can watch the northern lights, listen to the all-enveloping silence, and be deafened by wild geese touching down on the ice flows as they head south. And return home with photographs of the far north's "great whites."

For more information on this province, write Travel Manitoba, Dept 9035, 7th floor, 155 Carlton St., Winnipeg, Manitoba R3C 3H8. Telephone toll free 1-800-665-0040, extension 36.

THE CHANGING FACES
OF WINNIPEG

Winnipeg, Manitoba: I have to say I look forward to my visits to this prairie city. For one thing it's changing so fast there is always something new to see. For another it is culturally ahead of, or at least in step with, better known cities. My favorite museum is here, and a first rate zoo which is free so I don't feel obliged to stay all day, and a pot-pourri of cultures reflected in shops and restaurants. Well documented history is the stuff action movies used to be made of, telling about adventurers and buffalo hunts, scarlet coated Mounties and courageous pioneers who survived it all. Winnipeg has comfortable, centrally located hotels, friendly citizens and lots of green spaces to rest in. I ask no more of any city.

The first white man to come this way was French explorer and trader Pierre de la Verendrye who established a fort near the junction of the Red and Assiniboine Rivers in 1738. Other forts replaced it, the last being Upper Fort Garry in 1835 from which the Hudson's Bay Company administered its fur operations in Rupertsland. There is little physical evidence on site now to remind us of those times, except for a stone archway belonging to the Upper Fort. If walls could talk, it would have quite a tale to tell.

The Red River was the main highway then, and this junction a gateway to lucrative northern fur grounds. Hunters would bring pemmican into the fort, trappers came with furs, and Scottish immigrants farmed riverside lots to supply produce for both the fort and its distant trading posts.

Within walking distance of this site, the Museum of Man and Nature excites its patrons with displays pertinent to the fur trading era. One is a replica of *Nonsuch* berthed in a 17th-century London dock. Roughly 50 feet long it seems far too fragile for the open seas yet in 1688 the original *Nonsuch* sailed from England

to Hudson Bay, bypassing the French occupied St Lawrence
River. Voyageurs Radisson and Groseilleurs had convinced a
group of English businessmen to buy the ship and finance their
journey. They returned home with so many furs Charles II
granted a charter to "the Governor and Company of Adventurers
for trading into Hudson's Bay," and so gave birth to the Hudson's
Bay Company.

The museum has seven galleries portraying man's relation-
ship with the environment. Dioramas are so realistic I find myself shivering in the Arctic-Subarctic gallery. In the Boreal forest
I pause to mourn for this land before the white man plundered its
natural resources. And a buffalo hunt is so vivid, I can hear the
thundering hooves and catch terror in the beasts' eyes. Traditional lifestyles are depicted in sod huts and log cabins of early
settlers, to comfortable homes of the early 1900s. (The British
brought their teapots, just to be sure. . . .)

As the fur trade declined, focus of the Red River community
shifted to a new commercial center developing at the cross-roads
of two well-travelled fur trails. Interestingly Winnipeg's core has
never shifted from Portage and Main, reputedly the windiest corner in all of Canada. The 'windiest' story is thought to have got
its start around 1862 when the first two-storied store to open on
this corner required constant propping up against the ravaging
prairie winds. It survived, and soon there were more shops.
Within 10 years the commercial hub had spread to take in the
original Red River settlement and Upper Fort Garry. Now there
is no need to be windswept. A modern climate-controlled Portage
Place has a three-storied atrium to remind Winnipeggers of June
in January, numerous shops, restaurants and services, and an
award-winning Imax theater with a screen five and a half stories
high.

Far more colorful is the Chinese community's development of
eight downtown blocks as a tourist oriented center. Already a
colossal Chinese gate spans King Street. The Dynasty Building,
with its shiny green roofs, contains the Winnipeg Chinese Cultural Center. And an attractive Heritage Garden is scene of
Wednesday lunch-time entertainment in summer. Chinese shops,
a bakery and recreation room where dance and cooking classes

are held, are all part of the present scene. Even telephone booths are pagoda style, while dozens of Chinese restaurants are located in the area.

The thick red mud that sucked down wagon wheels of despairing settlers has finally relinquished its grip, giving way to public gardens and landscaped parkways along the river banks. Of particular interest to visitors is Kildonan Park, for its wooded paths and a public swimming pool, and in summer outdoor theater featuring popular musicals on its Rainbow Stage. And Assiniboine Park with 375 acres of treed lawns, formal gardens and a conservatory serving refreshments. Its zoo contains over 1,200 animals, including many species now endangered in the wild. Near the English gardens a Red River cart is sculpted in bronze, commemorating times when such carts provided land transportation for Red River settlers. Built from wood and fastened with buffalo hide, they could and often did carry loads in excess of 1,000 pounds.

Across the river, St Boniface is billed as the largest French Quarter west of Ottawa. Taché Promenade bordering the river is delightful for an evening stroll. The city's oldest structure is here, built for the Grey Nuns in 1846 as a convent, hospital, girls' school and orphanage. Now a museum, it has recreated spartan conditions under which the nuns lived in their dedication to "poverty in the service of misery." French-Indian Metis leader Louis Riel, executed in Regina for his part in the Northwest Rebellion, was born in St. Boniface and is buried here in the cathedral grounds. Riel memorabilia in the museum includes letters (one thanks a Judge Richardson for delaying the execution for 29 days until the birth of his baby—the infant, a boy, was stillborn), his will, photographs and such. Also what remains of a black box provided by the government for Riel's body. Friends brought the body home, laid it in a coffin more worthy of the man they deemed a martyr and gave him a hero's funeral. His tomb, inscribed simply "Louis Riel, President of the Provisional Government of 1869-70," is in the grounds where a Father Provencher built the first church in Western Canada in 1818. That log structure and several successors were destroyed by fire. The latest dates from 1972.

St Boniface, Winnipeg

Provencher, Louis Riel, Lord Selkirk (who brought Scottish immigrants to settle the land by the Red River) and other Manitoban figures from the past are among statues in the Provincial Legislative Building's gardens. Constructed of traditional fossilized tyndall stone, this handsome building is best known for its Golden Boy, a 12-foot-high statue sheathed in gold leaf standing atop the dome. If you don't have time for a guided tour, do at least peep into the main hall to see the massive bronze bison on either side of a marble staircase. Sculpted by Golden Boy's creator Frenchman Charles Gardet, each weighs two and a half tons.

As we hope for in a multi-cultural city such as this, Winnipeg has a tempting range of eating places. Chinese head the ethnic restaurants, but you will also find Greek, Ukrainian, French, Italian and Swiss, as well as French-Canadian in St Boniface. For a change you might try brunch or dinner on a riverboat cruising the Red River. I particularly enjoyed a quiet lunch in the rooftop sculpture garden of the Winnipeg Art Gallery, bubble and squeak in an English pub, and Sunday brunch to strains of Vivaldi in the Hotel Fort Garry's Provencher Room.

Winnipeg has first rate hotels, large and small, as well as an active B & B program. Campers are provided with secluded sites at Birds Hill Provincial Park 14 miles northeast of the city.

IF YOU GO: Winnipeg is mid-way between Canada's east and west coasts, 1300 miles from Toronto and 355 miles from Regina, Saskatchewan via the Trans Canada Highway. More information on Winnipeg is available from Tourism Winnipeg, 232-375 York Avenue, Winnipeg, Man., R3C 3J3, telephone 204-943-1970.

FORT GARRY HOTEL IS RESTORED TO ITS ORIGINAL SPLENDOR

Winnipeg, Manitoba: Around the turn of the century Canadian Pacific Railway constructed extraordinarily grand castle-like hotels across Canada, largely to accommodate its passengers touring by train. Soon the Grand Trunk Railway followed suit, starting its hotel chain with the Chateau Laurier in Ottawa. When plans for a second hotel were announced, they were for a 10-storied building in Winnipeg to be named the Selkirk. It materialized in 1913 with 14 floors, and was called Fort Garry.

Either name would have been appropriate. Lord Selkirk started the Red River settlement here that became the core of

Manitoba's capital city. Upper Fort Garry, a 19th century trading post across from the hotel site, was heartbeat of this outpost some 2,000 brave souls called home.

Like other railway hotels of the period, the Fort Garry is a massive fortress-style building with thick stone walls and a steep copper roof. From the beginning it was unusually self-contained, having its own butcher shop, bakery and printing press to produce menus and place cards daily. The laundry took care of fresh linens for trains on local runs, as well as the hotel's needs.

On a particularly frigid December 19 guests invited to the opening are said to have been dazzled by such splendor: the ceiling paintings and wall sculptures, crystal chandeliers, plush drapes and upholstery, and all those gleaming brass fittings typical of railway hotels the world over.

The 1920s and 30s were wonderful for the Fort Garry, a glorious setting for the city's most important social functions and a favorite with travellers who were brought in style from the station in an electric omnibus. But, post-war years brought a steady decline to these antiquated hotels. Some were purchased by provincial governments that spent millions of dollars nursing them back to good health. In 1979 the Fort Garry was sold to a Winnipeg businessman, eventually declared bankrupt and closed for two years.

In 1987 it was bought by Quebec hotelier Raymond Malenfant who achieved the seemingly impossible when he opened five months later, following very ambitious renovations. When he wasn't working as architect, interior designer and contractor, Malenfant found time to tour European castles seeking ideas for his prized hotel. At antique auctions he purchased furniture for suites and public rooms. Carpeting and matching wallpapers were commissioned, miles of soft grey velvet for drapes and upholstery ordered, original paintings purchased for every guest room. Heating and wiring systems were renewed, windows replaced, delicate ceiling art restored, and $12 million later the hotel opened on the scheduled date, May 20, 1988.

Now, the upbeat atmosphere is evident to everyone coming into the hotel—whether that's local traffic for Sunday's brunch accompanied by a string quartet or drinks in the opulent Oval Room and a meal in one of the two dining rooms, or travellers checking in for a few days. There are 270 rooms and 13 suites, all newly decorated, comfortably elegant and quiet. Prefer a suite? For $500 a day you will forget that this is downtown Winnipeg when ensconced here among ornate oriental art and furniture. A thousand dollars a day provides a split-level suite with traditional furnishings and a separate dining room.

The hotel's dining rooms have taken on a certain Frenchness in name and nature. The former coffee shop has become Café Piaf, a bright and cheerful room serving international fare. And what used to be the Factor's Table (reminding us of legendary hospitality at Lower Fort Garry where guests gathered around the factor's table) is now called Lautrec. Food is excellent, service attentive, and there's still some local flavor for diners wanting Winnipeg goldeye or prime rib or wild game. Even buffalo consomme with wild rice is listed among the frog legs and caviar.

More dramatic changes are in store later this year, according to manager Aziz Bocti, 22 years in Canada's hotel business, and as enthusiastic about the Fort Garry as a new father of his first-born. An indoor pool and health club are planned for summer's end. An even bigger splash is expected when a gambling casino is installed on the seventh floor. Two of the hotel's most spectacular rooms, a ballroom and concert hall, will be taken over for baccarat, blackjack and roulette. Slot machines will line the walls of the hallway connecting the two. The Manitoba government's lottery foundation is to operate the casino, Mr Bocti says, with proceeds going to hospitals and research. At time of writing, the opening date was tentatively planned for October 2, but Bocti rather fancied Friday the 13th, a day on which Lady Luck was bound to be present. In fact, it finally opened, to much fanfare, on another Friday—December 29, 1989.

IF YOU GO: The Fort Garry Hotel is at 222 Broadway, Winnipeg, Manitoba R3C OR3. Telephone 204-942-8251, or toll free 1-800-665-8088.

STEINBACH'S MENNONITES

Steinbach, Manitoba: It's a true labor of love, this Steinbach Mennonite Village Museum established by children and grandchildren of Manitoba's Mennonite settlers, 40 miles southeast of Winnipeg. Anxious to both preserve and share their heritage with outsiders, these descendents of the pioneers perform all the village chores. They take your admission, work the land, serve in the shop, keep the horses in shoes, cook and serve Mennonite meals to visitors. And when you show more than a passing interest in something, someone inevitably hurries on over to tell you, "my grandmother had one of those. I remember when . . . "

The long and often difficult road from 16th-century Holland where Menno Simons broke with the Catholic Church doctrine, to a tourist attraction in 20th-century Manitoba, is well documented at the museum. Here we learn that most of Canada's Mennonites came from South Russia; the first between 1874 and 1880, more in the 1920s and a third group following World War II. Persecuted during their early years, they had found religious freedom in what is now the Ukraine. For almost a century there, they were left alone in the chosen isolation of their farming settlements, but then new and threatening government rules were introduced. First, Russian was to be taught in all schools. Second, there would be no exemption from military conscription on grounds of religious beliefs.

And so the exodus began. The first Mennonites arrived in this area south of Winnipeg on August 1, 1874. By 1880 some 7,000 were established in Manitoba at a time when the provincial population was less than 70,000. Upon arrival, women and children were housed in government reception huts while the men located suitable sites for villages. Gruenfeld, the first ready for occupation, received 19 families. Nearby Steinbach, named for a village in South Russia, was second.

Mennonite Village, Steinbach

The re-created village at Steinbach typifies a Mennonite community in the late 1800s. These were street-villages, so called because their layout incorporated one main street, with dwellings on either side. Houses were built 200 feet apart and 100 feet back from the road, to leave plenty of room for fruit and vegetable gardens on each property. Houses of this period were inevitably of the same design: a living room overlooking the street, and an attached barn connected by a corridor which kept animal odors from family quarters. Each village had its own school. And of course a church, centrally located to symbolize religion as the core of these peoples' lives.

The village museum traces progress of Manitoba's settlers through different types of houses. Although accommodation improved greatly over the years, none is what you might consider luxurious because Mennonites believed that simplicity brings one closer to spiritual understanding. Their first shelter was in primitive sod huts constructed from natural materials available—sod, soil, wood and grass. Each hut measured only 29 feet by 12, yet often accommodated livestock as well as a family. Built two feet below ground, they had walls of wooden planks packed with sod on the outside, and roofs first plastered with clay, then covered with earth. Said to be snug enough in winter, these homes were painfully damp for days following a heavy rainfall. For anyone who was in wartime Britain, the furnished sod hut here will bring back memories of the garden air-raid shelter.

Log cabins with thatched roofs took over from the sod huts. Roomy, warm and dry, these were particularly handy in that they could be dismantled and moved to a new location. Numerals carved in the logs of the village's cabin illustrate how such markings were used to help with re-assembly.

Frame houses introduced by the late 1800s were so uniform in design, according to the guide: "If everyone opened his side door you could see the length of the street through them." Museum manager Peter Goertzen can tell you all about the village's frame house. It was the family home of his great-grandfather.

Steinbach's 19th-century church looks decidedly unfinished. There are no stained glass windows, or for that matter ornamentation of any kind. Interior walls are plastered white, wooden furnishings plain and simple. The pulpit is in the middle so that everyone could hear the preacher—men on one side, women on the other. Any form of music was banned. Actually, this quiet simplicity goes beyond religious beliefs to times of persecution when it was prudent to be unobtrusive.

While food tends to be stodgy and bland, you really can't leave Steinbach without sampling some. A barn on the main street has been converted to a restaurant. Typical meals which include vareniki, borscht, sausage, cole slaw, platz and coffee, cost five or six dollars. If you don't fancy a full lunch you might try the cold fruit soup called pluma moos. And some vareniki—a dough pocket stuffed with cottage cheese and served in sour cream sauce. The bread is baked from stone ground flour milled here daily. A hunk of it with homemade butter and cheese was the tastiest part of my Mennonite lunch.

Incongruous in its pioneer setting, the large and modern artifacts building was designed by the grandson of an early settler. Exhibits are accompanied by neatly printed cards where explanations are deemed necessary. From such a card, we learn that a Mennonite woman's first duty is to care for her children. Also that she must be proficient in cooking, gardening, sewing and cleaning her house.

Turn-of-the-century clothes, period furniture, books dating from the 16th century, clocks, coin collections, photographs and tools. One wonders how some survived the years, and journeys, and how they came to be chosen as treasures to be brought to the new world. You will see horns, with which the herdsmen signalled housewives to send out their cows for a day in the community pasture. And a rare Russian wicker trunk which once stored a family's valued possessions. Trunks such as this one also carried durable toasted buns as a source of food during the long voyage to Canada, since the emigrant decks of trans-Atlantic steamers had no dining facilities.

At the outset farming was the sole occupation of the Mennonites. In Manitoba it soon became practical for communities to have their own blacksmiths and printers, and eventually shopkeepers. This region's first real store opened in 1884 as a successor to the makeshift shop operated from Klaus Reimer's home. That store is now a village display. Another sells souvenirs, hand knitted garments, homemade candy, and copies of rules for 19th-century Mennonite teachers.

In addition to teaching, these noble souls had to fill the lamps, clean chimneys and bring buckets of water and coal to school daily. Male teachers were allowed one evening a week for courting purposes. After 10 hours in school, the teacher could spend his spare time reading the bible or other good books. Anyone who smoked, used liquor, frequented public halls or was shaved in a barber's shop, gave good reason to have his value, integrity, intention and honesty suspected. If he performed his labors faithfully for five years he received an increase of 25 cents a week—and you know what, guys? There's no mention of paid maternity leave or professional development days.

IF YOU GO: Steinbach is 40 miles southeast of Winnipeg, via the Trans-Canada Highway, then Highway 12 south. The village museum is open daily between May and September, from noon on Sundays. There is a modest admission charge.

RELIVE FUR TRADING YEARS AT FORT GARRY

Selkirk, Manitoba: Standing on the front porch to welcome visitors into his elegant home, Eden Colville looks very satisfied with life. And why not? He is associate Governor of the Hudson's Bay Company, has a lovely wife at home and a Métis mistress in town. It is a glorious summer's day, the gardens are a picture, and it's almost time for Sunday dinner.

Listening as he told me these things, a trio of German soldiers on leave from a nearby training camp fully understood the situation. But when the governor turned his attention to a woman from North Dakota she was thoroughly confused. After all, here is a young man dressed in formal attire, who claims to live here now, in the 1850s. He freely admits to having half-breed children in town, and in the same breath says he has just come from church. What's more he has an upper-crust British accent that she can't quite understand. With a shake of her head, and an exaggerated wink at me (implying this man surely has a screw loose) she suddenly remembers she must meet her daughter. The undaunted Colville, meantime, decides to stroll in the gardens, relishing his role as the Hudson's Bay Chief in residence here at Lower Fort Garry, 20 miles north of Winnipeg.

While the restored fort is an interesting introduction to the Hudson's Bay Company fur trade, the fun part for visitors lies in the role-playing costumed employees who converse in the present tense about their 19th-century lives. In the Big House, for instance, Mrs. Colville told me of lavish dinner parties she and the governor host for visiting dignitaries. A young man working on company books here said he had come from Scotland, and lives in rooms beside his office. In the retail store a woman was given the price of something in tokens. At no time will these actors revert to the 20th century. They are very convincing.

To fully appreciate what this is all about, visitors should first watch an audio visual presentation at the modern entrance building, a short walk from the fort itself. And then wait for a tour guide, who will escort you to the wall, explain the uses of the buildings and boats along the way, and leave you to explore on your own—with Colville and fellow students assisting you on your journey into the past.

In 1826, flooding of the Red River Settlement in what is now central Winnipeg, destroyed the first Fort Garry. A fort had stood at that junction of the Red and Assiniboine Rivers since the first white man came this way in 1738. By 1821, when the Northwest Company and Hudson's Bay Company united, Fort Garry was hub of the Red River colony.

In the early 1800s, Hudson's Bay Company governor George Simpson wasn't too thrilled with life in this rowdy commercial settlement. Planning to get married, he wanted a lifestyle more gracious than he and his bride could ever attain there. Following flooding of the fort in 1826, he saw an opportunity to relocate. To the directors in London it seemed a good idea. The new fort

Lower Fort Garry

would be made to last; it would stand on higher ground away from threat of floods, and it would be closer to Norway House and York Factory—the company's northern posts.

Construction of the stone fort began in 1830, and the Simpsons never did live there. (Following the death of their first child, they moved to Montreal.) Unfortunately, the location, so splendid for the governor and visiting big-wigs, was a whole day's journey by ox cart for settlers and plains herdsmen wanting to do business with the company. As sales dropped off, it was decided to re-open a shop on the old site for people of the settlement.

Next, the folly of conducting company affairs from the two forts 20 miles apart was realized, and reconstruction of the original fort was started. Now known as Upper Fort Garry, it reopened in 1837 as the administrative center for Hudson's Bay Company operations in Rupert's Land.

Although Lower Fort Garry lost much of its prestige, it was put to good use over the years. A hundred-acre farm was established to supply grain, peas and root crops for this and other posts. Beef cattle and pigs raised at the fort provided them with meat. Great supplies of pemmican, dried fish, flour and other foodstuffs were prepared or packed for shipment to outposts from here. In later life, Lower Fort Garry was many things: a military garrison, penitentiary, training center for the North West Mounted Police, lunatic asylum and country club. In 1951 it was given to the federal government, and carefully restored to the 1850s. Now it is the only stone fort of the fur trading era intact in North America.

Visitors are given a look at fort life through 20 exhibits and restored buildings. You will see one of the famed York Boats that used to leave from the fort each Spring—nine men per boat, nine boats per brigade—for the arduous journey to Hudson Bay and a rendezvous with ships bound for England. Theirs were terribly hard journeys. Bales of furs, weighing 80 to 100 pounds apiece had to be unloaded for each portage, one of which was 12 miles long. The average life of a York boat was four trips, and the men who powered them didn't last much longer.

Outside fort walls, the blacksmith is at work. His skills were so prized, he had his own home and an assistant, and 50 pounds in wages a year. By 1860 the company was using oxcarts, such as the one displayed here, to transport furs and trade goods. They must have presented quite a sight, travelling in brigades of 1,200 carts, on the road for 23 days to reach their Minnesota destination. At St Paul furs were loaded onto trains heading for Montreal's port. The carts, heavy with trade goods made their way back to Lower Fort Garry.

The fort's shop is stocked now as it was then, with commodities the settlers couldn't make for themselves—glass panes, pots and pans, dishes, Perry Davis Pain Killer, Lea and Perrins sauce. The loft, a hive of activity in its time, is hung with silky beaver pelts, fox furs and other skins I didn't recognize.

The Big House, set in landscaped gardens, was the scene of social functions so grand they were written about in Toronto and London newspapers. Furnished now to 1852, it has an attractive governor's suite with study, bedroom and parlor. The company's chief clerk and his assistant lived and worked in this house as did some of the servants.

Between 1846 and 1848 soldiers of the Royal Warwickshire (6th Foot) Regiment lived at Lower Fort Garry. Ostensibly they were brought in because of a possible American invasion. In fact, they were here to suppress trade with Hudson's Bay Company rivals. It is they who built the military style fortifications, for the battle that never came.

South of the fort, a modern visitors' reception center contains a good collection of Hudson's Bay Company and Indian artifacts. There is a bright cafeteria, picnic tables above the river, and ample parking space just off the highway.

IF YOU GO: Lower Fort Garry is open from mid-May to mid October. Located in Selkirk 20 miles north of Winnipeg, via Highway 9, or by cruise-boat on the Red River. There is a small admission charge, with special rate for families.

CANADA'S ICELANDIC COMMUNITY

Hecla Island, Manitoba: Crossing the causeway that connects Hecla to the mainland, we came upon the bleakest of scenes. On one side of us a small fishing boat was being tossed by monstrously high, steel-grey waves. On the other, flat, uninteresting farmlands were empty but for rolls of hay resembling giant soggy shredded wheats in some of the fields. There was no visible sign of life as we crossed the island. Then to make it worse, the heavens opened up, releasing a downpour of relentless, driving rain.

My first impression of Hecla, 110 miles north of Winnipeg, was of a hostile place. And yet it was to this apparently inhospitable environment that 19th-century Icelanders came with hope of improving their lives. In 1875, eruption of the volcanic Mt Hecla heaped unbearable hardships on the inhabitants of southern Iceland. And so they packed their few belongings and came to this island, which they named Hecla. It isn't big—just 26 by 6 1/2 miles—and most is too marshy for farming, but surrounding waters were filled with fish and they could create a lifestyle that had been no more than a dream back home.

It was the Icelanders who pioneered commercial fishing on Lake Winnipeg. Whitefish, goldeye, and pickerel were much sought after in those years. The men would be gone for months on end, living in fishing camps close to the most lucrative fishing grounds. Women and children stayed behind to look after family homesteads. Farming was never really successful because of floods and early frosts. Still they grew enough for their needs, raised cattle, and could afford to buy a few staples from the community store. Not that life was easy. When medical help was sought a patient had to be carried across the lake to Gimli, and in spring or fall when the ice was thin they didn't always make it.

By the 1920s, Icelandic residents of Hecla numbered 500. There was a well attended church, and a community hall where they would gather for meetings, amateur dramatics and dances that we're told went on until dawn. Many of the fishermen had built their own boats with money earned at island sawmills. And some families actually grew prosperous.

Only four families remain on Hecla now. Once the trees were used up, the sawmills closed. Fishing became unprofitable, and in fact the lake was closed to fishermen between 1970 and 1972 because of pollution. When the two-room school shut its doors, couples with young children moved away.

During the past two decades there have been dramatic changes here. In 1969 the entire island became a provincial park.

Six years later it opened to the public with a campground, cabin accommodation, nature trails and interpretive programs for visitors. The ferry service was replaced by a causeway, and the Manitoba government built a year-round resort Scandinavian in design and decor. Descendents of the Icelandic settlers have erected a modern monument to commemorate the centennial of their arrival at Hecla in 1876. Of more interest to visitors perhaps, some of the original buildings are being restored to form a pioneer village type of museum.

Already there is enough here to give a vivid picture of life around the turn of the century. A half-mile self-guiding trail, and buildings with descriptive plaques outside, will detain you for a couple of hours at least. From these you will learn that religion was all-important to the settlers. At first two ministers toured New Iceland conducting services in private homes. By 1890 Hecla had its first church, and would have had it 12 years earlier but for a dispute with the sawmill owner. It seems parishioners had cut and prepared the necessary lumber in 1878, only to have it siezed by the mill.

Some homes are repaired and painted, but have yet to be furnished and staffed. The Sigurgeirsson family obviously prospered here, as you will see from their spacious home which also served as a store and post office. In their spare time the Sigurgeirssons built boats and coffins. By 1913 they had a sawmill producing lumber for shipment to Winnipeg. And a box factory, making crates in which fish were packed and shipped in ice.

The red ice house on the lakeshore was used to preserve fish in summer. Huge blocks would be cut from the lake and hauled by horses to such sheds, in which walls were insulated with sawdust, and the loft filled with hay. Ice chipped from the blocks was spread on the fish, (packed in Sigurgeirsson boxes) and shipped twice a week to the mainland.

Alongside the Ice House, you will see a sturdy whitefish boat with a high bow to handle choppy lake waters, and enclosed cabin to protect the fishermen. Skiffs often built by the fishermen were an important part of the fleet, used by men who chose to fish close to home. Thomasson's boarding house is an attractive structure now, and a warming sight I'm sure for travellers who stayed here while doing business with island sawmills and fishing camps. A commemorative bell out front tells us that the owner was a devoted friend to the fishermen of Manitoba, and became the province's first Fishermens' Representative.

While the Icelandic settlement appeals to first-time visitors to Hecla, it is more likely that the park's resort, recreational facilities and wildlife bring them back time and again. Better than 180 species of birds and 24 animal species live on the island now, including a large population of moose.

At an interpretive center you can learn interesting trivia about the moose—how, for example, at the age of one week, an infant moose can outrun you—that springtime triggers growth of the young male's antlers—and that a mother moose often gives birth to twins. On the west quarry trail you may well see a moose or two for yourself, since this is an area rich in balsam, fir, poplar

Gulf Harbour Resort

and birch trees which they rather enjoy, as well as the dogwoods which they love.

A footpath leads to a 20-foot-high viewing platform from where the moose are usually sighted at sunset or sunrise as they cross between the marshlands and forests. At midday I saw only flying insects and birds, and an overall island view. (Sensible creatures that they are, the moose spend most of their days in the forest, out of the way of the insects.) Near a causeway I had better luck with a boardwalk over marshlands inhabited by great flocks of waterfowl, turtles and frogs.

Wet weather we experienced on arrival at Hecla was blamed for the huge number of mosquitoes that spoiled my walks, even around the resort and a path leading to the beach. Gulf Harbour Resort Hotel enhances the island tremendously for visitors requiring the comforts of home while away. Accommodation here is in brightly furnished rooms with glass doors opening to private patios and landscaped grounds. After only seven years of operation, a new wing has been added, bringing the total number of rooms to 93. The resort is well equipped for recreational pursuits: Tennis courts, an 18-hole golf course, a beach and access to the lake for swimming and sailing. A separate wing contains badminton courts, swimming pool, sauna and more. Winter brings cross-country skiing and ice skating.

Resort meals during my visit were adequate but not memorable. Breakfast and lunch are served in a cafeteria type hall. The dining room is more attractive, because of candlelight and table cloths, but I have to say the dinner menu seems too ambitious for the chef's capabilities. Another time I would pass up the duck à l' orange and veal cordon bleu, instead settling for local goldeye and pickerel which are well prepared and the Iceland vinarterta (prune layer cake with icing) which is delicious.

IF YOU GO: Hecla Island is 110 miles north of Winnipeg via Highway 8, then Provincial Road 233. For reservations at the Gulf Harbour Resort and Conference Center, write care of General Deliver, Riverton, Manitoba, ROC 2RO. Telephone 204-475-2354.

MANITOBA'S LANDLOCKED ISLAND OF CALM

Wasagaming, Manitoba: I must admit to flunking nature study at the interpretive center. Bear droppings in a jar I recognized because I found little piles around our campsite. And I could name most of the stuffed birds and animals displayed. But when it came to guessing what the parts of a buffalo were used for, I was stumped by the tail—a fly swatter, dummy, the sweet faced boy told his tiny brother.

All of the national parks I visited last summer have informative and entertaining programs to teach us more about our environment. Some are better than others. Here at Riding Mountain National Park, 60 miles north of Brandon, adult and childrens' programs are presented with such youthful zeal and obvious respect for nature, that it is difficult not to get involved.

Aptly described in brochures as "an island amid a sea of agricultural land," the park covers close to 1,160 square miles. Uniquely, the region is a cross-roads where habitats of eastern, western and northern Canada meet and mix harmoniously in forest and grasslands, hills and valleys. Elevated areas are forested with jackpine, balsam fir, aspen and birch trees. Along the escarpment base you will find low shrubs and vines and in summer wild flowers paint the western meadows.

Fur traders named Riding Mountain for its elevation 1,500 feet above surrounding lands, and because this is where they exchanged canoes for horses to continue their journey west.

In 1933, the preserve was declared a national park. As such, its development is limited, but sufficient to ensure home comforts for visitors not totally committed to the wilderness experience. Hub of the park is Wasagaming, on the southern shores of Clear

Lake. A short walk from this small community, our secluded campsite is carved out of the pine forest. Paved roads lead into town. Clean hot showers, toilets, full hook-ups and the essential bear-proof garbage cans are provided. Alternative Wasagaming accommodation is in cottages, motels and hotels.

Newcomers are well advised to make their first stop the Interpretive Centre, a stone and log facility crammed with interesting exhibits. Programs here include slide shows and demonstrations, and there is a comfortable lounge so you can sit and plan your day with brochures and maps from the information desk. A special section designed for children has hands-on exhibits, puzzles, quizzes, coloring games and more to acquaint youngsters with the park.

Campers who have been out of touch for a while will see Wasagaming as the pinnacle of civilization. Here we have a hairdresser, post office and liquor store. The laundrette has 16 washing machines and rattan armchairs to wait in. Eating places range from fast-food outlets and an ice-cream parlor with sidewalk tables to first-class dining rooms and restaurants.

Many of Wasagaming's buildings are made from logs. Dominating these is a wonderful old cinema constructed in the 1930s with emergency relief funds to generate employment during the Depression. Acclaimed the largest log theatre in North America (can there be others?), it is in two sections and has a good-sized auditorium. Peeled log construction was encouraged in the park because of the availability of logs and of local Scandinavian craftsmen skilled in log-building techniques. Current movies shown here are changed every couple of days.

Open all year, Riding Mountain National Park welcomes 750,000 visitors annually. Primarily they come to relax, explore and generally enjoy the environment. Man-made leisure pursuits include two golf courses, six hard-surface tennis courts and lawn bowling greens. Fishing for northern pike and trout is said to be excellent in Clear Lake and other lakes within the park boundaries.

Two hundred and fifty miles of trails are described in a guide distributed at the interpretive center. Long or short, all are designed for walking. Many are also recommended for horseback riders and cyclists. One of the most travelled (11 miles round trip) is to Beaver Lodge Lake and the log cabin where Grey Owl, controversial author and conservationist, lived before moving to Saskatchewan.

Landscapes within the park are so diverse you can take your pick. A casual stroll through mixed forest will bring you to an island where loons nest. Another, (only a mile long) leads to meadows decorated with prairie wild flowers. Some trails follow roads used by pioneers, some are original Indian paths, some above the escarpment are arduous to trek but reward with panoramic views. On the Ominnik Marsh boardwalk I hoped to see a beaver or two but had no such luck.

Although I saw no wildlife here, other than birds, sightings of bears, moose, elk, and beaver are recorded daily in the visitors' book. You can be reasonably sure of seeing buffalo by driving to the park's Lake Audy, where an enclosure contains 30 of these beasts and an on-site exhibit traces the fate of herds that once covered the plains.

For a taste of ranch life, trailhead outfitters will whet your appetite with a brief lunchtime or evening ride. Or you can join a pack trip lasting several days. Horse-drawn covered wagon excursions and evening barbecues ensure that even small children can enjoy a ranch experience. With so much to do in Wasagaming, I didn't see much of the wilderness beyond Clear Lake. Annual community events include frequent art exhibitions, a craft sale, merchants' fashion show and tea, outdoor concerts, photographic safaris for wild flowers and bison.

For everyday happenings I could have made good use of an appointment calendar. One evening, for example, I had the option of meeting Julie at the Lake Katherine fire circle, or Beth at Boat Cove. The next day, Jean Helene was scheduled to tell us all about native people inhabiting the park centuries ago, and Greg was to lead a car caravan. Then there was a two-hour river ramble through prime moose and elk habitat and a tour of an abandoned logging camp with Shelley. Or I could just gather some twigs for a fire and a private little cook-out and, by the light of the moon and dying embers, study park pamphlets so I'll be ready tomorrow for the know-it-all kid at the nature displays.

IF YOU GO: Riding Mountain National Park is 175 miles northwest of Winnipeg, or 60 miles north of Brandon, via Highway 10. For accommodation in the park, write Wasagaming Chamber of Commerce, Box 141, Onanole, Man., R0J IN0.

BED AND BREAKFAST WILL ADD INTEREST TO YOUR CANADIAN TOUR

Brandon, Manitoba: Maybe it was less pompous, but our welcome was definitely as royal as any during the Lieutenant Governor's years at the house he built here in the fertile farmlands of southern Manitoba. First, the dogs, all four of them, bounded up to the car, their tails swishing like motorized brushes as we pulled into the driveway. And then, in front of their gracious home, Joy and Keith Smith stood ready to invite us in for the night.

An hour or so earlier, over a Chinese dinner in downtown Brandon, we had telephoned the Smiths after selecting "Gwen Mar" from the Manitoba accommodation guide. Following eight days of criss-crossing the prairies, we had driven past several predictable hotels in town and agreed we were ready for something a little different.

According to the Smiths most of their paying guests telephone from Brandon, or a highway information center nearby, around late afternoon. Some come to drop off their luggage before going into town for an evening meal. Others, like us, arrive at around eight o'clock and settle in for the night. Almost all continue their journey next morning.

A newspaper advertisement ten years ago brought the Smiths into the world of B & Bs. Placed by someone compiling a guide to Canadian Bed and Breakfasts, it asked to hear from owners of such establishments. A telephone conversation with the editor convinced Keith he would like to give it a try. Gwen Mar was subsequently listed in that book and now, a decade later, he recalls only one couple he wouldn't gladly welcome back—and that's because they were so boring.

Keith and Joy say they invite strangers into their home not for the financial rewards but because it allows them to meet such interesting people. (At about $35 double, with cooked breakfast, it is hardly a money maker.) This is borne out by the guest book in which visitors write complementary comments about their hosts, and also say what they are doing here in the Brandon area. 1986 produced the largest crop of prairie visitors, stopping off on their way to and from Expo in Vancouver. Honeymooners on a camping trip wrote that it was a nice change from their tent. A young woman who teaches synchronised swimming throughout the province put that she was treated to "wonderful hospitality and an evening slide show." A mother and her young son have stayed at Gwen Mar twice during trips to Ottawa from the west coast. A musician touring with his wife and two children looks forward to future visits. Regulars include a couple from an old peoples' home in Brandon.

Obviously guests are not the only interesting parties here. Keith, an agrologist, can tell you all you want to know about agricultural problems in Canada and abroad. Joy is a home economist. With their four children living elsewhere, she has time for her enormous garden where currant bushes and raspberry canes, vegetables and flowers are flourishing this summer. Both Keith and Joy are active in community affairs.

Consulting assignments have taken the couple to live in Nigeria for six months and to Brazil; school exchange programs have brought overseas students to live with them. Once they escorted a school group to St Lucia, and more recently toured Europe visiting families of students they have hosted. On average they receive 50 or 60 paying guests a year.

The Smiths seldom accept more than one couple or family at a time, although they can accommodate several if necessary. Set in four and a half acres of peaceful countryside with not a solitary neighbor in sight, the house was designed and built by J.D. McGregor, Lieutenant Governor of Manitoba from 1929-34. Here he and his wife, and later his daughter Gwen (for whom the house is named) often entertained celebrated guests, including members of the Royal Family. It is thought that in 1929 Winston Churchill stayed at Gwen Mar during his cross-Canada tour.

Needless to say rooms are spacious. The lounge, warmed by a log fire as the evening turned chilly, is about the size of a Toronto apartment. The dining room is every large family's dream, the wrap-around porch reminiscent of TV commercials wanting to portray country life. Our bedroom is comfortably furnished, with personal knick-knacks around such as one might find when staying with friends or relatives. It has a washbasin on one wall, and the ground floor bathroom assigned to guests is so old fashioned in size it contains an armchair and magazines.

Breakfast—your choice of fruit or juice, cereal, bacon and eggs along with Joy's homemade bread and preserves—is served in the kitchen from where the view is of birds flitting about the trees. Currently there are four dogs joyfully playing on the lawn. All live outside, and they are ever ready to accompany you on an early morning walk. Indoors, a Siamese cat needs little encouragement to sit on a stranger's lap.

While we sat and talked until midnight, mostly about travel, other guest may well want to turn in earlier after a long day's drive. Either way it's fine with your hosts, who have private quarters on the second floor.

An important part of the vacation scene in Europe for as long as I can remember, B & Bs are becoming increasingly popular in Canada. Realizing the North American preference for private bathrooms, many offer ensuite facilities. Fancy rooms furnished

The Smiths at Gwen-Mar

with four poster beds, ensuite baths and duvet covers matching the curtains can cost as much as $80 a night for two. But for a good night's sleep and breakfast to send you on your way next morning there is no need to spend more than half that price.

Rules for B & Bs are a little different from those of hotels. Payment is usually by cash, you carry your own luggage, and shouldn't hang around for long after breakfast. Some have separate lounges and dining rooms for guests, others invite you to share with the family. These days some want only non-smokers or "discreet smokers," meaning I suppose that you can light up in the privacy of your room.

As more and more Canadians open up their homes to paying guests, travellers have a wider choice of locations. These include national parks, coastal villages, downtown residential areas in major cities and country homes convenient to highways. Many B & Bs reflect the owner's decorating talents, and often culinary skills that will produce a fine evening meal upon request. There are now hundreds of B & Bs on and off Canada's well travelled roads. With a bit of luck your travels will lead you to hosts like

Keith and Joy Smith, for whom hospitality is as natural as breathing the clean country air.

IF YOU GO: Located two and a half miles north of the Trans Canada Highway, Gwen Mar's mailing address is Box 59, R.R. 3, Brandon, Manitoba R7A 5Y3. Telephone 204-728-7339. In popular areas, especially during peak periods, it is advisable to book ahead. Provincial departments of tourism distribute free accommodation guides containing B & B listings as well as farms where overnight guests are welcomed.

SASKATCHEWAN

It has taken a while, but at last Saskatchewan has shed its unfair image of being one great field of wheat, a boring expanse wedged between Manitoba and Alberta, a place to hurry through on the way to better things. I am glad, because in reality this province has a proud and colorful past, brought to life with wonderful museums and historic parks. Cities are squeaky clean and modern, with space enough for doers and dreamers. It is a province of forested hills and beautiful valleys, millions of acres set aside as national and provincial parks. Summer days here are long, the humidity low and the sun shines brightly out of a broad blue sky.

Agriculture is the largest single source of income, a fact you won't dispute when driving for mile upon mile past a pale gold sea of wheat, interrupted by neat farm buildings and traditional grain elevators on railway sidings. But there are also lakes, nearly 100,000 of them, where you can swim and sail and fish. Manitou, known to early Indians as "the place of healing waters," is a lake with salt content three times greater than the Dead Sea. There are 200 golf courses, usually enhanced by their natural wooded settings. One at North Portal straddles the international border, so you will play your game in two countries.

Saskatchewan's cities are relaxed and friendly. Saskatoon, astride the South Saskatchewan River is a particularly gracious host to visitors, and obviously enjoyed by residents too. On a summer's day you will see them water skiing and sailing on the river, sunbathing and picnicking, attending a Shakespearean play or special show at the art gallery on its banks.

Regina was known to early Indian inhabitants as "Pile of Bones," for remains of buffalo slaughtered here. An important agricultural center because of its proximity to rail and road, it became the provincial capital at Saskatchewan's birth in 1905. Now visitors marvel at its Wascana Center, a 2,300-acre parkland with gardens, restaurants, museums and jogging trails around a picturesque lake right in the city core.

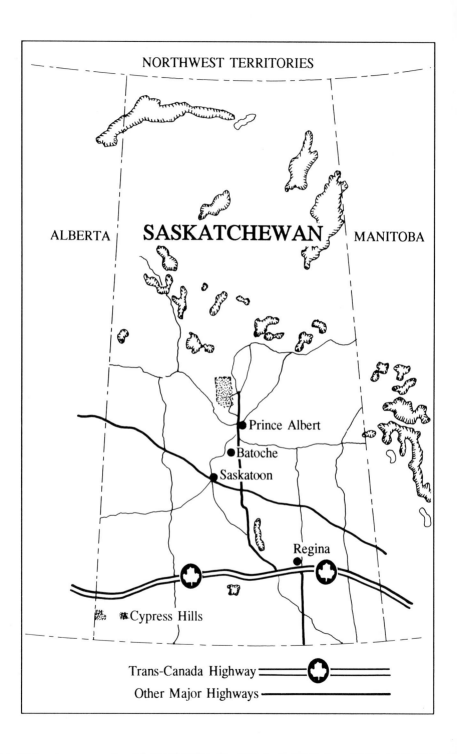

NORTHWEST TERRITORIES

ALBERTA

SASKATCHEWAN

MANITOBA

●Prince Albert

●Batoche

●Saskatoon

Regina

Cypress Hills

Trans-Canada Highway

Other Major Highways

Saskatchewan has more museums per capita than any other province. One of the most interesting displays a collection of Royal Canadian Mounted Police memorabilia at their training depot in Regina. The North West Mounted Police, now the Royal Canadian Mounted Police, were first established to bring order to the prairies. Recreated forts, trading posts and interpretive centers tell a fascinating tale of their pursuits. At these you will learn about traders who bartered with illegal whiskey, about Metis leaders, and courageous settlers, and legendary Indian chiefs such as Sitting Bull, Poundmaker and Big Bear.

In Saskatchewan you can join a hunt for Canadian geese in the south and black bear in the north. You can ride a covered wagon, pioneer-style for an hour, day or week. Follow historical routes, reliving the dreams and dramas of early settlers. Rent a houseboat, stay on a working farm. Enjoy back-country hospitality at a northern fishing camp. (If the comforts of home seem unnatural in the bush, you can be flown to an outpost and rough it on your own.)

Gateway to Saskatchewan's north country is Prince Albert National Park, with all essential visitor amenities, plus wilderness trails and remote lakes. Just two years ago a stretch of original North American prairie along the Frenchman River Valley (on the US border) was designated Saskatchewan's second, and Canada's 29th national park. Preserving the province's original mixed-grass prairie, it provides safe habitat for grassland creatures such as the rare pronghorn antelopes, prairie falcons, and colonies of black-tailed prairie dogs. Also it was in these grasslands that Sioux chief Sitting Bull sought refuge following the defeat of General Custer at the Battle of the Little Big Horn.

And all this time you thought Saskatchewan was nothing but wheat. . . .

More information is available from Tourism Saskatchewan, 1919 Saskatchewan Drive, Regina, Sask., S4P 3V7. Telephone toll free from USA and Canada: 1-800-667-7191.

A REGAL REGARD
FOR HISTORY

Regina, Saskatchewan: All too often I think, vacationers touring Canada head straight for its east and west coasts, missing out on a lot of good stuff in between. Even guide books tend to dismiss our prairie provinces as regions one must drive through to reach the Rockies. And yet this is where the west was won. This is where you can catch a glimpse into that dramatic era of the North West Mounted Police, the 1885 Rebellion, the illegal whiskey trade and triumph of pioneers who homesteaded on land that was not easily tamed.

Regina is one prairie city that records its heritage with pride. And so it should, because founders had foresight enough to create what is surely every urban planner's dream come true. In 1906, just one year after Regina was selected as the capital of the newly formed Province of Saskatchewan, they set aside a prime site for the Legislative Building on Wascana Creek's south shore. Then for added measure, further acreage on the creek's northern bank was designated a downtown public park, Over the years this site continued to grow, encompassing more and more cultural and educational buildings, recreational facilities and parklands. Now, as the 2,300-acre Wascana Center, it preserves a wonderful green oasis in the very core of the city.

Regina had its beginnings on the shores of Wascana Creek. Indians dried their buffalo skins and meat here, and bones piled up on the banks. They aptly called this place Oscana, which in the Cree language is Pile of Bones. In 1882, when the Canadian Pacific Railroad completed tracks across the prairies, Pile of Bones became a railway terminus. The North West Mounted Police established its headquarters in town and the North West Territories' capital was moved from Battleford. Befitting this status, a new name was provided by Princess Louise, wife of Canada's Governor General. Pile of Bones became Regina, for her mother, Queen Victoria.

Biggest surprise to first-time visitors is usually the Wascana Center. An orientation tour by double decker bus will show you what's where, after which you can drive, cycle or meander on your own. (Bicycles are for rent; helmets and child carriers are available.) Early immigrants solved their water shortages by damming the creek and creating Wascana Lake. Now there are boat tours, an attractive marina complex and ferry boats to Willow Island within the lake. Thousands of trees were planted and nurtured, destroying all evidence of the scorched and windswept prairies. For this you must travel beyond the city, or seek out some of its excellent museums.

Parliament building, Regina, Saskatchewan

The center's information booth is in Wascana Place. This is where you can watch a slide production, and on weekends see artists at work. Their creations, on sale in the gift shop, are interesting one-of-a-kind souvenirs. An art gallery on the fourth floor has changing exhibits.

Other attractions are as diverse as a bandshell featuring Sunday performances, waterfowl ponds and a Speakers' Corner enhanced by gas lamps from London and birch trees from Runnymede where King John signed the Magna Carta.

The center's most imposing structure is the Provincial Legislative Building set in glorious formal gardens. Final construction cost was $3 million, quite a sum in the early 1900s. We are told 300 men worked day and night for a year and a half to prepare the Tyndall stone facing, while the interior glistens with 34 different types of marble. Beneath the dome, a marble well within the rotunda is similar to Napoleon's tomb in Les Invalides. Original prairies inhabitants are remembered in a mural titled "Before the White Man Came," showing Indians preparing to attack a buffalo herd. Also in the Assiniboine Gallery, where pastel prints are of tribal chiefs. The 45-minute tours include this and other galleries, as well as the Legislative Chamber, library and rotunda.

A favorite with children is Wascana Center's Museum of Natural History which began as a small collection of wildlife specimens assembled for the 1906 Dominion Fair held in Halifax. Like the Legislative Building, its exterior is faced with Manitoba Tyndall stone recognized by its high fossil content. One of the two main galleries provides three-dimensional views of Saskatchewan's wildlife in their natural habitats. The other features educational displays. Both are equipped with an electronic system for self-guided tours, bringing visitors into the picture with genuine wildlife sounds and recorded information. Prehistoric creatures are great fun of course, especially a roaring dinosaur called Megamunch.

Human history is graphically recorded in the Plains Historical Museum. Its Regina Gallery recounts the city's beginnings. You will see a primitive sod hut, turn-of-the-century rooms furnished to period, exhibits of the Plains Indians including the 1885 Northwest Rebellion. During July and August visitors can be witness to the drama of Metis leader Louis Riel's trial, re-enacted in the ballroom at Government House. Based on transcripts of the five-day trial, the impassioned speech in which Riel refutes defense counsel's plea of insanity cannot help but leave you disturbed.

You will learn more about Riel at the RCMP Training Center's Centennial Museum. After the trial Riel was hanged here. The crucifix he carried to the gallows is among his personal belongings on show. The RCMP Depot is said to be Regina's No 1 visitor attraction. On week days guided tours are escorted by graduates, and shortly before 1 p.m. there's an impressive Sergeant Major's Parade.

IF YOU GO: Regina is 355 miles from Winnipeg, Man., and 470 miles from Calgary, Alberta via the Trans Canada Highway. More information on Regina is available from Tourism Regina, P.O. Box 3355, Regina, Sask., S4P 3H1, telephone 306-789-5099.

MOUNTIES IN TRAINING

Regina, Saskatchewan: Even in their work-day browns they are a stirring sight marching towards us, men and women of the Royal Canadian Mounted Police led by a brass band. It is a daily event, this Sergeant Major's Parade, well attended by visitors who have come to learn about the force, established in 1873 to bring law and order to western Canada with just 150 men.

Our walk-about at the RCMP Training Center was conducted by a young woman who had recently completed six months' basic training here, and would soon move to Quebec to study the field of drug-related crimes. To qualify for recruitment, she told us, applicants must be 19 to 50, in good health and of sterling character. Fluency in one of Canada's official languages, and a grade 12 education are required. These days recruits tend to be university graduates, with proficiency in both French and English. Women have been admitted since 1974.

First stop on the tour is a little chapel, constructed as a mess hall in 1883, later used as a canteen, and after damage by fire in 1895 rebuilt as a permanent chapel. Some of its stained glass windows are unique in that they relate to the force's history. Several were donated by an Englishwoman who had never been to Canada, but greatly admired our mounties.

Memorial plaques are everywhere, in the chapel and around the grounds. One is dedicated to the schooner *St Roche,* the RCMP's only floating detachment, and first ship to circumnavigate North America via the Panama Canal and the Northwest Passage. A Beechcraft airplane mounted in the grounds used to transport supplies to remote northern areas, and bring back prisoners for safe-keeping in the Regina guardhouse.

We are shown modern facilities: the administration building, residences, forensic and crime detection laboratories and D block in which female recruits are housed. Since physical fitness and stamina are essential to every mountie, the training center has several gymnasiums. One contains an indoor pool where they are taught to save themselves and others in the water. In another they learn karate, judo, ground defense techniques and prisoner handling. Sixty percent of a recruit's basic training though takes place in the Academic Building where law, human relations, drugs, weapons and use of computers are studied.

"You are leaving Rainbow Country" is a warning sign over the drill hall door. True enough, we found a troop inside practicing for graduation exercises as a drill corporal barked and bellowed better than any of his movieland counterparts. A disappointment for children in our group is the absence of horses. There used to be many, but now former stables are converted to an ice arena. The force's only horses perform in the musical ride, and they are stabled in Ottawa.

In a modern museum, dedicated by Queen Elizabeth in 1973, we were left to peruse some 25,000 artifacts. Focusing largely on RCMP history, and its contribution to the west's colorful past, this is one of Canada's most important and interesting museums.

Early exhibits include cannons dragged across the prairies in 1874 by members of what was then the North West Mounted Police. An officer's living room from 1890, and a 1914 police office have been reconstructed. Uniforms date to the very first, with its distinctive red coat, black boots, white trousers, long white gloves and pillbox hat. One display is devoted to Chief Sitting Bull who sought refuge in Canada after defeating George Armstrong Custer and a unit of the U.S. Seventh Cavalry at the Little Big Horn. Another recalls the 1885 rebellion with several items belonging to Louis Riel. In 1942 a Nazi spy came ashore off Canada's coast. Tools of his trade are every schoolchild's delight: a transmitter, slide rule used in figuring coded messages, chemical tipped matches for secret writing, a knife, pistol and copy of Mary Poppins.

Tales of the far north tell about heroic men of the dog patrol, and famous fugitives such as the Mad Trapper of Rat River who wore his snowshoes backwards to foil pursuers. Indian robes are magnificent. Nineteenth-century notices amuse. Movie posters show Hollywood's version of the men in red serge. In summer you can see the recruits in red serge at a weekly Sunset Ceremony, after which visitors are invited to talk with and photograph participants.

IF YOU GO: The RCMP Training Center and Museum at 6101 Dewdney Avenue, is open daily from 8 a.m. Admission is free. Summer's Sunset Ceremony is on Tuesdays, weather permitting, starting at 6:45 p.m.

THE LAND OF GREY OWL

Waskesiu, Saskatchewan: Grey Owl, the naturalist who is quoted often in this central Saskatchewan park, describes it best.

"The whole region," he wrote, "is one vast wilderness of lake and forest, and if 2,300 square miles is not enough for you, you may pass east and west without knowing the difference, and north as far as the Arctic Circle with little interruption except that provided by the trading post."

Traditional trading posts have since disappeared, but that small detail aside, most of the park remains unchanged, preserved for present and future generations to enjoy.

Over 60 years old, Prince Albert National Park is a great environmental mosaic that fairly teems with wildlife. Representative of Canada's southern boreal plains, its grassland region supports prairie animals, while northern forests are home to wolves, elks and bears. And in the far north, Lavallee Lake is nesting ground for Canada's second largest pelican colony.

An attractive feature of this, and most of Canada's national parks, is that you don't have to be gung-ho on hiking and canoeing to enjoy the wilderness experience. Gentle walking trails and waterways take one into regions where the power of nature is overwhelming. But then, if you so choose, at day's end you can return to a comfortable cottage, modern hotel room or motorhome within the park boundaries.

A few miles inside the park's eastern entrance, Waskesiu has all essential services and more. In the little townsite beside Waskesiu Lake you can have your hair set, buy a pizza or some Indian art. You can sit at a sidewalk cafe or in a licensed dining room, hire a canoe, houseboat or a horse. Play tennis or golf and brush up on your lawn bowling. Ride a paddlewheeler or a bicycle, sunbathe on a supervised beach, walk a quiet lakefront path or a wooded trail and expect to meet resident wildlife.

At the fully serviced trailer park here, we were allotted a sun-dappled site, its clipped grass studded with pine trees. A brief walk in one direction brought me to a grocery store, and in the other to Lake Waskesiu. Super-clean showers and toilets were minutes away. True naturalists may scoff at such modern conveniences in our wilderness, but for me the two worlds provide a perfect mix. By day there was hardly a soul around to disturb the quiet of the campground. Children had gone to the beach, adults were off fishing or golfing on the park's 18-hole course. My companions instead were black billed magpies, beautiful birds with a brilliant blue sheen to their black coats, fronted with whiter-than-white bibs. Later, tall pines rustled at my back as I sat beside the lake, choppy as the Atlantic in winter and trimmed with a sandy beach unmarked by human prints.

At Waskesiu's interpretive center, slide presentations are both informative and entertaining. One shows this million-acre preserve in all seasons. Another introduces us to the legendary Grey Owl: impostor, trapper, conservationist, who lived and died in Prince Albert National Park. Until 50 years ago Grey Owl was Canada's best know naturalist, a colorful spokesman for preser-

Prince Albert National Park

vation of our wilderness and its inhabitants. An impressive figure with his plaited hair and buckskins, he lectured in Europe as an Indian, the son of an Apache woman and a Scot who had served as a scout with the U.S. Cavalry.

For years he earned his living as a trapper in Northern Ontario and Quebec. His wife, Anahereo, turned him around when she adopted two beaver kits orphaned by one of his traps. As the beavers grew to win a place in his heart, Grey Owl was transformed from trapper to conservationist. His first nature article was published in 1929 and followed two years later by the first of several books. As resident naturalist of Prince Albert National Park between 1931 and 1938, he lived in a log cabin at Ajawaan Lake. "Far enough away to gain seclusion, yet within reach of those whose genuine interests prompt them to make the trip," he said.

These days some 700 visitors a year are interested enough to make the trip to Grey Owl's cabin, which is no more accessible now than when he lived there. Built on the lake's shore, it allowed the beavers entry under a wall to an indoors beaver lodge. Living with them this way, Grey Owl had a unique opportunity to study the creatures at close range. Through his writings, two of his beaver friends, Rawhide and Jellyroll, became almost as famous as the author.

After an exhaustive lecture tour, Grey Owl contracted pneumonia and died here in his cabin on April 13, 1938. Almost immediately the story of his real identity broke in the North Bay Nugget. It turns out he was an Englishman, Archibald Belaney, raised in Hastings by two maiden aunts. During an unhappy childhood his dreams were nourished with tales of the Canadian wilderness and, at 17, he emigrated to Northern Ontario to make them a reality. Not even his native wife Anahereo suspected the masquerade.

It was years before the impact of Grey Owl's work as a naturalist outweighed the shock of his fake pedigree. Now he is remembered only as a man who lived with the beavers and promoted their preservation. His cabin has been restored. Grey Owl, Anahereo, and daughter Shirley Dawn are buried nearby.

If an overnight trip to Ajawaan sounds a little too rugged, you can join a modern day naturalist on a wolf howl or star gazing expedition. Or take yourself on one of the many backwoods trails that weave through aspen and spruce forests. Or go fishing. Few easterners think of Saskatchewan when planning a fishing trip, yet a third of the park is water—much of it enjoyed by fishermen.

Wildlife abounds here, even close to populated areas. We didn't see any bears, but each morning found fresh evidence of their campground visits. Campers are advised to keep food away from their tents, because lingering odors will attract scavenging bears. All garbage cans are bear-proof. Pamphlets distributed at the park entrance counsel visitors on how to act when faced by a black or grizzly bear. This sobering advice reduces us to size, reminding us again of Grey Owl. "Remember you belong to nature," he told us, "not it to you."

IF YOU GO: Located in the center of Saskatchewan, Prince Albert National Park is about 50 miles north of Prince Albert. Grey Owl's cabin can be reached via a 12-mile hike, or by canoe and a two-mile walk. The park operates several campgrounds, ranging from primitive to those with full hook-ups suitable for recreational vehicles. Waskesiu accommodation includes motels, cottages, and a hotel. For more information on the park, write Superintendent, Prince Albert National Park, P.O. Box 100, Waskesiu Lake, Sask., S0J 2Y0, telephone 306-663-5322. Information on accommodation is available from the Waskesiu Chamber of Commerce, telephone 306-663-5410 in summer, 306-922-3232 in winter.

CYPRESS HILLS, A HISTORIC PRAIRIE OASIS

Fort Walsh, Saskatchewan: School children sat wide eyed listening to a park guide telling about the North West Mounted Police and the great Sioux Chief Sitting Bull, about the Chief's victory at the Little Big Horn and how he was shown around Fort Walsh just as they are today. Later, during a games period, these jubilant youngsters formed teams representing the police, before settling down to their picnic lunches. Few I think will easily forget their school outing to Fort Walsh, or the important slice of Canadian history played out here in these Cypress Hills.

Located in the southwest corner of Saskatchewan, the hills are unique, a geological oddity in that they form a wide plateau 2,000 feet higher than surrounding plains and are covered in tall bald pines. (Voyageurs mistook forests of pines for cypress trees, hence the misnomer.) When John Palliser and his expedition camped in these hills back in 1859 he wrote that he had found "a perfect oasis in the desert we have travelled." Modern visitors can say the same, for this is an area draped in lush scenery, still rich in wildlife and steeped in history, enhanced now by a 400-site campground and a resort in the Cypress Hills Provincial Park.

For thousands of years the vast plains were home to various Indian tribes who gathered every spring to hunt the buffalo herds. Nomadic people, they followed the buffalo and lived in teepees made from pine poles covered with hides. They sewed clothes from skins and furs, and made pemmican from dried meat pounded with animal fat and Saskatoon berries. The late 1700s brought the gun and the horse to these Cypress Hills, and everything changed. Within a hundred years the buffalo had been hunted to extinction. White settlers came to fence in the open spaces. Trading expanded to include guns, wolf skins and whiskey.

Several trading posts in the Cypress Hills were operated by Americans from Montana. History tells us that in the winter of 1872 a band of Assiniboine Indians were camped near the Farwell trading post, when a group of American wolf hunters came in saying their horses had been stolen. After a few jugs of firewater, the wolfers decided the Assiniboines had taken their horses. They attacked and destroyed the camp, and when they were through some 20 Indians and one wolfer had been killed in what became known as the Cypress Hills Massacre. When news of the senseless slaughter reached Ottawa, it hastened creation of the North West Mounted Police to keep order in the west and rid the region of illegal whiskey trading. Fort Walsh, two miles from the massacre site, became headquarters for the police. Now it and the trading post form a national historic park.

As is usual in most of Canada's historical replications, an interpretive center and attendant staff do an excellent job in explaining historical reasons for preservation of the site. Several movies are offered. I chose one called Bitter Brew, and learned of the massacre.

By the fall of 1873, 150 men were recruited into the North West Mounted Police. Displays in the center show uniforms and weapons, and tools from the original fort. Increased concern over whiskey trading in this region caused NWMP headquarters to be transferred here from Fort MacLeod in 1878. This was an unhealthy and uncomfortable place, hot in summer and cold in winter. Nevertheless the town that grew up around it became the largest between Winnipeg and Vancouver. A real frontier town with two hotels, pool halls, a dance hall, photography studio, laundry, several resident bootleggers and prostitutes. The fort commander was James Walsh, a charismatic character by all accounts who rode into Chief Sitting Bull's camp of 5,000 with only four constables. In doing so he earned respect of the Sioux chief (who had moved to Saskatchewan following his victory over General Custer at the Little Big Horn south of the border) and his own men.

Now rebuilt dwellings include the commissioner's house, NCO's quarters, officers' mess and cramped constables' barracks shared by as many as 50 men sleeping on crude wooden bunks.

The number of men in residence fluctuated as patrols came and went. In 1881 there were five officers, 16 NCOs and 76 constables plus 80 horses. Daily rations posted on a wall show generous meals which included one and a half pounds each of bread and beef, but only a half ounce of tea and coffee and three ounces of sugar. A constable's wage at that time was a dollar a day, while in the canteen a can of fruit cost $1.50. There was little free time. As well as police duty the men performed foot and mounted drills, and target practice. When through with all that they had to clean their kits, cut wood and ice.

From the fort visitors can ride a covered wagon to Farwell's trading post. By 1873 there were at least 30 such posts in these hills. The "fire water" they sold contained some rather unconventional ingredients—like pepper, tobacco, ginger, strichnine, and gunpowder to give it that little extra kick. Friction over hunting and trading escalated until disaster appeared imminent. It struck with the stolen horses and ensuing massacre (during which the chief's head was cut off and stuck on a pole.) None of the white men involved was ever convicted for murder.

Four buildings are reconstructed at the post, including the store stocked with beads and cloth and similar trade goods. A wagon will take you back to the fort, from where a short walk past the NWMP cemetery brings you to the parking lot.

Try to allow two days minimum in the Cypress Hills. That's one for Fort Walsh and Farwell's, another to enjoy the provincial park. The park is divided into two. The Western Block is kept as a wilderness preserve. In the Center Block you can play tennis and golf, rent a boat on the trout-stocked lake, swim in an outdoor pool, take a scenic drive past the beaver ponds and meadows dotted with colorful wild flowers. Here, campsites cut from the forest are well maintained and comfortable accommodation at the Cypress Four Seasons Resort costs $64 plus tax for a double room.

IF YOU GO: Cypress Hills Provincial Park is 25 miles south of the Trans-Canada Highway via Highway 21 through Maple Creek. Fort Walsh is open from mid-May through Thanksgiving, between 9 and 5:30 daily. Sometimes the road through the park to Fort Walsh is washed out, in which case you can drive paved Highway 271 from

Maple Creek. Park campsites may be reserved by calling 306-662-4411. For resort rooms and suites call 306-662-4477.

VISIT THE PAST IN SASKATCHEWAN'S WESTERN DEVELOPMENT MUSEUMS

Saskatoon, Saskatchewan: Back in the sixties, in our boxy little houses on the tree-less streets of outer suburbia two important arrivals told us it would soon be Spring. One was the eagerly awaited seed catalogue which germinated grandiose ideas about creating a miniature Kew Gardens from our backyard clay. The other, landing with a welcome thud on the front step, was Eaton's catalogue. While still surrounded by snow, it enabled us to drool over glossy pictures of gingham prints and cotton shirt-waisters, sun-dresses for toddlers, garden furniture and barbecues. We got to know the contents by heart. When my neighbor, Marie, asked whether I thought she should buy a certain number in mint green or rose pink, I knew exactly which "pretty as a picture" dress she was talking about. Actually she would order both colors. The drivers were as obliging about pick-ups as they were about deliveries, and often both dresses were returned, but not before we had each tried them on.

Eaton's and Simpson's catalogues played an essential role in our lives at that time because the nearest mall with stores worth the drive was an hour away by car, and none of us had wheels anyway. I can sympathize, then, with isolated families who relied on the "wish book" for just about everything but food.

All of this is brought vividly to mind in Saskatoon's Western Development Museum where one display is devoted to catalogue shopping. Others take us on a walk through Boomtown 1910, transportation and agricultural equipment used in this province since the turn of the century.

There are four Western Development Museums in Saskatchewan, each one recording a different aspect of provincial heritage. Last year the museums celebrated their 40th anniversary, and to more readily distinguish one from the other, they were given new names. Moose Jaw now has WDW's "History of Transportation." In North Battleford, there is a "Heritage Farm and Village." Yorkton's is "Story of People," and here in Saskatoon memories are relived in "Boomtown 1910."

These museums were founded following World War II when a group of citizens in Battleford expressed concerns over the scrap-

Prairie scene, Saskatchewan

ping of vintage farm equipment. They began collecting it, aided by a government grant to pay for storage space in an aircraft hanger. As the public became aware of the collections, more and more items were contributed and new buildings constructed to hold them. Recently North Battleford added a Saskatchewan Wheat Pool elevator, a barn and two houses to its 1920's village. Yorkton has expanded its outdoor exhibit of farm machinery. 1988 brought a restored Cessna Crane aircraft to the Moose Jaw museum, while work continues on an Avro Anson aircraft. Saskatoon added buildings to its Boomtown 1910 street last year. Everything is in working order, and in fact often used in demonstrations at fairs and festivals. All of Saskatoon's exhibits are indoors, which makes it an ideal place for browsing during inclement weather.

This is an authentic recreation of a prairie town's main street during the early 1900s. Sidewalks are wooden, horse-drawn wagons and carriages stand waiting outside the stores. In the pharmacy window medicines include catarrh balm and Rexall's throat gargle, a linament for aching muscles, ointment used for barbed wire poisoning. Hair dyes cost 16¢ a bottle. And because this is farm country, there is a large stock of veterinary medications and instruments. Upstairs in the physician's surgery, Dr. W.P. John charges two to five dollars for a consultation, two for a disability certificate, five and up for an anesthetic. House calls were three dollars, very much more in rural areas.

It would seem that Mr. Wing Lee was one of the busiest men in town. His laundry is well equipped with a wringer and flat irons, and a big old stove on which the washing is boiled. A wall poster at the real estate office invites us to a barn dance; fox trots, hoe down, waltzes, square dances, come one come all . . . The Live Wire Pool Hall and Barbershop was the place where the boys hung out while the girls tried on hats and high button shoes in the milliner's shop.

An adjoining agricultural pavilion is filled with threshing machines and gas tractors, choppers, horse-drawn drills and harrows and potato planters which evoked cries of recognition and chuckles from three old gents during my visit. I can't get excited over farm equipment, but the transportation gallery's cars are quite wonderful, from the Model T, to no-nonsense no-frills auto-mobiles made by farm implement manufacturers and flashy cars half a block long from the '50s.

The mail order exhibit is bound to bring a smile if you used to outfit the family from its shiny pages. The T. Eaton Company began the service in 1884 in Toronto, and by 1905 catered to westerners from a Winnipeg mail order warehouse. Here in the prairies people bought not only clothes, household appliances, toys and sporting goods, but also houses and barns for which they received all plans and building materials. Viking products (Eaton's in-house brand) became known for their reliability, especially appliances such as the washing machine here with its safety rollers, timer and fast acting drain for $5 down and $8 per month. The catalogue service closed in 1976.

The annual summer catalogue of course generated its own excitement, because goods we couldn't manage in Spring sometimes became affordable. Early catalogues on display now advertise little boys' suits for $2.62 down from $3.50, and a man's single breasted tweed suit (with Italian cloth lining) for $3.95, originally $5.00. A disadvantage of catalogue shopping is that you were likely to meet your outfit several times over at the local barn dance. If that proved an embarrassment, you could always settle on fabric from the catalogue and a Viking sewing machine.

Between them, the four Western Development Museums have in excess of 70,000 exhibits. Here in Saskatoon, the "Modern Café" is part of the Main Street Hotel, serving a full breakfast for three dollars and nutritious lunches.

IF YOU GO: Located on the exhibition grounds at 2610 Lorne Ave. South, telephone 306-931-1910, the museum is open May 15 to September 15, 9 to 9, with reduced hours in winter. There is a modest admission charge.

HISTORIC BATOCHE INVITES VISITORS

Batoche, Saskatchewan: The name of 19th-century Metis leader Louis Riel is one you hear often while touring historic sites in the prairies. In Winnipeg you can see where he was born and is buried, and where in 1869 he led the Red River Rebellion resulting in a tiny new province called Manitoba. At Regina's mountie barracks where Riel was hanged in 1889, his personal belongings are displayed in an outstanding museum, and while in Regina you can watch a re-enactment of his trial presented every summer. Battle sites of the 1885 North West Rebellion in the South Saskatchewan River valley are preserved. Most important of these is Batoche, scene of the last battle ever fought on Canadian soil, won by the militia after four days of fighting.

1985, centennial of the North West Rebellion, provided impetus for improving and expanding interpretation facilities at these sites. Batoche, 55 miles north of Saskatoon is an excellent example of what the province is doing to interest visitors in its past. Even though I arrived here during torrential rain, exhibits and a movie in the Reception Center were enough to make my drive from the city worthwhile. Moreover, when I was through there, my interest was sufficiently piqued for me to slosh around outside.

Of five significant battles fought during the North West Rebellion, only Batoche was a decisive victory for the Canadian government. It was fought over the period May 9 to 12, 1885, with fewer than 300 Metis and Indians led by Riel and Gabriel Dumont, and better than 800 government militia.

Residents of Batoche, and leading figures in the battle are introduced to us via a 45-minute movie. We learn that the village was established in the early 1870s by Xavier Letendre (also known as "Batoche") and became a small commercial center for Metis settlers along the river. By 1885 they had a church, and a rectory, a store and ferry across the river. Central figures in the final conflict are Gabriel Dumont (buffalo hunter and Metis military leader), Louis Riel (brought back from exile to represent the Metis), General Middleton leading the Canadian militia, and of course Prime Minister Sir John A. MacDonald who tells us in his Scottish accent, "I do not want to steal their miserable little plots, but have to get on with running the country." The film details strategic points during the battle, and surrender of Riel a few days later. From here visitors are invited to take a self-guided tour of exhibits before going onto the site.

Political and social events leading to the rebellion have had many different interpretations these past 100 years. In a capsule, the Metis (a people resulting from the union of early voyageurs and traders with Indian women) were originally buffalo hunters. As the herds diminished they became interpreters in the York boat brigades, and worked on the cart trains. They farmed their Red River plots in Manitoba and they fished.

In the 1870s many moved to the South Saskatchewan River valley where they had hunted for years, leaving behind squabbling white settlers and government surveyors. But they couldn't escape "progress." In Saskatchewan the buffalo herds became hunted to extinction, and more settlers arrived from the east. Metis who had sold their Manitoba plots (usually for ridiculously low prices) now found they didn't qualify for a second land grant and in consequence didn't own their land here. In 1884 they sent for Louis Riel, who was living in exile in Montana following his part in the successful Red River Rebellion. Petitions to Ottawa were ignored. At Duck Lake a skirmish between Metis and North West Mounted Police ended with policemen being killed. Galvanized into action, Ottawa dispatched troops under Major General Middleton. Luckily for them, gaps in the Canadian Pacific Railway could be hurriedly completed, allowing a well equipped Dominion military force to arrive at Qu'appelle Station in the Saskatchewan Valley within 11 days. From there they travelled overland and by steamboat.

At first the battle went well for the Metis and Indians, who fought from a series of pits lined with wood and camouflaged with clumps of trees. On the first day Middleton sent some of his

Qu'appelle Valley

men down river on the steamship *Northcote*. This strategy failed when the Metis lowered a ferry cable, decapitating the vessel's smokestacks and leaving it to drift aimlessly on the river. It was never a fair fight. By the fourth day Middleton was using a nine-pounder Gatling, predecessor of the machine gun. The Metis were down to firing nails and stones from their rifles.

Retracing the battle now you can determine most of the strategic battle locations, starting with the church and rectory around which the first fighting took place. The church, which wasn't quite finished in 1885, contains some original pews. The rectory, furnished to period, has a priest's office and bedroom, and a second bedroom used by the bishop. Its ground floor provides accommodation for boys from the area who boarded, while an annex represents living quarters for girl pupils and the District of Saskatchewan's first school teacher. Bullet holes from the battle remain above the rectory's top window.

A brief walk from these buildings brings you to the cemetery, with individual graves of Gabriel Dumont and Xavier Letendre, and a mass grave of Metis who died on the final day of the battle. Ridges still outline the militia's camp, or zareba, and the rifle pits. Nearby is a farmhouse constructed to replace one destroyed by the militia. Up the hill you will find a Metis rifle pit. Guaranteed to ignite the imagination of school-aged children, Batoche is an interesting family trip for a day's outing from Saskatoon. In July, Back to Batoche Days feature Metis dancers, fiddling and jigging contests, a pow-wow, etc.

IF YOU GO: Batoche National Historic Park is 55 miles north of Saskatoon via Highways 11 and 312. It is open between the second Sunday in May and Thanksgiving weekend. Admission is free. Telephone 306-423-6227 for hours of operation.

ALBERTA

More than once visitors to Canada have told me Alberta is why they are here—that long before their trip they were inspired by pictures of snow-capped mountains reflected in turquoise lakes, images of trail riding cowboys and castle-like hotels in magical settings. They are not disappointed. This is a province that's larger than life, its scenery more majestic than any picture can depict.

Mountain climbers, skiers, hunters and fisherman are naturally drawn to Alberta. For the rest of us, less demanding adventures await. Since the 1800s outfitters have organized horseback safaris for experienced and novice riders. Some are trips of a few hours arranged for ranch and hotel guests. Others have you sleeping under the stars, bathing in natural pools, eating meals cooked over a camp fire. You can even fish in glacial lakes, inaccessible except on foot or horseback.

The adventure doesn't stop there. We can walk alpine paths reached by cablecar. Or better yet be deposited by helicopter on more remote peaks for a guided hike. Mountain bike tours requiring no special skills lead to emerald lakes and hot springs far from roads and highways. Raft, canoe and kayak excursions are geared to various levels of fitness and experience.

Canada's first national park was established at Banff in 1885 to safeguard sulphur hot springs discovered by railroad workers. Now the province has five such preserves, chosen for their unique beauty and natural phenomena. Maligne, Louise and Minnewanka Lakes are just three of many sensational panoramas within Banff and Jasper parks. Waterton Lakes National Park is as lovely as its more famous neighbors, and far less busy in summer. The relatively small Elk Island National Park provides a sanctuary for elk and bison. In addition to the usual facilities, towers here enable visitors to watch resident marshbirds, while trails lead to beaver colonies. In the north, Wood Buffalo is the country's largest national park. Home to 5,000 buffalo, and the last known breed-

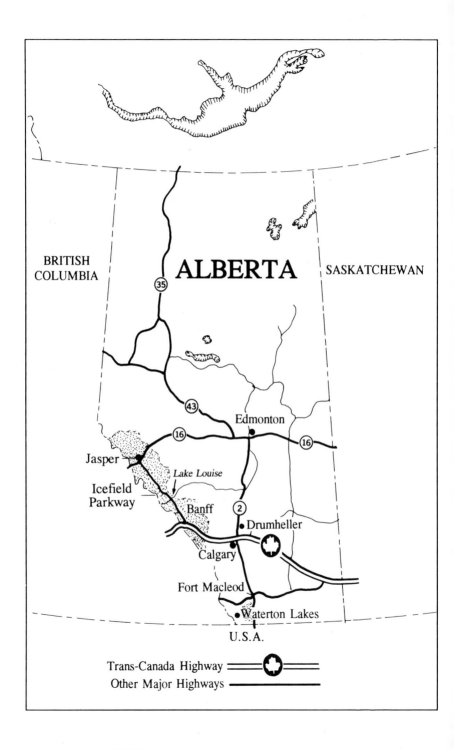

BRITISH COLUMBIA

ALBERTA

SASKATCHEWAN

35

43

16

Edmonton

16

Jasper

Lake Louise

Icefield Parkway

Banff

2

Drumheller

Calgary

Fort Macleod

Waterton Lakes

U.S.A.

Trans-Canada Highway

Other Major Highways

ing grounds for rare whooping cranes, it is reached from Fort Smith across the border in the North West Territories.

Modern as Alberta's oil-rich cities have become, they are reluctant to completely shed their cow-town beginnings. Calgary has enclosed walkways offering respite from winter's cold weather, a stunning center for the performing arts, an interesting heritage park, sports and recreational facilities built for the '88 Winter Olympics, but still tourists know it as site of the annual Exhibition and Stampede. That's when, for two weeks every July, the entire city is involved with rodeos, chuckwagon races, grandstand shows and more. Store clerks wear western outfits, and almost every visitor dons a stetson.

In the same manner Edmonton recalls its wild west reputation during Klondike Days, a 10-day festival where you can pan for gold, gamble in temporary casinos and generally kick up your heels with costumed residents. Panning for gold and casino gambling are about the only things you can't do at West Edmonton Mall which, along with 800 shops, 100 eateries, 19 cinemas and other essentials, boasts a skating rink, water park, tropical bird aviary, fantasyland and miniature golf course. The Guinness Book of World Records lists this as the largest shopping mall.

Fort Edmonton in a ravine by the North Saskatchewan River better demonstrates city growth with a series of communities from original fort to provincial capital. Edmonton's Provincial Museum of Alberta does a wonderful job in presenting human and natural history.

More of Alberta's past is often vividly portrayed in museums and interpretive centers built on site. Two that should not be missed are fairly new: Head-Smashed-In Buffalo Jump is constructed on the side of a cliff over which thousands of buffalo used to be lured to their deaths. Tyrrell Museum of Paleontology brings us dinosaurs of every description, with skeletons reconstructed from bones located in the surrounding Badlands they once inhabited.

Regional museums and memorials tell of local heroes and characters. Such are "Kootenai" Brown, an adventurer from England who eventually settled down to be Waterton's first park

superintendent. Father Albert Lacombe who dedicated 60 years of his life to prairie Indians and Metis established a log mission in St. Albert which is now a museum. At Rocky Mountain House, Alberta's only national historic park, you will hear about trappers and traders. Fort Macleod is named for James Farquharson Macleod, first commissioner of the North West Mounted Police who brought his men on a grueling trek from Manitoba to stop the illegal whiskey trade. And let's not forget Twelve Foot Davis, a prospector who filed a 12-foot claim between two much larger claims and managed to remove $15,000 worth of gold from it. Not bad, in times when a dollar was worth something.

More information is available from Travel Alberta, P.O. Box 2500, Edmonton, Alberta, T5J 2Z4. Telephone toll free from Alberta 1–800–222–6501; Canada and US 1–800–661–8888.

AUTUMN IN BANFF

Banff, Alberta: Last August, Banff was so unbearably crowded I literally took to the hills, coming down only for essentials such as money and food. Sidewalks then were jammed with tourists wandering from one shop to the next, restaurants appeared to be filled all the time, and mid-week lineups at the banks rivalled those of big city branches on a Friday evening. Tour busses and camping vehicles clogged the streets. Parking was a nightmare. "How do you stand the pace?" I asked the saleswoman bagging my warm croissants. "Well, this summer beats most," she said, "but two weeks from now I'll start to wind down. September and October is when I catch my breath and really enjoy the park. Unless you ski, I reckon fall is the best time to visit Banff."

I am sure she is right. With the tourist flood reduced to a trickle, or even a steady flow, the townsite would be a delight.

Alberta, along the Trans-Canada Highway

Surrounding mountains, dressed in autumn colors can only be glorious. Off-season rates are in effect for visitor accommodation. And experts tell us that spring and fall are the best seasons for viewing park wildlife.

This is Banff National Park, established in 1885 as the first link in a chain of magnificent nature preserves across Canada. It was here, two years before, that three intrepid Canadian Pacific Railroad workers descended a tree trunk ladder into a cave and came upon sulphurous hot springs. Realizing their commercial possibilities, they erected a cabin nearby hoping to establish squatters' rights. Within a year, several small hotels were accommodating guests who came to test the springs' curative powers. And so, to safekeep the springs for public use, the government stepped in and created a national park around them. Known at first as Rocky Mountain Park, it covered little more than a square mile. Over the years boundaries were extended to take in more and more scenic phenomena, and now as Banff National Park it covers 2,575 square miles of spectacular mountain scenery.

Today, modern Banff, in a mountain-rimmed valley through which the Bow River so prettily winds, has a year-round population numbering approximately 5,500. Banff Avenue, stretching from one end of town to the other, is lined with souvenir and speciality shops. Restaurants will satisfy almost every taste. Museums fascinate with regional wildlife and historical exhibits. The Banff Center, founded in 1933, presents year-round entertainment.

Hot springs may no longer be the area's biggest draw but still they shouldn't be missed. In 1914 an enormous outdoor pool (Canada's largest at the time) was built at the Cave, fed by the hot springs those railroad workers discovered. It fell into disrepair and was rebuilt in 1985 as part of a grand Centennial Center commemorating the National Park's 100th birthday. While the new pool (a replica of the original) closes at summer's end, the center's other attractions remain open. These include the original foul-smelling cave with hot water still spurting through its rocky walls. And the basin, a second thermal spring with an average temperature of 93 °F. Once a popular swimming hole, the basin has reverted to its 19th-century appearance now, and for safety reasons is off limits to bathers. Exhibits, plaques explaining various events connected with the springs and a slide show will give you an interesting couple of hours. A boardwalk above the centennial center leads past the opening in the cave's roof. Benches along the trail invite you to sit and enjoy the view. A licensed restaurant with seating indoors and out serves appetizing lunches and snacks.

Three miles from Banff townsite, Sulphur Mountain's outdoor pool, served by the hottest of that mountain's five springs, is open all year. A car park nearby allows you to drive to this 5,250-foot level for a soak and a massage. Then, if you aren't too drowsy, you might ride in one of the glass-enclosed gondolas to the 7,500-foot peak. At the top full meals are offered in the Summit Restaurant; walking footpaths lead to the quieter spots.

Walking has always been a favorite pastime here, in part because it brings you to beauty spots inaccessible by car. What's more, you don't have to be a long-distance hiker to enjoy. Short self-guiding, interpretive trails from the townsite are attractive to anyone interested in nature. The one-and-a-half-mile Fenland trail, for example, will take you through marsh and forest inhabited by beaver, muskrat and waterfowl. Campers at Tunnel Mountain invariably follow the asphalt path leading to unusual rock formations (hoodoos) and explanatory plaques. Almost any of the trails cut through Tunnel Mountain are great for bird watching, at the same time opening up terrific alpine vistas. The paved Sundance trail from the Cave and Basin allows for easy walking and cycling alongside the Bow River. Follow a mile-long path that starts behind the park's administrative building and you will come to yet another cave spurting thermal water. These and more walks are described in brochures distributed by Banff's visitor information officers.

Unless you are prepared to take on day-long hikes, you will have to drive to the park's most famous scenic sites and then locate their footpaths. Among my favorites are Moraine Lake (nine miles off the Trans-Canada Highway north of Banff) where you may leave your car and walk for a half a mile to the top of the rockpile, for a wonderful view of lake and mountain peaks—as depicted on the back of our $20 bills. In August, Lake Louise, 34 miles north of Banff, was as busy as downtown Toronto. A gentle

Lake Louise

walk will take you around the lake. A more arduous two-mile hike, uphill all the way there, brings you to Lake Agnes Teahouse named for the wife of Sir John A. MacDonald after she came to visit. Johnston Canyon is reached via a mile-and-a-half trail and suspended catwalk, once you have driven the 16 miles from Banff townsite.

On this visit I saw very little wildlife, considering the great variety of species living in the park. Several elk and deer visited our Tunnel Mountain campground in early mornings, and magpies hung around for crumbs. Alongside the Trans-Canada Highway I saw a coyote who appeared to be counting passing cars. But that's about it. Chipmunks are everywhere, but they're not exactly wild, and most are so tame they will eat from your hand. Bears are noticeably absent. These days everyone entering the park is handed a pamphlet explaining the behavioural characteristics of resident black bears. Garbage cans are "bear proofed" and campers urged to pack away food so as to eliminate odors that attract bears. The campaign to discourage them from inhabited areas seems to be working. Even the traditional drive around Vermillion Lakes at dusk brought no success in locating bears, where I have always seen them before.

Holiday accommodation in and around Banff offers an unusually wide choice, including as it does modern hotels and motels, rustic cottages, mountain resorts and two of Canadian Pacific's castle-like hotels established in the late 1800s. Some campgrounds remain open all year, often with limited facilities. Banff Springs Hotel on the outskirts of town, and the Chateau Lake Louise were both revamped in time for guests attending the recent Winter Olympics. If you are lodged elsewhere, you might like to visit them anyway. Both hotels have public lounges, bars and restaurants open to non-residents. Need I add that views from their picture windows are nothing short of sensational?

IF YOU GO: Banff townsite is 75 miles west of Calgary. More information is available from the Superintendent, Banff National Park, P.O. Box 900, Banff, Alta., TOL OCO, telephone 403-762-3324.

BANFF SPRINGS HOTEL FITS A MAJESTIC SETTING

Banff, Alberta: Well, he certainly recognized a powerful view when he saw one, this William Cornelius Van Horne, general manager of the Canadian Pacific Railway in 1882 and its president six years later. "Since we can't export the scenery, we'll have to import the tourists," he said, then went about doing just that by building vacation resorts in the most scenic spots along his railway's route. Within a year of completing its trans-Canada line, CPR had three mountain resorts in British Columbia. Next came the big one. In June, 1888, the five storey Banff Springs Hotel opened as a summer resort in the eastern Rockies.

Van Horne personally chose this site, overlooking the Spray River Valley, with snow-wrapped mountains all around. A century later the view is intoxicating. It's as if the artist fusses over it continuously—a little more green to the river this morning, a pinkish tinge to the mountains, perhaps another layer of white sparkle on those peaks tonight . . .

Stare at it long enough, and you will find your thoughts slipping back to events here in the 1880s. You can all but taste the excitement of railway workers who stumbled upon hot springs spouting through the mountainside, and hear the noisy squabbling over ownership before the government stepped in to create a national park around them. And understand Van Horne's zeal as he planned, not for a simple hostel where people could rest their travel-weary bones, but for a grand hotel to equal the majesty of this setting.

From the outset it was a resort designed to attract guests of royal caliber. This it did with luxurious lodgings, sulphur hot

springs and a promise of adventure-packed holidays in the Rockies. From day one it was a sell-out. Every winter after the first, construction crews added more rooms. Every summer, more would-be guests had to be turned away. Finally in 1910 the add-on approach to the original wooden structure was abandoned. Plans were drawn up for a new Banff Springs—a great baronial castle of local stone with rooms for 1,100 guests, facilities to rival any on the continent.

Construction was completed after 18 years, at a cost of nine million dollars—in an era when room and full board was only three dollars. Nothing had been skimped. Not time, money, skills, materials or imagination. Stonemasons were brought in from Scotland, cutters from Italy to work on the exterior facing.

Building supplies were carried in by rail: oak from Michigan, flagstones from Indiana, the pale fossilized Tyndall stone, used extensively for stairs and fireplaces, from Manitoba. Arched picture windows in the Riverview Lounge were manufactured in Czechoslovakia. A special baggage car was built to bring them from Quebec.

Surrounded by majestic pines, the hotel is as stark as a medieval castle in remote Scottish highlands. Interior decor is severe, with heavy oak ceiling beams and wall panels, stone floors and enormous arches. Public spaces, vast as football fields, are made comfortable with solid furnishings copied from antique pieces seen in European castles. Reminders of Scotland are everywhere, in the hotel and in the town named at the request of Lord Strathcona, because it reminded him of his Scottish home.

Since most of the hotel's early guests crossed oceans and continents to get here, they looked for more than mere comforts of home. Their every whim was anticipated. Swiss guides were imported for the mountain climbers. Riding trails were rendered dust-free. The valley's 18-hole golf course was laid out with the finest turf. There were fishing expeditions to nearby lakes, boat excursions on the Bow River. Private baths fed by the hot springs were attended by European masseurs. Evening entertainment included formal dining and dancing and classical concerts in the great halls.

As an example of hotel service, we were told of an American in 1888 who asked for goat's milk for his breakfast. On the first day it was unavailable. By the second, a maitre d' had bought a goat and taught a waiter to milk her, so that Dr. Fowler could enjoy future breakfasts at the Banff Springs. The manager proved equally enterprising a year later when guests were detained at the hotel by a disruption of train service. He invited Indians of the Stoney Tribe to put on a show and from that beginning, Banff Indian Days has been an annual festival ever since.

During the rich and royal period between world wars, many Banff Springs guests came back year after year, and settled in for most of the summer. Now they arrive in tour busses (at a special entrance to avoid congestion of the front lobby), dine on meal plans and stay for an average of two nights. They have rooms with private bath, consume 6,000 meals a day and ride into town on the Happy Bus. Last summer's occupancy rate was 120 percent with tour guides sleeping in suite lounges. I wouldn't have taken bets on your chances of getting goat's milk then. Still service was efficient and cheerful, from a staff young enough to enjoy the crowds.

In spite of such heavy traffic, the hotel positively shines after its five-year renovation plan. Recreational facilities, continuously upgraded, include indoor and outdoor swimming pools. At the stables guests can sign up for an hour on the trails or overnight pack trips into the mountains. There are putting greens and tennis courts, electric carts nipping around the golf course. Rubber rafts have replaced the *Mountain Belle* on the Bow, a cable car will whip you up to the mountain peak, and heli-hiking is in vogue.

After 90 years as a summer resort, the Banff Springs became a year-round operation. In winter months the scene is pure Christmas card,with ice skating, toboganning and cross country skiing. Bus transportation takes downhill skiers to the slopes. Christmas brings Santa in his horse-drawn sleigh, a present in his sack for each young guest. This is a time of feasts and dances, decorated trees in the public halls, a poinsettia in every room.

Management is so proud of the refurbished hotel it offers public tours at 2:30 daily. They don't divulge anything startling to discuss over dinner, but you are peppered with interesting trivia, such as: those magnificent bronze doors leading to the Alhambra Dining Room cost $30,000 originally and are insured now for a quarter-million dollars. The two-storey Mount Stephen Hall is the scene of medieval banquets on winter evenings. Guests used to bring newspapers from their home towns and leave them in the lovely little oak-panelled library for others to read. Brass in public places is polished twice a day, chandeliers cleaned by hand every two months. Names of celebrities who have stayed here these past 100 years could fill volumes. Of show-business personalities we learned that Jack Benny gave out silver dollars as tips. Benny Goodman required a landing strip for his airplane before he could come to visit. (One was established beside the Buffalo Paddocks, and is used still.) Marilyn Monroe broke her leg while filming *River of No Return* at Bow Falls, and so extended her stay at the hotel. Every morning bellboys gathered to draw straws, the winner getting to push Marilyn in her wheelchair for the day.

An occasional, and less welcome guest, is the ghost of former employee Sam McCauley. The story goes that in the 1930s Sam drove a coach between the hotel and railway station. As travel patterns changed and his lucrative job eventually disappeared, the embittered man vowed to haunt the hotel after his death. Well now, there are no ledges on ninth floor windows, but guess who has been standing outside swinging a lantern? Then, there's the incident of a woman who locked herself out of a ninth floor room without her key. She telephoned for a bellman to bring a spare, which he did, only to find her happily inside her room. The elderly bellman came to her rescue, she said. His description fitted that of the aged Sam. A lookalike? Not really. Average age of bellboys at the Banff Springs is 19.

IF YOU GO: For reservations, write Banff Springs Hotel, P.O. Box 960, Banff, Alta TOL OCO, telephone 403–762–2211. CP Hotels toll free numbers are: US 1–800–828–7447. Ontario & Quebec 1–800–268–9420, elsewhere in Canada 1–800–268–9411.

TRAVELLING THE ICEFIELD PARKWAY

JASPER, ALBERTA: In the light of grim winters experienced these past few years, it is hard to believe I was disappointed by lack of ice and snow encountered in September. But then there's snow and snow. That pretty white fluff lodged on mountains and reflected in translucent green lakes is no relation to the soggy mess we were shoveling at home in late March.

Heaven knows it was stunningly beautiful last autumn. My disappointment was prompted by memories of another time, when snow was prettily wedged in the mountain's lower crevices and spindly fingers of glaciers reached down almost to touch us. But what's in a little ice recession? International travel authorities continue to recognize this as one of the world's most beautiful drives. For here in the shadow of the Great Divide, motorists are embraced on either side by an unbroken chain of mountains. At times the road climbs to 7,000 feet; it winds around mountains and forges through passes, opening up fantastic vistas for motorists where only hikers and pack trains travelled before.

You can drive the 178 miles between Banff and Jasper in three to four hours, but nobody does. Even in unfriendly weather you will want to stop often, for photographs or to simply stand and stare at the achingly beautiful scenes. Side roads and walking trails from the Parkway are bound to detain you further, leading as they do to canyons and waterfalls and secluded spots where wild larkspur and violets prosper.

Some 60 years ago only the hardiest of tourists attempted this journey, and it took them at least two weeks. The first road connecting Banff to Jasper was undertaken as a relief work project during the Depression, while the current Parkway was completed in the early 1960s. On a family camping trip in 1968, we saw curly horned mountain sheep posed imperiously on rocky crags above this highway and a moose drinking from a roadside lake. A mother bear and her two cubs crossed in front of our car at the Vermillion Lakes. At the Jasper campground, a velvety deer walked with me from a washroom to our site. Then at Miette Hot Springs so many raggedy sheep came begging we packed up and left our picnic table to them.

On this recent trip, I saw nothing of park wildlife. Probably you won't either unless you venture from the well-travelled Parkway. A word of caution from Parks Canada on this. Those colorful pamphlets handed out at park entrances telling us we're in Bear Country? The pictures and paw prints and advice on whether to climb a tree or play dead when threatened by a bear seem ludicrous if the only wildlife you've seen has been worked on by a taxidermist. The fact is, bears are alive and well in these wilderness preserves, and it's important to know how to act on meeting one. The brochures aren't printed and distributed as a lark.

Driving north from Banff, our first stop is Num-ti-Jah Lodge. Its Bow Lake setting—a green lake reflecting snow-dipped mountains, tall pines sprinkled with frost this early morning—rivals any in the Canadian Rockies. Accommodation, dining room and coffee-cum-gift shop are in a rambling old log structure a few minutes from the Parkway's knobby wood sign.

We pass mountains and lakes named for traders, trappers or courageous pioneers; and the North Saskatchewan River, where canoeists thrash about in the fast flowing water, as two park wardens on horseback watch. A cluster of modern buildings includes motels, gas station and cafeteria, and a sign telling that the Columbia Icefield is 32 miles away. Soon the road climbs rapidly for a thousand feet. Drivers must be attentive. Passengers can look back to a fabulous view of the Saskatchewan Valley.

Three of the Columbia Icefield's major glaciers—the Athabasca, Dome and Stutfield—are visible from the Parkway. Straddling the boundaries of Banff and Jasper National Parks, hemmed in by mountains in the 12,000-foot range, this huge cap of ice with fingers dipping into the valleys covers 125 square miles. If you have always wanted to send a message to sea in a bottle, this may well be your big chance because meltwaters end up in the Pacific, Atlantic and Arctic Oceans.

A side road off the highway takes you almost to the foot of the Athabasca Glacier. You can park there and walk to the tip, where you will learn that the ice is receding at a rate of 200 feet a year. Or you can drive up the mountain-side to another parking lot and terminal. Here, a bus designed especially for this terrain will take you into the thick of things. Adventurers searching for peaks rumoured to be in the 16,000-foot range stumbled upon the Athabasca glacier in 1898. The first public tours onto it involved horses equipped with non-slip shoes. Then came the "snow cats," tank-like vehicles which, from the highway, resembled colored bugs crawling on a damask cloth. Excitement they generated is somewhat lost to progress, since full-sized busses now carry 40 to 50 passengers each on a road cut across the glacier.

Because this is the world's only glacier ride you may well consider it worth the fare. For me it proved a waste of time and money. I should have settled for memories of the small tank-like snowmobiles. In those days we had to wait for the ice to be churned up before setting off. Our driver pointed out the moraines, ice falls and glacier tables. Then he rested the vehicle across a cavernous crevice, opened its door and invited us to peer into the 700-foot depth. At a turnabout point we sampled water from a crystal clear stream and made snow balls, it being summer and all.

You can still make summer snow balls, but it's difficult to capture a sense of adventure in a crowded bus travelling a road like many another. For starters, our driver tells us this vehicle cost his company $250,000, then recalls a recent mountain climb made with a friend. Later we are shown photographs. A hundred and ten years ago, he says, the ice was high as the ticket office. I believe him. Ten years ago I know it covered the ugly grey expanse of the parking lot.

At the turnabout point we leave the bus and watch a Japanese film crew trying to work without artificial lights. From time to time the pretty star sits demurely on the ice, her hairdresser slipping about behind her. Camera men gingerly crawl into position, study the sky and glumly shake their heads. They have been here for hours. We photograph them, and each other, and make our snowballs, then pile back into the bus.

In summer, line-ups for the snow ride can be lengthy over the noon hour. Earlier and later in the day, there is usually no more than a 15- to 20-minute wait. There are no restrooms up there. Facilities, gift shop, cafeteria and gas pumps are about two miles down the hill beside the Parkway.

After close encounters with the ice age, we are almost blasé about further mountain scenes. Pinkish boulders by the road are most disconcerting, even though the landslide that put them there occured seventy years ago. A footbridge leads to a silvery waterfall and canyon. There are raft tours on the Athabasca River now, where trappers and traders travelled 150 years before. Whistlers Mountain, named for resident marmots, has rugged camp grounds such as you see in advertisements but seldom find in reality.

The Parkway ends at Jasper Townsite, but your park visit doesn't have to. Let's entice you to stay, with talk of day trips to Maligne Lake, so fabulous the national park was established around it in 1907. And alpine meadows atop Whistlers Mountain, reached by the Jasper Tramway. Or golfing at Jasper Park Lodge where the course's every hole is lined up with a mountain view, so your day will be memorable even if your game isn't. At the Miette Hot Springs a public pool is fed by the naturally hot water. Horseback safaris into the mountains from Jasper are for a couple of hours, a day or longer.

The luxurious Jasper Park Lodge is one of Canada's finest resorts. Comfortable accommodation in bungalows, chalets and housekeeping apartments is available in and around Jasper. There is a campsite at Whistlers Mountain and others, some quite primitive, along the Parkway.

IF YOU GO: Officially the Icefield Parkway (Highway 93) starts at Lake Louise, 35 miles north of Banff. It is open all year. Athabasca Glacier tours are operated from mid-May to mid-September. The Jasper Tramway is open from late March to mid-October. The Miette Hot Springs pool is open mid-May to Labor Day. For more information on Canada's Rocky Mountain National Parks, write Parks Canada, 220, Fourth Avenue S.E., Calgary, Alta., T2P 3H8, telephone 403–292–4440.

FORT EDMONTON PARK

Edmonton, Alberta: Malcolm was pretty pleased with life that August morning. His feet, in worn moose-hide moccasins, were completely dry and warm even though he had no socks. Mine on the other hand were soaking wet. But then, as he was quick to tell me, he is an all round lucky man. As a 19th century carpenter living in Fort Edmonton he is steadily employed by the Hudson's Bay Co. And he has an Indian wife who knows how to look after him during the cold Albertan winters. She does all the heavy work, makes his clothes, cooks the pemmican, cares for their children and in her spare time teaches him native languages.

He readily agrees the married quarters are cramped, with several families in one room and children sleeping in the attic, but assures me he is far better off now than he ever was in Britain. Here, he says, the air is fresh and so is the water. There is no crime, food is plentiful, and didn't the chief factor, John Rowand, give permission for him to marry a hard-working woman?

I met John Rowand, an impressive looking gentleman with a Metis wife and three daughters. His home is even more impressive, all 8,000 square feet of it, with solid pine furnishings and glass windows brought from England in kegs of molasses so they wouldn't break. Company clerks have offices in the house. Visiting Indian chiefs, among others, are entertained in its Great Hall.

Based on meticulous research, the palisaded Hudson's Bay Fort is 99 percent accurate in replicating buildings and everyday life here in 1848. On a wet day, with few tourists to spoil the illusion, it is easy to put myself back in time, especially when employees like Malcolm insist in talking in the present tense about 19th century events.

Similarly in the trading center, an enthusiastic young man tells me how he never refuses poor quality skins, because he doesn't want them taken to American trading posts. Some tribes, he says, arrive in the thousands and set up camp outside the fort. Blankets, guns, tinware and beads are the most popular trade goods. Seven beaver pelts will buy a blanket, 14 a musket and you'll need another fur for a quarter pound of shot.

The fort is a self-contained community recreated on the banks of the Saskatchewan River. Approximately 150 Hudson's Bay Co. employees lived here with their families. Men had company business to attend to. Wives cultivated gardens, did the harvesting, smoked fish and venison. It's all here now: married and bachelor quarters, a kitchen with ice house and outdoors oven, workshops, watchtower, blockhouses in the palisades.

Loathe as I was to leave the log fires and chatty fort residents, I had to move on because there are more steps along the way to Edmonton's city status.

Jasper Avenue, for example, represents the pre-railway era around 1885. Wooden sidewalks are lined with shops selling medicines, hardware and other necessities of life in a farming settlement. There is a blacksmith's shop, saloon and bakery. A little wooden church was in 1873 Alberta's first Protestant house of worship. Vehicles in a barn of that period include a stagecoach that used to do the Calgary-Edmonton run. Return fare was $25, including a 100-pound baggage allowance.

Its Stopping House must have been a welcome sight for prairie travellers. Still it seems a bit of a stretch to advertise "private bed and bath" for a bed, tin footbath and chamber pot all in the same room. Most men stayed in an upstairs dormitory for $1 a night and received a large cooked breakfast next morning. Others were packed into a bunkhouse that provided free lodgings, and a stove on which to cook their own food.

By 1905 life was so civilized an artist set up shop, doubling as a photographer specializing in family portraits. These days he will supply you with period clothes to snap you in the early 1900s. In 1892 when Edmonton was officially incorporated as a town, the newly elected council established a volunteer fire brigade. As you will see, its headquarters also housed the police department with a courtroom and cell block at the rear of the building.

1920 brought a little leisure time, so the Ukranian Bookshop did well. Farms prospered too as indicated from one here, complete with livestock and a windmill. Farm implements range from pitchforks to agricultural steam engines. The family home of Alberta's first premier, Alexander Rutherford, has been relocated to the park.

Visitors are brought to the historic streets aboard a steam train or streetcar. The train was out of action when we were here, so we rode the streetcar, beautifully restored by members of the Edmonton Radial Railway Society. Retired in 1951 after 43 years of service in downtown Edmonton, it now looks very much at home travelling along the 1905 and 1920 streets.

Special events at Fort Edmonton include Sunday afternoon's arrival of a York boat with supplies for the fort, and a cannon salute from the chief factor. Concerts are held in the 1905 Street bandshell. Cooking and handicraft demonstrations and a harvest fair, stagecoach and wagon rides provides added interest.

IF YOU GO: Fort Edmonton Park is located, within the city limits, on the south bank of the North Saskatchewan River, immediately west of the Whitemud Freeway. It is open daily from late May to Labor Day, then Sundays to mid-October. More details are available by calling 403–435–0755.

THE DINOSAURS OF DRUMHELLER

Drumheller, Alberta: Dinosaurs are definitely in vogue these days. You see them as soft toys and home decor accessories, fashioned into costume jewelry and grinning from children's school gear. But believe me, nothing is as exciting as the real thing exhibited in natural habitats recreated here at the Tyrrell Museum of Paleontology. If you come through these doors feeling lukewarm about prehistoric monsters, be assured you will leave hopelessly hooked.

The Red Deer River valley has been world famous for its dinosaurs since the first remains were found accidentally by Joseph Tyrrell in the spring of 1884. Leading an expedition for the Geological Survey of Canada he was here to study coal seams. In addition to large coal beds, he came across a 70-million-year-old dinosaur skull. (It was later named Albertosaurus.) Although no expert, he realized its value and looked around for more. Soon his wagon was so loaded down it broke an axle, necessitating several trips to cart the fossilized specimens out of the valley. Once they were verified, paleontologists arrived on the scene to claim the best specimens for natural history museums around the world. The great dinosaur rush was on.

With more bones being found all the time, and an ever-growing knowledge of dinosaurs, a permanent storage and display facility was required. In 1987 this huge museum was built with nearly 48,000 square feet of display space, a 200-seat auditorium, research library, storage areas and laboratories. It is named for the man who discovered that first skull: Joseph Burr Tyrrell. The workshop currently contains between 85,000 and 95,000 bones, identified and tagged. During its first year the museum received 600,000 visitors.

The supply of bones appears never-ending. Whenever farmers or hikers telephone to say they have found something, museum employees are sent to investigate. If it belongs to a dinosaur it is brought to the museum. In 1988 most of a small dinosaur with razor sharp claws was located. A year before, the first dinosaur nesting site in Canada (second in the world) with eggs containing embryos was discovered. Needless to say these are heady times for Dino fans.

Located in Midland Provincial Park, this is the first Canadian institution devoted entirely to paleontology, i.e. study of life through fossils. Its display of 200 dinosaurs is the largest under one roof, anywhere. Presentations are fascinating, taking us back to life on earth over three billion year ago. For $3 you can rent a cassette player and taped commentary to guide you on your museum tour. First off you will see the preparation laboratory to which fossils are brought from the field. And tools used to separate fossils from their rock beds, drills and chisels for hard stuff, dental picks and brushes to pry fragile samples from their ancient cocoons.

Stimulated dig sites contain a jumble of unconnected bones and fossils of huge Cretaceous fish. The skeleton of one large fish actually has a smaller one inside. In all probability the small fish was swallowed, got caught in the larger one's gills and caused it to drown. Sinking to the sea's bottom, it was soon covered with layers of silt.

During the Devonian period, 350 million years ago, the land we know as Alberta was covered by oceans. All classes of fish developed. Some were small, others over 30 feet long. The heads and parts of the bodies of some were covered with bony armor, while bony plates acted as crude teeth. It was from such fish that amphibians and reptiles developed. As fresh water pools began to dry up, the fish learned to struggle onto land and take their first gulps of air.

The most spectacular development occurred during the era when reptiles dominated both land and sea 150 million years ago. Hadrosaurs, known as duckbills, were commonplace here 70 million years ago. It's amazing what has been learned from their remains. Known plant eaters, they were anything from two to 80 feet long and weighed up to 60 tons. They appear to have moved with ease on land and in water. Some had paddle-like webbed hands and rudder tails to navigate in water. Specimens preserved with stomach contents indicate a diet of coniferous leaves and branches. Oblong eggs of a hadrosaurus were larger than a human hand, and more like an emu's egg than that of a reptile. Recent finds indicate they were laid in double rows of 12 to 24 eggs, beneath an incubating bed of rotting vegetation.

Plant life too has changed through the ages. A conservatory houses more than 100 species of plants that grew in Alberta during the dinosaur era, and still thrive in tropical climates such as existed here then. Magnolias were among the few flowering plants of 80 million years ago. There was no grass. When dinosaurs disappeared, mammals with whom they had co-existed took over. Only then did grass appear. Animals developed hooves for walking on hard prairie grasslands, high crowned teeth and complicated digestive systems to eat the grass.

It is now believed dinosaurs and birds developed from a common ancestor since each has similar characteristics. Some of the dinosaurs were carnivorous, others herbivorous. Some were fast, some clumsy. Some had body armor, some were thin skinned. Some had small heads, others enormous heads that made them look top heavy.

When touring Alberta do allow two days minimum for the Drumheller area, and the museum's field station in Dinosaur Provincial Park a two-hour journey from here. Before leaving Drumheller, I should tell you about two interesting drives. One is the 30-mile circular Dinosaur Trail starting near the museum. It takes you to high points for viewing the valley, once the bed of a great inland sea—past oilfields where pumps resemble prehistoric birds pecking at the ground—on to the grandeur of Horse Thief Canyon, then across the river by ferry to dinosaur graveyards and the road home. The second (about 37 miles round trip) is through numerous small or abandoned mining communities. At one time there were as many as 40 mines here, and a Calgary-Drumheller rail line to ship the coal out. A side road from Rosedale takes you to Wayne, and the Last Chance Saloon. Highlight of this drive is a cluster of hoodoos, those strange capped rock formations by the side of the road.

If you see any fossilized bones, remember that it is illegal to carry them off. Instead telephone the museum (403–378–4342) for someone to check on the site. It was an amateur prospector's discovery of a petrified eggshell that led to the extraordinary find of eggs containing intact embryos. She later joined a volunteer group working on an official dig in the park.

IF YOU GO: Drumheller is 87 miles northeast of Calgary, 180 miles south of Edmonton. Museum admission and parking is free. Hours: daily 9 to 9 in summer. Daily (except Mondays) 10 to 5 the rest of the year. More information is available by calling

403–823–7707. For information on area motels and campgrounds contact Big Country Tourist Association, P.O. Box 2308, Drumheller, Alta TOJ OYO, telephone 403–823–5885.

GOOD DIGGING IN THE BADLANDS

Dinosaur Provincial Park, Alberta: Unless you have been to the moon, I would think the scene before you is unlike anything you have witnessed before. In places it is starkly devoid of vegetation. Intricately sculpted into hills and gullies now, the area was a series of deltas and river flood plains millions of years ago. These are Alberta's Badlands, their name derived from the time when early French trappers knew the region as "mauvaise terre." Natural erosion has created unbelievable sculptures, sink holes, striking multi-colored layers of rock accumulated over millions of years. For good reason then this 30-square-mile Dinosaur Provincial Park was declared a UNESCO World Heritage Site in 1979.

Within the park a field station, satellite of the Tyrrell Museum of Paleontology, opened just three years ago. In its reception center you will find dinosaur exhibits and photographs, slide shows on the park, and a staff eager to talk about it.

Most of the museum's bones were found within the park. Important fossils are wrapped in burlap and plaster of Paris for their journey into Drumheller, often by helicopter because of the bundle's size and weight.

A two-mile drive through the park leads to outdoors exhibits, including a hadrosaurus skeleton on the site where it was discovered by the park's first ranger in 1959. Essentially complete, it has part of the skull missing which inhibits precise identification as to what kind of hadrosaurus it might be. There are walking

Hoodoos, Alberta Badlands

trails from the Field Station. On the Cottonwood Flats you are almost guaranteed to see deer by the river. If not, well the wild flowers are pretty and a scent of sagebrush fills the air.

Most exciting is the 75-minute bus tour departing the field station at 10 a.m., 1 and 3 p.m. daily (unless rain has temporarily washed out the dirt road) into areas otherwise inaccessible to visitors. Maximum number of passengers per trip is 17, so you must be here early to get your ticket. During the tour you will stop at unforgettable sand and rock formations. Your ranger escort will show you fossilized dinosaur bones still on site, and with a bit of luck you will see some wildlife.

Since it gets very hot and dry here in summer, you may want to bring some cold drinks. Or even a picnic lunch because there is no cafeteria or refreshment stand and you will want to spend several hours in the park, especially if waiting for the afternoon tour.

Volunteers 18 years and over are invited to work on dinosaur digs in the park for three week periods during summer. For further information contact the Volunteer Coordinator, Tyrrell Museum of Paleontology, P.O. Box 7500, Drumheller, Alberta, T0J 0Y0.

IF YOU GO: The Dinosaur Provincial Park is 120 miles southeast of Drumheller by road, 30 miles north of Brooks. Day use of the park is free. A campground across from the field station accepts reservations: (403–378–4587). More campgrounds and inexpensive motels are located in Brooks.

HEAD-SMASHED-IN BUFFALO JUMP

Fort Macleod, Alberta: I guess most of us heard about Head-Smashed-In Buffalo Jump when the Duke and Duchess of York joked about spending their first wedding anniversary here. It was July 1987, and the royal couple came to officially open the $10-million interpretive center at a site where buffalo herds were once lured to their deaths. On a Sunday morning, three weeks after that ceremony, I found wall-to-wall people jostling around the exhibits. It didn't take long to see why. This is one of Canada's most exciting museums, commemorating a culture that goes back at least 5,500 years. Leading archeologists agree. UNESCO has declared this a World Heritage Site, putting it in the same league as the Pyramids, the Parthenon and Stonehenge.

Although the jump was in almost continuous use for millennia, it was named by Indians only 150 years ago. During one of their hunts, in which hundreds of buffalo crashed to their deaths from the 36-foot-high cliff, a young man of the Peigan Blackfoot stood below (as one might behind a waterfall) for an unusual view of the kill. It was a particularly successful hunt. Bodies of the beasts piled up thick and fast, and when his people came to butcher them they found the youth with his skull crushed.

In his memory they named the place Estipah-Sikikini-Kots, in the Blackfoot language, "where he got his head smashed in."

The center's exterior is as deceptive to us as was the jump to the hapless buffalo all those years ago. A single-story entrance embedded in the cliff looks only marginally enticing. But once inside, the heart quickens, for here we are faced with the sheer cliff, 33 feet high, atop which three buffalo are about to crash to their deaths. Dynamited out of the cliff, the seven-tiered museum is an architectural showpiece. The story it unfolds about the cultures of the plains people since 4,000 BC is even more spine tingling. Tempting as it is to dally, essentially one must start at the top where an orientation movie portrays what is believed to have been an annual hunt, and the elaborate preparations for it.

Head-Smashed-In may well be the oldest buffalo jump in North America. Evidence uncovered so far shows that it was in use for 5,500 years, with the exception of 1,200 years when it seems to have been abandoned. However, spearheads such as were used 9,000 years ago have been found at the site.

Arrival of Europeans in the 1700s spelled doom for the herds. An estimated 60 million buffalo had inhabited the plains but by the mid-1800s they were virtually wiped out.

The hunts, which probably involved 300 to 400 people were planned and executed with the precision of a military assault. When conditions appeared favorable, preparations got under way. The herd was stalked for days. Drive lanes, some extending for six miles from the cliff's edge, were marked with stone cairns. These funnelled the beasts to a point where they could do nothing but gallop right over the edge. Runners, young men dressed in buffalo and wolf skins, were sent to lure them into the lanes. Knowing the herd was led by dominant females, and that when upset the buffalo would stampede under direction of the lead cows, the runners attracted them with imitation calls of a calf in distress.

Religious rituals, an important part of the hunt before it began, continued at camp as it progressed. There were even alternative jumps made ready in case the wind direction changed. Buffalo have weak eyesight and a keen sense of smell, so pursuers had to keep downwind of the herd. Dried buffalo dung was burned to rid the air of human scent. These were fast and intelligent creatures. It is thought the lead animals became aware of the trap as they approached the cliff's edge, but couldn't turn back. Not when they were followed by several hundred others, thundering along head to tail at 30 miles an hour. And any that weren't killed from the fall were clubbed to death. Butchering was something of a celebration following a good hunt. Favorite snacks then included tongues, eyeballs, fresh blood and bone marrow.

Descending the museum floor by floor, visitors are led through the ages of prehistoric times to present archeological work at the slaughter site. Artifacts, dioramas, photographs and more bring it all spectacularly to life. We learn that the plains people collected plants for food, spices, dyes and incense. And we see how they lived in tepees made from buffalo hides sewn with sinew and draped over pine poles. Usually travelling in groups of 50 to 60, they moved each season and in summer joined with other groups for the great hunt. This was a time for religious ceremonies, arranged marriages, renewed friendships.

A successful hunt meant everything to these people. Bones, rich in grease and marrow, provided nutritious fats. Meat was boiled in skin lined pots or roasted over a fire. Hides were stretched and scraped clean with stone or bone scrapers. Bones were packed and stored for winter, when they would be fashioned into tools. Meat for future use would be cut into strips and dried on wooden racks. Later, beaten to a powder, mixed with fat and berries, it became pemmican.

Arrival of Europeans with guns heralded an end to the great buffalo herds. Small hunting crews would kill 100 beasts a day. For a few dollars they could shoot from the comfort of a seat in a railway car. Usually they took no more than the skins, and perhaps humps and tongues, since these are particularly tender.

Outdoors, a footpath leads along the cliff top. Escorted walks take visitors to original cairns made from stones. Probably used as anchors for brush and branches, they marked out the V-shaped channels leading to the jump. Below the cliff during summer, visitors will see archeologists at work on the dig that has produced a pile of bones over 30 feet high.

By the turn of the century the plains buffalo had disappeared. Miners dug the kill sites indiscriminately, often with bulldozers. Important clues to the area's past were shipped to fertilizer and munitions factories. Part of the cliff was quarried for sandstone by Fort Macleod builders. Serious collectors and souvenir hunters had a field day.

Now preservation is assured. Remains of village camps have been found below the cliffs. Circles of stones that once held tepee walls are visible. So are boiling pits and scatters of butchered bones.

Plan to spend several hours here when visiting southern Alberta. This is an opportunity to examine the culture of a people who inhabited this country more than 500 years before the Pharaoh Cheops ordered his great pyramid at Giza.

IF YOU GO: Head-Smashed-In Buffalo Jump is 11 miles northwest of Fort Macleod on Secondary Highway 785, 95 miles south of Calgary. The Interpretive Center is open daily from 9 a.m. to 8 p.m. in summer, and Thursdays through Sundays 9 a.m. to 5 p.m. in winter. For more information, write the Facility Manager, Head-Smashed-In Buffalo Jump, P.O. Box 1977, Fort Macleod, Alta., TOL OZO, telephone 403–553–2731.

LAND OF THE SHINING MOUNTAINS

Waterton Townsite, Alberta: In spite of heavy rain, the bride looked radiant stepping from her horse-drawn carriage to a canopy of umbrellas, and she later drank champagne with her guests on a cruise boat in the harbor instead of out on the lake. At the park information office, hikers, warned of a probable snowfall at campgrounds in higher altitudes, set off anyway. A bird watcher, rain dripping off her nose, earnestly inquired about the name of a particularly brilliant blue jay she had just seen at Cameron Lake.

That's how it is in our wilderness parks, where more than inclement weather is needed to keep visitors from their pursuits. At Wateron Lakes National Park for only two days, I am naturally disappointed with the rain, non-stop one day and dogging the sun for most of the next. But I am thrilled at it all anyway—its grandeur, its wildlife, its wilderness beauty and a solitude reminiscent of our other Rocky Mountain parks decades ago.

On the eastern slopes of the Rockies, Waterton's western boundary is the crest of the Rocky Mountain Divide, its eastern border the foothills of Alberta while in the south it joins Montana's Glacier National Park. Unlike Banff and Jasper, Waterton was never served by rail so it received little publicity in the early years. Even now there is no major highway slicing through the preserve. Therefore it remains strictly a destination park, unspoiled and undeveloped except for a small townsite, roads and trails.

Encompassing 205 square miles where the prairies and mountains meet, the region was known to Indians as Land of Shining Mountains. The first white men to come through were members of a fur trading party led by David Thompson in 1800. The first white inhabitant was the legendary Kootenai Brown, who declared it one of the most beautiful spots in Western Canada. He should know. He saw most of the west before settling here. A remarkable man, educated at Eton and Oxford, he served in India as a military officer before being lured into America's gold strikes. He eventually left the Caribou goldfields, where he made and lost what he called "a little fortune," with 50¢, a good pair of boots and an indefatigable spirit.

Kootenai became a Pony Express rider and frontiersman, and had many scrapes with death. On his way to Fort Edmonton one time an arrow in his back almost killed him, till a friend poured half a pint of turpentine into the open wound! Once when carrying mail he was captured by Chief Sitting Bull and an even more painful death appeared likely. This time he escaped by jumping into a lake, arriving at his destination (Fort Stevenson) some time later with no mail, no clothes and every inch of his naked body bitten by mosquitoes. Brown was married twice, each time to a Cree woman. The second wife, Blue Flash of Lightning, was so beautiful he exchanged five horses for her on sight, then reputedly won them back during festivities that followed. John George "Kootenai" Brown, 1839–1916, is buried in the park alongside his two wives, on the shore of Lower Waterton Lake he loved so well.

Kootenai Brown was instrumental in getting the area set aside as a forest reserve in 1895, and in 1911 as a national park. By this time he had built a log cabin here and settled in with his family. The Dominion government made him the park's forest ranger. In his report to Ottawa two years later he noted that, "in spite of much rain and competition from the Calgary Stampede, the park received 1,794 visitors."

Most prominent building in the park today is the seven-storied chalet-style Prince of Wales Hotel, erected on a knoll outside the townsite in 1927. Every window they say frames a lake view. I believe it. Views from the lofty Windsor Lounge and Maple Leaf Dining Room are wonderful. And those vintage busses out front? They carry guests who arrive at the town's dock by boat from the American side of the lake.

Snuggled cosily between the mountains, the townsite could be likened to a Swiss alpine village. Largest of its hotels is Bayshore Inn hugging the lake's edge. A two-storied modern motel-type complex, it has large welcoming rooms. (Honeymoon suites have heart-shaped whirlpool tubs and showers for two.) In town you'll find several restaurants and cafés, craft and souvenir shops, movie theatre, laundrette and a campground, solar heated swimming pool and free tennis courts.

Prince of Wales Hotel, Waterton Lakes Park

But townsite amenities are incidental to the park's natural wonders—the mountains and lakes, wild flowers that proliferate so in early July, the stillness disturbed only by birds and rushing waterfalls, and footsteps of a deer wanting to lick your hand.

In the village, sidewalk flower boxes are covered with wire to protect them from deer. Not that flowers are their prime target. They wander into the parking lots at dusk to lick salt off car tires. Mountain sheep are plentiful, bear sightings frequent within the park. Although grizzlies as well as black bears live here, you aren't likely to come across one. Even so it is recommended that hikers on wilderness trails walk with a friend or two.

Incidentally, if you think junior will be bored on the nature trails, first drop by the Heritage Center in town. Here you can rent a nylon backpack filled with goodies for a Nature Day. Puzzles and games in the backpack are designed to keep youngsters busy looking for signs of nature on park walks. At this same center, a family room is furnished for story telling, puppet theater and games themed to nature. Your child is invited to cut out a green paper leaf, write his or her name and home town on it, then attach it to a huge tree.

Waterton's high country, reached by trails, is studded with ice blue lakes and streams. In all there are 20 trails. Conducted hikes in summer last from one hour to 10, so there is something for everyone. A two-hour walk around Cameron Lake at the foot of snow-covered Mount Custer is very popular. So is the fairly easy mile-and-half trail to Bertha Falls. The area is a haven for birds and their observers. Majestic red-tailed hawks and golden eagles often seen gliding over the mountains are among 228 bird species recorded in the park.

Two memorable drives are to Cameron Lake and Red Rock Canyon. The first, 10 miles from the townsite, is on a road bordered by flowers. Once here you can hire a boat, walk the trail, use up rolls of film on the sensational view. En route you will pass a sign commemorating the site of Oil City. Incongruous as it seems, this was where the first oil well in western Canada was drilled. As park booklets tell it, a prospector had an injured leg treated by an Indian woman who used thick oil as a healing agent. He mentioned the incident to a Dominion land surveyor and together they traced what they thought to be the oil's source. Wells were drilled and houses built. Several attempts to retrieve the oil in any quantity failed, and finally in 1929 the "city" was abandoned. Geologists later explained that surface pools causing the excitement probably seeped from a reserve well beyond the park.

Red Rock Canyon (11 miles) is even more dramatic. Here mountain slopes wear a velvety green cloak patched with dark green pines, its hem embroidered with alpine flowers—golden daisies the size of saucers, purple, pink, yellow, white and mauve blooms. Long thin waterfalls hang like silver ribbons on a bride's bouquet. Canyon walls are brick red.

Slowed down by the rain, (it caused me to hang around a lot for photographs), I missed the cruise boat departing from a dock in town for its one-and-a-half-hour ride which crosses the American border into Glacier Park. I haven't sought out the 18-hole golf course either.

Rain or shine, my favorite evening walk is a lakefront path from Bayshore Inn to the outskirts of town. The view from this path is what the park is about, with snow-fringed mountains rising from the shimmering moonlit water. The turnabout point is a little park frequented by deer, the route home through the campground and town. Back in my room if I leave the balcony door open I can hear a loon's woeful cry as I read about the courageous, foolhardy, daring and caring Kootenai Brown.

IF YOU GO: Waterton Lakes National Park is 165 miles south of Calgary, via Highways 2 and 5. The park information center is open from mid-May to Labor day weekend, tel. 403–859–2445, and serviced and semi-serviced campsites are available on a first-come basis. Accommodation information is available from the Waterton Park Chamber of Commerce and Visitors Association, P.O. Box 55–5 Tamarack Mall, Waterton Lakes National Park, Alta, TOK 2MO, telephone 403–859–2203. Double rooms at the Bayshore Inn will cost $84 this summer (tel 403–859–2211 for reservations). At the Prince of Wales Hotel (tel 403–859–2231) double rooms are $90 to $110 per day.

YUKON

U.S.A.

NORTHWEST
TERRITORIES

Alaska Highway

BRITISH
COLUMBIA

97

ALBERTA

16

Pacific
Ocean

97

Nanaimo

Vancouver

Okanagan
Valley

Victoria

Seattle

Trans-Canada Highway ═══ 🍁 ═══ Other Major Highways ━━━

BRITISH
COLUMBIA

British Columbia is big, bold and beautiful, seducing its visitors with a coastline bordering the Pacific Ocean and fine beaches, mountains that attract skiers long after spring is heralded by blossoming fruit trees in valleys below, dramatic fjords and hauntingly beautiful landscapes. It is a province that beckons with sophisticated cities and sumptuous resorts, and an exciting past filled with tales of adventurers and prospectors and explorers looking for a short cut between the Atlantic and Pacific.

You won't be looking for short cuts. This is a province where you will want to stay longer than planned. (If you decide to move here after a brief vacation you won't be the first.) Water sports off the Pacific coast include untold opportunities for scuba divers. Fishing is a year-round pursuit. Ranches cater to leisure cowboys, spas promote relaxation in pools fed by hot springs. White water rafting is popular on rapid moving rivers. Heli-hiking and mountain biking demand no special skills in return for their thrills. And the coastal ferry system is so extensive, it could keep you travelling for a week. (An inexpensive alternative to a luxury cruise of the fabled Inside Passage is a 15-hour daylight trip aboard a B.C. ferry.)

Vancouver is a dynamic metropolis prettily wedged between mountains and the sea. A multi-cultured city, it welcomes visitors to international shops on Robson Street and the second largest Chinatown on the Pacific coast, to historic Gastown and modern waterfront buildings erected for Expo '86.

First settled in 1886, Vancouver became firmly established a year later when the first passenger train steamed in from eastern Canada. Four years after that it received the first of the Canadian Pacific fleet's ships from the Orient, stamping it as an international port.

Most of downtown Vancouver is accessible on foot, but if you require a lift then busses are conveniently frequent. (An all day pass, $3.50 per adult, gives unlimited travel.) Museums and galleries are excellent. For anyone interested in Northwest Indian art, the University of British Columbia's Museum of Anthropology and recreated Haida Village outside should head their "must see" list. Dining out is an adventure in this city. Pacific salmon and Okanagan fruit and vegetables harvested in abundance are served in most city restaurants. European fare is offered in the intimate cafés of Robson Street. Oriental food is the best. For a table with a view you might try the Harbor Center Tower's restaurant or the Grouse Nest in the Grouse Mountain Chalet 3,700 feet above the sea.

Because of its mild, often damp, climate, Vancouver is enhanced by the lushest parks and gardens. Not so well known are the University of British Columbia's Botanical Gardens containing six different teaching gardens. Dr. Sun Yat-Sen Classical Chinese Garden is the only one of its kind outside China. In northern Vancouver the Capilano Suspension Bridge swings above gardens and waterfalls in a mountain setting. Pride and joy of Vancouverites though is the 970-acre Stanley Park.

Vancouver Island visitors often get no further than the provincial capital of Victoria. There is much more. A drive "up island" brings you to the beaches of Pacific Rim National Park where sea lions and grey whales cavort offshore. And ferry routes to the Gulf Islands, a haven of sheltered coves and scenery that's heaven blessed.

In this province you can follow in the steps of legendary gold rush characters, be a cowboy at a guest ranch, watch a rodeo, rent a houseboat and search for a mysterious monster called Ogopogo. Go "north by northwest" to a region of staggering beauty. While up there hop a ferry to the Queen Charlotte Islands, home of Haida art and culture. Follow the Alaska Highway from Dawson Creek. It will take you through mountain passes and alpine meadows, past glacial lakes and native history and culture that goes back 9,000 years.

For more information on BC Ferries' 24 routes contact BC Ferries, 1112 Fort Street, Victoria, B.C. V8V 4V2. Telephone 604–386–3431 or 206–441–6865 in Seattle, Wa. For general information in British Columbia write Tourism British Columbia, 1117 Wharf Street, Victoria, B.C. V8V 1X4, telephone 604–683–2000. Toll free number 1–800–663–6000 in Canada and USA.

PARADISE IS THE OKANAGAN VALLEY

Kelowna, British Columbia: "Our region is recommended for anyone who enjoys being in paradise. Life's a picnic of beaches and peaches during our endless summers. And our winters are easy to take, especially if you're up to great skiing. . . . " So begins a highway storyboard welcoming visitors to the Okanagan Valley, a year-round, super-scenic vacationland covering 110 miles from Vernon to Osoyoos, in a region roughly halfway between Calgary and Vancouver.

The advertisement doesn't lie. It doesn't even exaggerate, for this is a place endowed with hundreds of lakes and silken beaches, a climate as friendly as its people, rodeos and regattas and wine festivals, and more sunshine than Hawaii. There are lakeside resorts and holiday villages on mountain tops. Wineries to tour, hot springs to soak in, and golfing in the blossom-filled valley as skiers rejoice in thick fluffy snow on upper mountain slopes.

We came here in early October, a special time when luscious red apples weigh down the trees in orchards stretching for miles. Formal wine tasting dinners and hilarious grape stomps are hosted by local vintners celebrating yet another successful year. And during these golden days of Indian summer, the entire valley appears to be ripe for harvesting.

It is possible to drive through the valley in a day, but I wouldn't recommend it. A better idea is to come for a week, or two, enjoy some fishing or houseboating, camping in the provincial parks. Dazzling jewel in the valley's crown is Lake Okanagan, all of 90 miles long, a breathtaking sight beneath the afternoon sun with surrounding hills and vineyards mirrored in its turquoise water. But, before you rush off to Kelowna or Penticton to book your houseboat for a week on the lake, perhaps I should mention its resident monster "Ogopogo". Like its name, Ogopogo is the same at both ends. Sightings have pegged him at anywhere between 30 and 70 feet in length, and according to Indian legend the two-headed creature is a demon-possessed man being punished for murdering a respected native.

Some of the most glorious lake views are to be had from wineries high in the hills, their vineyards spread like fine ribbed skirts all around them. Between May and October a dozen or so offer conducted tours, on the hour, seven days a week. If you don't want a tour you are invited to drop by anyway, to taste and shop and drink in that heady scene below.

According to a local guide, one third of all Canada's fruit shipments originate in the Okanagan region. What is now a $165 million industry virtually grew out of an apple tree planted 130 years ago by an Oblate priest who established the first non-native settlement in Kelowna. Referred to now as "our Johnny Appleseed," Father Pandosy came to the valley in October 1860. In addition to spreading his religious beliefs, he acted as doctor, lawyer and sports coach to settlers who arrived close on his heels. He opened a school and farmed the land, and planted that first apple tree.

Some of the Pandosy Mission's original buildings have been restored on site, others were brought here because they are representative of the period. Most poignant is the tiny log chapel made of hand-hewn logs and handmade nails. Needless to say living quarters were cramped, containing no more than bare essentials, but for what he lacked in physical comfort Father Pandosy was compensated with a gentle land and climate.

Doubtless the valley had its share of colorful characters in the late 1800s. Some, like Cornelius O'Keefe who settled at the northern end of Lake Okanagan, came this way in search of gold. Concluding more money could be made from feeding miners than being one, in 1867 Cornelius and his partner drove a herd of cattle from Oregon to the valley. Four decades later their cattle was grazing on some 15,000 acres of prime land.

When he wanted to start a family, O'Keefe returned to his Ontario childhood home for a bride, brought her back to Vernon, and the couple produced nine children. In 1899 Mrs. O'Keefe died, and 63 year-old Cornelius again went to his Ontario home town looking for a wife. This time he chose a girl forty years his junior. More children were born, the youngest of whom lived in the ranch's main house until 1977.

An important visitor attraction now, this O'Keefe Historic Ranch is explored on a self-guided tour. Exception is the comfortable home O'Keefe built for his ever-growing family, shown by an enthusiastic guide well versed in area history. Still it is the early log structures that evoke pictures of life here a century ago—the Chinese cooks' bunkhouse, the original log home of Cornelius and Mary Anne constructed from trees cut on the property. St Anne's church, oldest surviving Catholic church in the British Columbia interior, was erected in 1888 by public subscription. And a small hillside cemetery where the grave of O'Keefe is flanked on either side by those of his two wives.

The valley's visitor accommodation is varied enough to suit everyone. In-town hotels and motels advertise double rooms for $50, interesting looking B & Bs cost less. Ranch and farm holidays are popular here. So is camping in provincial parks, where serviced sites cost around $16 a day. Way above Vernon on Silver Star Mountain some half dozen hotels form a year-round resort. Condos and cottages, fishing lodges and deluxe resorts, they are all part of the valley's vacation scene rightly promoted as paradise.

IF YOU GO: Driving time from Calgary or Vancouver to Kelowna, about midway through the valley, is six hours. Canadian

Airlines International operates flights from both Vancouver and Calgary to Kelowna. For more information about the Okanagan Valley, contact the Okanagan–Similkameen Tourist Association, Suite #104, 515 Highway 97 South, Kelowna, B.C. V1Z 3J2, telephone 604–769–5959.

LAKE OKANAGAN RESORT

Kelowna, British Columbia: When we first came upon it following a magical drive from downtown Kelowna, I would have pegged this as a posh French Riviera hotel, or a luxurious resort on the scenic shores of Lake Geneva. Wearing summer clothes this October afternoon, guests lingered over lunch on the terrace. Immediately below, sun-worshippers lazed on chaises around the pools, and a sight-seeing boat had just departed the marina for an excursion on the turquoise lake. But this is not a European resort of international acclaim. It is one of Canada's little-publicized gems, where holiday accommodation, restaurants and leisure facilities are attractively nestled in landscaped gardens around Lake Okanagan in southern British Columbia.

Opened in 1980 as the Okanagan Park Country Club Resort, the Lake Okanagan Resort has had a short but eventful life to date. Some years it has remained open in winter, and some years it has not. Once a tugboat collided with and destroyed much of its dock. In the fall of 1984 a fire gutted the dining rooms and kitchens, so the resort opened the following spring without them. It has changed hands several times. Some years saw construction of additional accommodation. 1986 brought more recreational facilities.

But to the convention delegates and vacationers here now, the resort's past vicissitudes are no longer in evidence. What they

Lake Okanagan Resort

see is a luxurious, smoothly operated resort, attractive for family vacations and weekend escapes from city pressures. In October I met several Americans on their annual pilgrimage to the Okanagan's wine festival which has functions scheduled throughout the valley.

Relaxation is definitely the name of the game. Sports enthusiasts can be kept busy with horseback safaris geared for novice as well as seasoned riders. Of seven tennis courts, three are lit for night play. There is a nine-hole golf course and boat rentals at the marina, where water skiing and board sailing instruction is offered. The rest of us have horse-drawn carriages to take us on scenic rides, pools to lounge by, hot tubs and Jacuzzis, and walks along the lakefront.

Dining rooms are surprisingly affordable for a resort of this caliber. Lunch or dinner at the Eidelweiss can be had for seven to nine dollars for say the Plowman's (Scotch egg, cheddar, chicken breast, grapes, melon and strawberries,) chicken with blackberry sauce, or tasty pork schnitzel. The main dining room is a beauty, its huge windows on three sides taking full advantage of the panoramic lake view. Imaginatively presented dinners are created from local produce where possible. A full meal, with Okanagan wine, runs to $70 for two people, and in this balmy climate there is often dancing beneath the stars.

Accommodation is deluxe, whether you decide on a chalet, condominium or room at one of the two inns. At Kingfisher Inn our suite is so spacious it would have been comfortable as a permanent home. The living room has a kitchenette, adequate for making snacks and light meals. Outside, a wide furnished balcony looks out over the lake. Bedroom closets cover an entire wall, and there are enough toiletries in the bathroom to cause me to disappear for hours. Chalets may be rented by the room, or with family and friends you can take an entire two or three bedroom unit.

Room rates are as attractive as everything else here. In 1990, at the height of the summer, our Kingfisher suite will cost $125 a day, single or double occupancy, plus 8 percent provincial tax. In spring and fall it is reduced to $85 to $105. Specials such as the Festival of Wines during September and early October are worth looking into. Last fall this package included two nights accommodation, a wine lecture and tasting, dinner in the main dining room, Sunday brunch, water transportation to and from the Grey Monk Winery for a tour, tax and gratuities. Cost based on double occupancy was only $129 per person, for a really super couple of days.

When we left on Sunday morning, rain was steady, the temperature cool and the lake had turned the color of wet lead. My regret at having to move on had dissipated along with yesterday's sunshine. That is until I watched a man in front of me at reception. Gathering up a selection of video cassettes he inquired about the upcoming brunch and cheerfully asked "who cares if it's raining?" He said the weather gave him a chance to be lazy without guilt, that he planned to eat and sleep and stare into the fire, and catch up on movies he never had time for at home. Setting off for a dismal drive to Vancouver, I decided his day would be better than mine.

IF YOU GO: Lake Okanagan Resort is open April to mid-
October. Inquiries should be made to P.O. Box 1321, Station A.
Kelowna, B.C., V1Y 7V8., telephone 604–769–3511.

SILVER STAR SHINES BRIGHTLY ALL YEAR

Silver Star Mtn., British Columbia: I don't quite know what I
expected, but certainly not this. On a sun-drenched October
afternoon we had driven up, up and around Silver Star Mountain
rising from the Okanagan Valley. Below us grapes were being
harvested for the wineries and rosy-red apples still clung to trees
in orderly rows beside the highway. Now, with the horse ranches
and farms behind us we were met by the raw beauty of the pine
forests stretching into the distance beneath a broad blue sky, and
never a soul in sight. There were signs of habitation of course.
Houses, built to give owners the best of views, good looking bed
and breakfast places, Cedar Hot Springs where we soaked in the
public pool next day. Then 14 miles from the valley town of Vernon, 5,000 feet above sea level, we came to what I first took to be
a movie set for a 19th-century frontier town.

In reality it is Silver Star Mountain Resort, a place for all
seasons, built in the wild west tradition of the gaslight era. Clustered around the main street, its wooden buildings include a
town hall, an opera house and the Vance Creek Saloon. Hotels
have names like Kickwillie Inn, Putnam Station, Vance Creek
and Silver Lode.

When we arrived it resembled a ghost town, or one of those
scenes where everyone's taken cover because the gunfighter has
arrived in town. Next day a women's group moved their workshop

outdoors and gave it a bit of a lived-in look. But so far as I could tell we were the only independent guests, and as such had the ghosts of abandoned mines, the mountain trails and the hot tubs to ourselves.

On this warm day it was hard to believe that within a month those alpine meadows would be blanketed in snow. If I had any doubts, they were dispelled after a visit to the little wooden office of Charli Erker, as she enthusiastically pored over maps of Putnam Creek, a brand new area being developed for limited skiing this winter and which is expected to be fully operative in the 1990/91 winter season.

I had called into Charli's office to inquire about doing some mountain bike riding. Turned out the bikes were sold on Labor Day (new ones will be purchased for next summer) but by the time I left I was ready to take up skiing. I was even tempted to buy one of her lots, on which purchasers are building their own chalets next spring.

It is an interesting concept. Here on this plateau are six hotels and some private chalets. Largest hotel is the Vance Creek where I stayed. Oldest is Putnam Station, built in 1984. Guests of any of the hotels, the chalets and recreational vehicle park have use of all resort facilities. Day visitors are also welcomed.

As some of the better known resorts have become too popular for their own good, Silver Star shines brighter than ever. Skiers know they will spend most of their time here on the slopes, and not standing in line for lifts. Many come from Calgary and Vancouver regions for this reason. At present, six lifts take them to the 6,710-foot summit for 35 different downhill runs. Cross country skiers have six miles of trails starting from the village and a further 30 miles at nearby Sovereign Lakes, which can be reached by connector trails.

In summer some of these trails are used by mountain bikers. Introduced only last year, tours start from the summit and take participants down to Vernon on an 18-mile run. The all-inclusive $30 cost includes use of a bicycle, helmet, safety vest and gloves, plus chairlift to the summit and transportation back to the resort from Vernon. In eight weeks last summer, with virtually no advertising, 350 guests joined the cycling groups. Some brought their own bicycles, most promised to come back next year. Routes taken are as simple or challenging as befits a rider's experience. Travelling through the forests and orchards, past waterfalls and hot springs, they complete a vertical drop of more than 5000 feet. Happily you don't have to cycle back up the mountain.

Still, Silver Mountain Resort's raison d'etre is its superb skiing. Less severe than the weather in the Canadian Rockies and colder than Vancouver, it has an average winter temperature of 23° F, with lots of sunshine and deep powdery snow. The ski season is a long one, starting in mid-November and finishing towards the end of April, not through lack of snow but because the apple blossoms are out and golf courses in the valley have been busy since March. (One of the resort's most unusual programs offers a morning skiing on the mountain, and afternoon golf in Vernon.) Conditions here are considered so ideal that nine countries sent skiers for several weeks' practice on Silver Mountain prior to Calgary's Winter Olympics.

An appealing aspect of this resort is that everything is within a brief walk. You can park your car for the week, or even leave it at home since flights to Kelowna are met. This winter there will be a bus service into Vernon should you need anything in town. Such easy access on foot means that families can split up for their lessons, trails and runs that demand different levels of ability. Even junior, if three years or older, can learn to ski, while babies are provided with sitters.

The resort's new winter brochures will fill you in on their different programs and packages. A ski week includes two hours' instruction each day. Night skiing continues to 10 o'clock; Christmas and New Year bring torchlight parades and seasonal festivities. In February, Vernon holds its winter carnival, and a ski event on Silver Star has families entered as teams.

Come evening if you aren't too bushed for more than hot cocoa by the fire there are live bands to dance to, a revue performed by hotel managers and staff, can-can dancers and a casino. The resort's aquatic center has a 50-foot indoor pool. Hot tubs are located on hotel roofs.

So far as possible, local produce is served in hotel dining rooms, which means fresh Okanagan meat, cheese and most noticeably wines. A good mix of European and Canadian dishes are served. Accommodation has been thoughtfully planned to cover everybody's needs. For example, 12 of Vance Creek's 51 spacious rooms are equipped with kitchenettes. Aberdeen Hotel, owned by mountain guide Klaus Flux (formerly of Zermatt), has 13 one- and two-bedroom apartments. The Silver Lode, owned by a Swiss family, has 20 European-style rooms. Both Kickwillie Inn and The Pinnacles provide ski-to-your-door suites with full kitchens, ensuite baths, sundecks and interior access to roof hot tubs. Hotels are all owner-operated, to ensure first class and friendly service. Also privately owned chalets with fireplaces and every home comfort are available for short-term rentals.

IF YOU GO: Driving time from Vancouver or Calgary is about six hours and do ask for a car with winter tires if you are renting. The resort can provide ground transportation from Kelowna airport. Costs are reasonable but vary considerably, depending upon season and number of persons sharing accommodation (some suites can hold eight people). A number of packages, including meals, lessons and use of ski-lifts, are available. For details and reservations, contact Silver Star Mountain Resort, Ltd., P.O. Box 7000, Vernon, B.C., V1T 8X5, telephone 604–542–0224, toll free from Alberta and British Columbia 1–800–663–4431.

GETTING AWAY FROM IT ALL IN DOWNTOWN VANCOUVER

Vancouver, British Columbia: You can rest easy Lord Stanley, sir. That park you dedicated in 1889 "to use and enjoyment of all people of all colors, creeds and customs for all time" received around two million visitors last year. They wore saris, blue jeans, jogging suits and cricketers' whites. They came with groups and teams, in families and on their own. And each and every one of them, I am sure, enjoyed your park.

Bounded by sea on three sides, the remarkable Stanley Park contains 970 acres of prime land within 10 to 15 minutes' walk of downtown Vancouver. Roughly 700 acres is primitive forest, with Douglas firs so tall they disappear into the sky, and so dense you can walk the trails beneath them in pouring rain without getting wet. Fifty acres of formal gardens lead to open fields where children run and tumble and urge parents to perform handstands. There's a zoo, an aquarium and a miniature railroad. Recreation facilities include tennis courts, playing fields, a harbor for small craft, swimming pools and beaches and miles of trails for pedestrians and cyclists. Memorials are to poets, heroes, Indian legends, and to Governor General Lord Stanley whose statue welcomes us with open arms to the park named for him.

A couple of Saturdays ago, the warm April sun enticed winter-weary crowds to Stanley Park. It was a triumph of color. Flowering trees along the paths were smothered in pink and white blossoms, rich green lawns wore patches of blue from masses of tiny birdseye. Beds of daffodils, of the brightest gold, nodded heads in unison at the bidding of the wind. Tulips were a blaze of fiery reds, oranges and yellows. There were scraps of mauve heather beside some paths, velvety wallflowers and sturdy evergreens—all against a back-drop of mountains capped with snow.

On this cool spring day joggers were out in force, and a few cyclists battled the wind, but for most the visit was a family outing. Toddlers, confident they could catch a pigeon, stumbled along with tiny hands outstretched. Some babies were so bundled up they couldn't have known if they were indoors or out. Older kids chased after kites and frisbees. Popcorn vendors sold out.

The zoo was the park's busiest spot. Resident animals, perhaps appreciating the first large audience of the year, entertained with zeal. Everybody's favorites, the penguins resembled me-

Vancouver skyline, from Stanley Park

chanical toys waddling across a rock, dropping into the pool then swimming around to the rear to start all over again. Sea lions were super show-offs too. One, flippers planted like feet on the pool's floor, repeatedly turned its head from left to right. With a whiskered face and huge expressive eyes, he could have been a middle-aged man waiting for a bus.

While the zoo is free, there is an admission fee at the adjoining Vancouver Public Aquarium. If you're the least bit interested in sea life, this is a must, containing as it does over 8,000 aquatic creatures from around the world. Killer whale and dolphin shows are said to be among the finest.

Jogging takes on a new dimension, and probably new enthusiasts, in a park where a paved path follows the sea wall for seven miles. It winds past such notable landmarks as the Nine O'Clock Gun, lighthouses, totem poles and the harbor entrance. It takes you to Prospect Point, from which Vancouverites used to wave goodbye to friends leaving on trans-Pacific liners. And to Siwash Rock, named for the Indian tribe whose princess hurled herself from it to follow her lover in death.

Totem groves hold a particular fascination for Easterners. Unique to tribes on British Columbia's north west coast and lower Alaska, the totem is likened to a family coat of arms. Cut from red cedar, totems come in any size, each carving telling of a real or mythical event. The Thunderbird at the top of the pole, for example, is "Giver of Light, crafty and wise." Grizzly Bear symbolizes brute force on land. Killer Whale is king of the ocean, salmon a sign of abundance and prosperity. Little books sold in local gift shops explain the totems.

For centuries, Salish Indians inhabited this region. Shells from their refuse heaps actually paved the park's first roads, and their trails still criss-cross its central forest. In 1863 the wooded peninsula was claimed as a military reserve to protect New Westminster from possible American attack, and after the war threat had passed its military status continued to keep it intact. When in 1886 Vancouver became a city, one of the first items of business was a request for this prime city land to become a public park.

Native poet Pauline Johnson named the park's Lost Lagoon. While sitting in her canoe watching the receding tide, we are told, she began her poem "it is dusk on the Lost Lagoon . . ." It was almost dusk when I got around to it, this lovely surprisingly peaceful spot at the park's rim where swans and ducks nest undisturbed in the reeds little more than a stone's throw from the city proper.

IF YOU GO: Stanley Park's Georgia Street entrance is minutes from the city's central hotels. The #11 bus along Georgia or Pender Streets will get you there in a jiffy. Across from the entrance bicycles, strollers, roller skates, and just about anything you might need for a family outing can be rented. More information on the city is available from the Vancouver Travel InfoCenter, Suite 4, Bentall Center, 1055 Dunsmuir Street, P.O. Box 49296, Vancouver, B.C., V7X 1L3, telephone 604–683–2000.

VICTORIA, OUR EVER SO BRITISH CITY

Victoria, British Columbia: Slipping into town soon after Christmas, spring comes early to Victoria. By February the flower count is on, with citizens phoning the Chamber of Commerce to report blooms in their backyards. In mid-March a Victorian told me he had already cut his grass five times this year, that his tulips and hyacinths were in full bloom, fruit trees dressed in frothy pinks and whites, and his neighbor's garden has a rose or two in bud. To me that's what this city is all about. They can send the double deckers back to Blighty, and do away with all the replicas in miniature. Their "little piece of Britain" image will never tarnish so long as daffodils nod their beautiful brassy heads on Beacon Hill while the rest of the country is buried in snow.

Tacky though it can sometimes be, Victoria came by her British image honestly. Located on Vancouver Island's southern tip, her climate is similar to that of southern England inasmuch as temperatures seldom drop below freezing or rise to uncomfortable heights. The moderate weather, with an annual precipitation less than London's, has attracted British immigrants for years, especially retirees from the colonial service in India and the Far East during the early 1900s.

Here, after all, they can walk by the sea and in spacious parklands or enjoy a round of golf at any time of the year. In summer outdoor activities and events are so plentiful there's always something to watch. They take great pride in their gardens, some of which resemble London's Kew in miniature. And wherever they are, come mid-afternoon they can stop for tea.

Victoria's British roots go back to the 1840s when the Hudson's Bay Company established Fort Victoria in the vicinity of the present Bastion Square. The 1860s saw this as a rough and tumble outfitting center for prospectors heading towards the Fraser River gold fields. In that same decade the community (by now a population of 2,000) became incorporated as the City of Victoria, capital of the crown colony of British Columbia.

Double decker busses and tally-ho wagons aside, Victoria's character is also markedly Canadian. You will see it right away in the ponderous buildings, typical of so many constructed across the country in the early 1900s. And native artifacts in parks, museums and shops, remind us that west coast Indians were once the island's sole inhabitants.

Because of the mild climate tourism is big business here at any time of the year. So is the flower industry with local seeds as well as blooms being shipped across the country and overseas. In summer, flowers are everywhere: in colorful beds cut from emerald green lawns surrounding public buildings, flourishing untended on cliffs hugging the Juan de Fuca strait, providing joy for walkers in Beacon Hill Park. They tumble from 650 baskets draped over city lamp posts, and from office window boxes. Cruise passengers coming ashore here receive roses from young women in Victorian costumes. Then let's not forget the Chamber of Commerce's annual bloom count. Last February, it totalled 23 million.

Unless you are continuing up-island from Victoria, you might consider leaving your car at home or on the mainland, since this is one great little city to explore on foot. Sight-seeing busses travel the scenic Marine Drive, stopping at various attractions along the way. Departures are frequent, from stands in front of the Empress Hotel. The city is so compact, you could happily spend a whole day around the inner harbor dominated by the Empress on one side, Parliament Buildings on another, and with much to interest the visitor in between.

Original government buildings nicknamed "the bird cages" went up here in 1859. When they became inadequate, an architectural competition was held and new Parliament Buildings constructed from the winning design began in 1893. The chosen entry was submitted by Francis Mawson Rattenbury, a young man who moved to British Columbia from Britain a year before and went on to make a name for himself throughout Canada. (He came to a sticky end alas, murdered by his wife's young lover.)

At night the multi-domed buildings are outlined with more than 3,300 lights. By day, their grounds make for very pleasant strolling among flower beds and statues. A youthful looking Queen Victoria sits out in front, scepter in hand. On the highest dome is Captain Vancouver, first British navigator to sail around the island. Free public tours are conducted every 15 minutes, daily in summer and on weekdays during the rest of the year. In recent years, the buildings have been fully restored according to Rattenbury's original drawings, and are quite magnificent now with gilt trimmed plaster, stained glass windows and historical murals depicting provincial events and industries.

Several museums are contained within a city block of the Parliament Buildings. Most important is the fabulous Provincial Museum, guaranteed to transport you back in time through its realistic settings enhanced by sounds and smells. Telling the history of Canada's Pacific coast native peoples, its Indian displays are the best I have ever seen.

There's no way I could take in all of Victoria's visitor attractions during my three days here. I enjoyed the promise of summer at Butchart Gardens, and signs of spring in the 154-acre Beacon Hill Park. I visited countless shops in restored buildings, including those of Bastion Square where Fort Victoria was established in 1843. Some of the stores are in Victoria's first brick building, Burnes House, "once an opulent hotel, later a brothel, then a warehouse," according to the guidebooks. Bastion Square's Maritime Museum is worth some time for the handsome 19th-century Court House it used to be, as well as current exhibits. Among paraphernalia connected with the city's seafaring past, you will see a dugout canoe named *Tilikum*. Fitted with three short masts at the turn of the century, the 38-foot canoe sailed around most of the world.

Victoria's Chinatown is over a century old. Chinese laborers brought to British Columbia for construction of the trans-Canada railway started the community which rivalled San Francisco's in its heyday. Now reduced to two or three blocks, its entrance at Fisgard and Government Streets is marked by a bright red Gate of Harmonious Interest. Walk beneath that wondrous piece of oriental architecture and you are into a colorful little world of pungent spices, inexpensive restaurants, cheap souvenirs and costly Chinese art.

Upon reflection, I spent far too long in the shops and allowed too little time for the city's natural attributes—which says something for the immense variety of merchandise offered. Local souvenirs can be quite special, if you consider seeds packaged and sold at Butchart Gardens, or an Emily Carr print, or an Indian carving. Native handicrafts here are the best, ranging in price from around $50 for a small totem pole without much detail, to thousands of dollars for a ceremonial mask. Traditional Cowichan sweaters are extremely popular. Using undyed wool which retains its water repellancy, knitters work designs that have been in their families for generations. Natural colors are usually grey, black or brown on white. Cowichan toques, mittens, socks and ponchos are also available. For addresses of stores equipped to fill mail orders, contact Victoria's Visitor Information Center.

If your background is British, the English Sweet Shop will surely awaken dormant memories of treacle toffee and pomfret cakes, aniseed balls and gob-stoppers. More lasting souvenirs from Britain are tweeds, tartans, china and linens, all of which please visiting Americans.

IF YOU GO: In summer, car ferries from the mainland depart every hour on the hour, less frequently in winter. Pacific Coach lines will take you by bus and ferry from downtown Vancouver to downtown Victoria. Ferry services also connect the city with Washington state. For more information, contact Tourism Victoria, 6th Floor, 612 View Street, Victoria, B.C., V8W 1J5, telephone 604–382–1131, toll free anywhere in North America 1–800–663–3883.

THE EVER GROWING LEGACY OF JENNY BUTCHART

Victoria, British Columbia: "Gardens," the old man said softly, "are like women. They improve with age." I had joined him on the seat to change my film, not to get into a philosophical discussion. Nonetheless I agreed that the garden spread before us was far more beautiful than I had remembered. Maturity, autumnal colors spotlighted by an Indian summer sun and absence of summer crowds all contributed to the magic of Butchart Gardens that October afternoon.

Located on Tod Inlet, some 12 miles from downtown Victoria, the gardens cover 50 acres of the 130-acre Butchart estate. At this time of the year they are awash with copper and brass colored chrysanthemums nudging their tousled heads; marigolds, like thick bands of gold bordering a green scarf; dahlias, single and double blooms in purples and pinks, magentas and mauves, swaying with the slightest breeze. The rose garden isn't at its best right now but the perfume lingers. It's like walking through a great bowl of pot-pourri freshly released from plastic wrap.

Almost all of the flowers here are commonal garden types: hydrangeas and hollyhocks, deep blue delphiniums, brown eyed daisies, carnations and asters, sunflowers nodding imperiously over delicate little lobelia. There are no labels to identify them, no seed packages spiked on popsicle sticks in the soil, no Latin names, because this is not your average botanical garden. And that's the beauty of it. To come here is like visiting somebody's private garden. Part of the pleasure is in remembering flowers long forgotten that used to grow in your grandmother's backyard.

Absolutely everything you want to know about gardening will be explained by experts at the horticultural center, or you can ask the gardeners. There are 35 on permanent staff. I asked one young woman deftly removing dead-heads what a ground cover with an enticing scent was called. She told me it was heliotrope, also known as "the cherry pie plant"—because that's exactly what it smells like.

Legend has it that when Jenny Butchart started her garden in 1904, she hardly knew a daisy from a daffodil. What you see now originated with a 50-foot mud hole from which her husband's company had quarried limestone. When the limestone was finished Jenny decided to beautify the ugly scar by creating a sunken garden. Eventually it became one of the world's finest.

First she collected rocks into piles for her raised flower beds. One particularly messy puddle became a lake. Tons and tons of topsoil were carted in from neighboring farms. Sites for trees were carefully selected. Then, when the pit's floor was decently covered, the valiant Mrs. B. clothed its naked walls by dangling over the side in a bosun's chair and tucking ivy into crevices.

The estate was named Benvenuto, or "Welcome" in Italian, and the Butcharts lost no time in putting action to the word. First friends and then strangers came to admire the transformation. When annual outings for the blind were hosted, Jenny personally identified and described her flowers to them. She often provided boiling water from her kitchen for picnickers, and even made them tea until the crowds became too large. In the early years there was no thought of charging admission. Now half a million visitors a year happily pay for the privilege.

As the gardens were extended, the Butcharts travelled to far off lands in search for new plants, seeds, bulbs, sculptures and ornaments for Benvenuto. Italian and Japanese Gardens were created.

There is a wonderful rose garden and a concert lawn, fountains and a waterfall, and an area reserved for summer fireworks.

The gardens are open in all seasons, in all weather. On summer evenings they are illuminated by hundreds of hidden lights. By December wallflowers and pansies will be in bloom, along with colorful berry trees and shrubs. The new year brings spring heather and witch hazel; February the primroses and pansies; and by March daffodils in the thousands herald arrival of spring. Some say April is best, being a time of hyacinths, tulips and rhododendrons, and 550 cherry trees in full flower along Benvenuto Avenue leading to the estate.

Don't be deterred by rain. All year, flowers in the greenhouses get a jump on the season outside and, while your photos may not be the greatest, the gardens themselves are still a picture.

Lunch and afternoon tea are served daily in the Butcharts' original house. (At present dinner service is limited to Thursdays, Fridays and Saturdays.) There is also a self-service cafeteria, The Blue Poppy, in a giant greenhouse with tables cushioned between potted plants and hanging baskets. Prices in both restaurants are reasonable.

Already the gift shop is well stocked with Christmas ideas. Botanical calendars and cards, wreaths and handicrafts are popular mementos. Packages of seeds from the gardens hold more promise than a lottery ticket. Encouraged by Jenny's success I always leave the gardens with packages of seeds and grandiose ideas for my garden at home. For insurance, I rub the already gleaming snout of Tacca, the bronze boar brought back from Florence by the Butcharts. Such gesture supposedly brings good luck, but I can't truthfully say that it works for me.

IF YOU GO: For more information telephone 604–652–5256 for a recording 24 hours a day, or 604–652–4422 during business hours. The gardens open at 9 a.m. daily, and close at 11:00 p.m. in July and August, 9:00 p.m. in June and 5:00 p.m. in the other months. Admission during the peak season is $9.50 for adults, $5 for juniors, $1 for children, less at other times.

HER MAJESTY HAS RETURNED

Victoria, British Columbia: The Empress is back. The grand-dame of Canadian hotels presiding so nobly over Victoria's inner harbor closed in the autumn of '88. Employees who had worked here week-in week-out for decades suddenly found themselves with time on their hands. Chamber music gave way to noise from hammers and electric saws in the 12-foot-wide halls, and I can visualize many a lost soul wondering whether to brave it out or seek an alternative venue for afternoon tea. In April 1989, six months and $45 million later, the hotel re-opened with most of its former staff, an added wing, modern facilities and a brand new look to enhance the original character which, to put it kindly, had become a mite dowdy over the past 80 years.

Reminiscent of Canada's other castle-like hotels built by railway companies in the early 1900s, The Empress is still owned and operated by Canadian Pacific. It received its first guests in 1908. Instant success caused a new wing to be added two years later, and a further addition in 1929 increased the original 160 rooms to 570. Unfortunately for this and other grand hotels, tourism changed direction following the Second World War. The 1950s saw many of the Empress' rooms permanently closed; the '60s brought talk of closing down completely. Instead it was decided to upgrade. Rooms and suites were decorated, facilities updated, and when all was done 75-year-old band leader Billy Tickle, an Empress fixture for so long, was coaxed out of retirement to join in week-long celebrations.

This time around the dowager hotel has received more than cosmetic surgery. Architects and designers have done a champion job in blending new and modern features to enhance the old. At first I found the layout confusing. A wing built on what used to be the parking lot now houses a bright, lofty reception area. In this same wing a 40-foot indoor pool (plus a shallow pool for children), saunas, and gymnasium are for the exclusive use of hotel guests. Gardens viewed from almost every ground floor window will be a treat in early March, when the rest of the country is in

The Empress Hotel

deep freeze. Public areas have shed their heavy, turn-of-the-century look. As bright and sunny as a summer's day, they are furnished in light mauves, lemons and pale greens. Great oriental vases are stuffed with fresh flowers. Even the carpeting has rosy blooms woven onto a pale green background, while antique desks and bureaus, vases and sculptures shine from every corner.

Large spaces are artfully broken up by pillars and potted plants. Lounge seating is arranged for private conversation. Armchairs, in twos and threes facing the harbor view, were inevitably occupied when I passed by. Pursuing the idea that "small is better" the main dining room is literally cut in half, reducing the seating to 72 from an original 184.

Several features long since forgotten or hidden have come to light during the recent restoration. One is the Palm Court's stained glass dome. Damaged in the 1960s by a freak snowstorm, it was covered over until this year. Now beautifully restored to original glory, it is protected by an outer shell of plexiglass. Next to the Palm Court, the Crystal Ballroom is as magnificent as ever, its pink and green decor reflected in a mirrored ceiling hung with huge antique crystal balls. The slate-floored conservatory, to which former guests have occasionally willed their plants, is now a link between hotel and a new two-storeyed convention center.

To see the Empress in her former life, you must seek out the archives on a lower floor. Here, in an alcove bricked in for years, a small museum displays photographs of the hotel when first built. Memorabilia includes a 1908 register showing that guests came from other provinces, Europe and the United States from the very start. Invitations and programs illustrate the Empress' place in city history, as a glittering setting for royal occasions and gala events. Hotel prices tell their own story. Sixty years ago a dollar would buy you Afternoon Tea, seven dollars, a double room with harbor view.

All of Canada's heritage hotels are steeped in tales of eccentric guests, devoted employees and even resident ghosts. Here we learn about the woman who booked into the same room every Christmas, then sat there talking to her dead husband. And the military chap who relived old battles with thousands of lead soldiers set up in his room. One couple ordered cod steaks for dinner every night for six years. Painter Emily Carr used to bring her pet monkey in a pram to Afternoon Tea.

Saddest stories are of the dollar-a-day guests, usually widows, who lived here in style until their fortunes changed with the 1929 stock market crash. Some moved away. Others were given attic rooms for a dollar a day, and learned to survive with their dignity intact. I am reminded of them in my attic room now, on the seventh floor beyond the reach of elevators. Tucked away from the usual hotel traffic, and altered beyond recognition, these are a special few rooms often requested by honeymooners. Spacious, luxuriously appointed, mine has sloping ceilings and a walk-in closet, a four poster bed and cushioned window seats where I sit and watch the harbor sights. Balloon curtains, television sets and mini-bars hidden in armoires, and antique furniture are featured in all of the upgraded rooms. Handicapped guests are planned for with wheelchair access, elevators signed in braille, and special guest rooms equipped with visual fire alarms for the hearing impaired.

The hotel's three restaurants have been remodelled. Most formal is the Empress Room, offering an exciting menu, attentive yet friendly service and excellent food. A dinner of say, game consommé en croute, lamb with black currant and mint glaze with garden fresh vegetables, and a dessert selected from assorted fruits, tortes and trifles, costs in the region of $65–75 for two plus wine. The more casual Bengal Lounge and Bar provides a good curry, buffet style for lunch or dinner. Decor is Indian-style from the days of the Raj. A tiger skin is stretched above the fireplace, and ceiling fans are augmented by electrically driven punkahs. The Garden Café is transformed from a traditionally gloomy hotel coffee shop to a modern bistro. Open all day, its menu is guaranteed to perk up jaded appetites. (If you have always wanted a croissant filled with grilled tomato, bacon and alfalfa sprouts for breakfast, here's your chance.)

I hope the air of excitement that permeates the new Empress is here to stay. Already the enthusiasm of bellboys and waitresses, receptionists, shop assistants and manager Ian Balfour has spread to the guests. So far business has exceeded expectations. The 95 percent occupancy rate of last summer has dropped only slightly this fall. A Christmas package (five days of feasting, carolling and seasonal celebrations) was sold out last spring. On a weekday evening this month I saw would-be diners turned away from the Empress Room because it was fully booked, and the only vacancy for Afternoon Tea on the day I inquired was at 12:30 p.m. According to Balfour, the biggest compliment paid by locals is that they now use the hotel as their "regular," whereas in the past, they tended to look on it as the place to come to on special occasions.

IF YOU GO: Located in the inner harbor, the Empress is convenient to downtown attractions. Seaplanes from Vancouver touch down across from the hotel. An inexpensive bus and ferry service from downtown Vancouver to a terminal beside the hotel takes three and a quarter hours. A superior room is about $155 double in summer, less at other times. For reservations telephone 604–384–8111, or CP Hotels toll free numbers: US, 1–800–828–7447, Ontario & Quebec 1–800–268–9420, elsewhere in Canada 1–800–268–9411.

INDEX